HOW TO GROW
ANNUALS

Ann Roe Robbins

HOW TO GROW ANNUALS

REVISED EDITION

Illustrated by L. J. Robbins

DOVER PUBLICATIONS, INC.
NEW YORK

Published in Canada by General Publishing Company, Ltd., 30 Lesmill Road, Don Mills, Toronto, Ontario.
Published in the United Kingdom by Constable and Company, Ltd., 10 Orange Street, London WC2H 7EG.

This Dover edition, first published in 1977, is a completely revised edition of the work first published by The Macmillan Company, New York, in 1949.

International Standard Book Number: 0-486-23272-7
Library of Congress Catalog Card Number: 76-51612

Manufactured in the United States of America
Dover Publications, Inc.
180 Varick Street
New York, N.Y. 10014

This is a revision of a book with the same title published in 1949.

Much of the description of each of the annuals in the main group of twenty-five and in the general list is unchanged. Time does not alter the general appearance, the basic habits of growth, and the dependence on climatic conditions of annual flowering plants.

However, during the last three decades, seedsmen, growers and supply houses have produced and introduced on the market a number of new varieties of most annuals, having different colors, new flower shapes, resistance to heat, longer length of bloom, and other desirable qualities. Some older varieties are no longer commercially grown. The specific information on varieties has therefore been brought up to date.

In addition, improved and ingenious gardening materials, tools and labor saving devices are now available; where suitable, these and their sources are referred to. Naturally, previous mentions of the costs of seeds and other items have had to be changed to indicate that inflation has reached the garden—although, I might add, not nearly as much as it has in other areas.

I do not think the revisions will affect the implied message in the original text—that the pleasure and satisfaction resulting from the successful cultivation of annual flowers in gardens of all sizes depend on intelligent selection of what to grow and manual labor to make it grow.

The reference books I have used for checking botanical facts are *Hortus Second* by L. H. Bailey and Ethel Zoe

Bailey, *The Standard Cyclopedia of Horticulture* by L. H. Bailey, and *The Garden Dictionary* edited by Norman Taylor. The pronunciations are based on the information in *The Garden Dictionary,* in a little book called *The Home Garden Self-Pronouncing Dictionary of Plant Names* (published by the American Garden Guild, Inc.,) and in *Webster's Collegiate Dictionary*—and occasionally my own interpretation of these authorities.

The seed catalogues referred to are:

W. Atlee Burpee Co., 300 Park Avenue, Warminster, Pa. 18974

Burnett Brothers, Inc., 92 Chambers Street, New York, N.Y. 10007

Comstock, Ferre & Co., 263 Main Street, Wethersfield, Conn. 06109

Joseph Harris Company, Moreton Farm, Rochester, N.Y. 14624

Olds Seed Company, 2901 Packers Avenue, P.O. Box 1069, Madison, Wisc. 73701

Geo. W. Park Seed Co. Inc., Box 31, Greenwood, S.C. 29647

Stokes Seeds Inc., Box 548, Buffalo, N.Y. 14240

INTRODUCTION

"And I beseech you, forget not to inform yourselves **diligently** as may be, in things that belong to gardening."

John Evelyn (1620–1706)

Since numerous books on growing annual flowers are available, I should like to explain how this one differs from the others. Ever since I started gardening about fifteen years ago it has seemed to me that most gardeners need something that simplifies the subject. The information in the many excellent general books is so all-inclusive that it is perplexing to anyone who knows little about gardening, or for that matter even to the seasoned gardener. No one can possibly hope to grow all the flowers there are, and it is difficult to know how to make a choice. It is also difficult to plan a garden so that the effect is harmonious and the bloom continuous. So I have done two things. The first is to limit the choice, the second to try to guide the reader into making well planned gardens for both color and season of bloom.

There are at least 150 annual flowers. I have chosen 25 annuals which for various reasons seem the best to me, and treated them separately and in detail. Several years ago I did the same thing with vegetables, and found from many letters that people who are not experienced gardeners want concrete information. Each of these 25 annuals is discussed in this way: History, description, classification and recommended varieties, culture, when to plant, how to plant, care and cultivation, uses and planting combinations. In each instance I hope I have answered the questions which can be so baffling to a novice—what is the color range? the height? how long does it take to bloom from seed? how long will it bloom? will it stand heat? when to plant? However, conditions vary in different localities and no one can be dogmatic about all of the answers. Heat dwarfs many plants, and may cause variation of a foot or more in height depending upon whether the summers are hot or reasonably cool. Heat also either retards or stops the flowering of certain annuals, so the season of bloom may be considerably shorter in some hot parts of the country. Some seeds will not germinate if the weather is cool, others only get a good start before summer sets in. Zinnias, for instance, will flower in 40–50 days from planting when both soil and weather are really warm, but require a month longer if you try to force them in cool weather. So most of the figures are relative and a guide, rather than a flat statement of fact. This is the real reason why more such figures are not given in seed catalogues and garden literature. In a country as vast as ours and with such deviation in climate and soil, it is difficult to be precise on almost any statistic except color—and even that often fades in intense sun.

My choice of annuals was, of necessity, an arbitrary one, and many people probably will not agree with me. There were certain self-imposed limitations. I have assumed that the reader does not have greenhouse facilities for early planting. Only a few annuals in my group require an early start, and that can be accomplished in a window of southern exposure. Practically all these annuals are easy to raise, do not take too long a time to flower, and the large majority bloom for a long time. They are all flowers I have often grown myself and that I like. Calliopsis, for instance, is easy to raise but to me not especially attractive, so it is not on the list. I have also tried to include annuals for every use such as cutting, edging, window boxes, and trellises, as well as general bedding.

If you are garden-minded and ride around almost any town in almost any part of the country, you will probably be surprised to see how few homes have flower gardens, and how badly planned are the gardens that do exist. Even in a relatively prosperous country community like New Canaan, Connecticut, where I live, there are beautiful trees and lawns but very few flower gardens, and almost none planned for good color combinations. In a ten thousand mile trip to the West Coast and back this summer, it was depressing to notice the prevalence of beds full of clashing pinks and oranges, or the total absence of gardens.

Most beginners worry primarily about raising flowers from seed, and do not give much thought to planning good color arrangements. Therefore, to try to help along this line, simple planting combinations are suggested with each of my 25 annuals.

I have tried very hard to recommend good varieties. Many gardeners do not understand just how important it is to buy by variety, and to get the right one. Many varieties are listed, and there is often much difference between them in color, size, and habit of growth. Many of us go into a seed store and ask for Ageratum seed to use for a low edging—only to find when the plants bloom they are 18 inches high, just because we didn't ask for a dwarf variety.

Like many other problems, selecting good varieties isn't easy. Catalogue descriptions are not infallible, and there is general confusion about classifications and color. Asters are often called blue in catalogues although the color is usually lavender. In the rose, pink, red, crimson, scarlet, carmine color groups, it is often almost impossible to define the color so that a reader can visualize it. I had hoped to be specific, by referring to two of the standard color charts. But the one used by most seedsmen, issued by the Royal Horticultural Society in England, has about 200 separate colors, with 4 tones of each (about 800 possibilities in all). So there are obvious obstacles to finding the proper color, and in identifying it to anyone who does not own a color chart. As Louis Agassiz said: "If you study nature in books, when you go out of doors you cannot find her." Even the seedsmen disagree among themselves about naming colors. So the only way to be sure of the color of a flower is to see it growing.

With this in mind I have not only grown hundreds of varieties myself, but have visited the trial gardens at State College, Pennsylvania, where over 300 annuals are grown; I have seen some of the commercial seed farms in California where hundreds of acres of flowers are raised, and noted good varieties in private gardens. In almost every instance where I recommend a given variety, I have seen it in bloom, and believe that my description will give you a better mental picture of the plant than some of the catalogues with their grandiose ideas about color and size. Like all personal choices, no doubt many people will take issue with some of mine.

This book also has simple basic sections on garden procedure and practices. I am a dirt gardener, and write mostly from my own experience. My interest is in growing flowers and producing an attractive garden, and I hope this book will help prospective and present gardeners to have beautiful gardens and all the fun and satisfaction that gardening can bring.

As I once read somewhere: "If you want to be happy an hour, get intoxicated. If you want to be happy three days, get married. If you want to be happy eight days, kill a pig and eat it. But if you want to be happy forever, become a gardener."

CONTENTS

HOW TO GROW ANNUALS

What Is an Annual? An annual is a plant which completes its life cycle from seed to natural death in one growing season. The seed is sown, the plant flowers, produces seed and dies all within a few months, usually between the last spring frost and the first fall one.

Most gardens contain annuals, biennials and perennials. Biennials flower the following year after the seed is sown and then usually die or flower so poorly another year that it is not worth while to give them garden space. Perennials live for several or many years. They die down in the fall but the roots live over and new growth starts again in the spring. They generally do not flower until the year after the seed is sown, although there are exceptions to this rule.

Climate often determines whether a plant is an annual or perennial. Many plants which live for years in a warm tropical climate, die in parts of the world where there are frosts and cold winters. Some so-called annuals in this book are actually tender perennials. Also many annuals are perennial in our gardens, not because the plants themselves live over the winter, but because their self-sown seeds do, and germinate in the spring to produce new flowering plants.

Advantages of Annuals. Although perennials live for years while most annuals have to be sown anew each spring, the latter have several distinct advantages that more than justify their place in the garden.

Most annuals are of the easiest possible culture. If the seed is sown at the right time in a moderately decent soil, in a spot that receives at least 5–6 hours of sun a day, the plants, given minimum care and attention, will flower profusely and, often, for months. Perennials take much longer to produce flowers and many are difficult to grow.

Annuals are the cheapest garden flowers. A package of seed generally costs 30¢–80¢ and will produce dozens of plants. Even a package of the most expensive seed, like fancy hybrid Petunias, costs only 75¢–$1.25, often the price of a plant or two from a nurseryman. For what you pay for a good rose bush, you can fill a large bed with long-blooming annuals.

Annuals flower in a relatively short time, and continue in bloom much longer than most perennials. A majority of annuals flower 6–10 weeks after seed is sown, and many stay in bloom throughout summer and fall. With proper planning, annuals can supply the garden and house with flowers from the middle of June until frost—all from seed. In temperate climates, annuals are in bloom throughout the whole year.

Because of the variety of color, form, and foliage, there is a good annual for every conceivable use. The height varies from 3 inches to 10–12 feet; the foliage from dark green to almost white; and if you want plants solely for their foliage, you can have them in variegated tones of green, yellow, white and red. The color range of the flowers is complete, with every possible hue and tone.

Annuals are almost without exception both disease and pest free. This is an important factor for the novice, or for that matter, for any gardener. Many annuals self-sow and come up for years, so that they are a permanent addition to the garden.

When you start to list the advantages of growing annuals, the tendency is to forget, perhaps, the most important reason, and that is that they can be so beautiful. Their exquisite colors and forms make them a profound pleasure to grow and have in the garden and house. My descriptions aren't full of ecstatic phrases, but I hope you will try growing many of these flowers and see for yourself just how lovely they can be.

Uses of Annuals. In new or rented homes: for quick and inexpensive wealth of bloom.

With shrubs: to plant between new shrubs or in front of well established ones. New shrubs should always be given sufficient space to grow to maturity without crowding, and annuals are very useful for filling in the gaps. Also, since the majority of shrubs are spring blooming, annuals planted in front of them will provide summer and fall bloom to continue the color.

With bulbs: to hide fading bulb foliage. Sow in fall or early spring. See page 287 for suggestions.

With perennials: to fill in gaps in perennial beds, and supply a variety of color during summer when few perennials are in bloom. The foliage of some perennials, such as Oriental Poppies and Bleeding Heart, entirely disappears in summer. Also most perennials are either spring or fall blooming, so that even in the most carefully planned borders there is a dearth of summer bloom without annuals.

By themselves: annuals are also excellent in beds and borders by themselves; and if you have space, in a cutting garden. Most annuals bloom longer and more abundantly than perennials, and are actually benefited by constant cutting. So many colors are available in such a diversity of form that beautiful beds can be planned in any desired color, size, or height.

Classification of Annuals. Annuals are classified as hardy, half-hardy, and tender. The difference is a matter of response to frost. Hardy annuals can stand some frost which means that hardy seeds can be sown in the open ground well before the last frost date (there is a spring Frost Zone Map on page 282). The young seedlings are not affected by an unexpected late frost, and in the fall the plants will not be killed by a light frost. Hardy annuals can usually be fall sown to produce very early spring flowers. And since the seeds of some hardy annuals live over the winter, they also self-sow although the colors are sometimes less desirable in self-sown seedlings, especially with new hybrid plants which tend to revert to type.

Half-hardy annuals will survive a light frost but are usually planted in the open about the last frost date or a little later, while the weather is still cool but not when there is much risk of a spell of frost. In the spring Frost Zone Map on page 282 the first of the two dates is the usual one for last spring frosts, the second date an outside chance. In other words, if the dates are April 15–May 1st, you can expect frost on April 15th but it is most unlikely by May 1st. So half-hardy annuals could be planted April 15–April 22nd. In the fall they will survive a very light frost, but are not as frost resistant as hardy annuals.

Tender annuals, on the other hand, are warm-weather plants which cannot stand any frost at all. They should never be planted until you are reasonably sure that frosts are over as they will be killed by the first touch of frost in spring. Most tender annuals, like Zinnias, need warm weather to germinate and flourish, and if you try to hasten the bloom by early planting you will waste your time because they will stand still when the weather is cool or perhaps be permanently checked in growth. So tender annuals, which take a long time to bloom from seed, should be started in a greenhouse or indoors where it is warm.

Many annuals are difficult to classify precisely; often the line between hardy and half-hardy is slim, and even established garden authorities differ in their classifications. But, to the practical gardener, it is important to know what type each annual is because of the planting time. Some hardy annuals, like Larkspur and Sweet Peas, do well only if sown very early, two weeks or so before the last frost date. If you delay planting Sweet Peas you won't have any flowers. On the other hand, a light frost or cool weather has an adverse effect on tender annuals, preventing germination or killing young seedlings.

There are some gardeners who hoot at this business of regulating planting dates, and say they just plant everything the first of May and it turns out all right. But this is only true if you plant a few die-hards like Petunias, Nasturtiums, and Marigolds. For success with a variety of annuals, knowing the types and planting at the proper time is the keynote. When to plant is discussed more fully on page 28.

Plant names. Anyone writing about flowers is in somewhat of a quandary when it comes to names. Should you use the botanical or the common name?

Prior to the eighteenth century there was a great deal of confusion about plant names. Plants were being carried all over the world by navigators and were of great medical importance to doctors, but there was no standard procedure for naming them. Luckily this situation was remedied by Linnaeus, a Swedish doctor and naturalist, who lived from 1707–1778. He instituted a binomial system of plant names which is now used all over the world.

The basis of the names is either Greek, Latin, or a latinized form of words in other languages. Each plant is given at least two names. The genus or family name is equivalent to a person's surname. The second or species name is like the given name in a family group. A third name is often added which is the name of a particular variety. For example, a name like *Centaurea americana alba* means that the family name is *Centaurea*, that this particular member of the family is from America, and the flowers are white. The plant names have many sources; people's names, classical and mythical references, geographical localities, religious references, allusions to animals, and sometimes the origin is unknown.

The advantage of having a botanical name which is used the world over is obvious. There are more than 350,000 species of plants in the world, to say nothing of the thousands of varieties and strains within these groups. It is important for the botanists, and anyone working professionally with flowers, to be able to identify any plant in any part of the world; therefore plants must have names that are understood in any language. In time they also acquire common names in individual countries. *Eschscholzia,* for instance, is named in honor of a Russian Dr. Eschscholtz, but since it is a native California plant it is often called California Poppy. *Antirrhinums* are called Snapdragons so frequently that most gardeners don't even know how to pronounce the botanical name.

So which name should a writer use, writing for American amateur gardeners? The use of plant names varies considerably in all written material about flowers except in the standard reference books. Seed catalogues certainly have no standard practice and neither do most authors of so-called popular books. I have no desire to appear "long-haired" and pedantic; on the other hand books and pamphlets which use strictly local common names are confusing because half the time you do not even know which plant is being referred to.

What I have tried to do is use the name that would be most readily understood, holding to the botanical names as often as seems feasible. In many cases the botanical name is also the common name: *Ageratum, Alyssum* and *Phlox* for instance. In some cases the botanical name is so rarely used that most readers would be baffled: *Tropaeolum* (Nasturtium) and *Lathyrus odorata* (Sweet Peas) for example. In some cases where the genus has several species which I wanted to include, I have given the botanical name although it may not often be used; for instance, I have discussed five species of *Centaurea,* so Bachelor's Buttons or Cornflowers are called *Centaurea cyanus.*

Hybridizing. This simple drawing of the make-up of a flower shows all the essential parts.

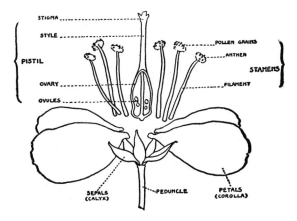

Pollen, produced in the anther (the male reproductive part of the flower), must reach the stigma and travel down the style to fertilize the ovules in the ovary. From this union, seed is produced.

Plants normally are self-fertilizing, and their seeds produce plants similar to the original. For over two centuries botanists have been trying to improve on nature by hybridizing plants; that is, by crossing strains. According to the records the first hybridist was Thomas Fairchild, who produced Fairchild's Sweet William in 1719 by artificial pollination. Since then hybridists have been very active in increasing the size of flowers, the color range, doubling the form, waving and fringing the petals, increasing the resistance to heat and drought, and even removing the.odor from Marigolds! You can realize just what they have accomplished when you look at the present lists of such flowers as Petunias, Zinnias, and Marigolds and consider the original flowers.

The principle of hybridizing is simple enough. You start with two plants you wish to cross. Then you remove all the male organs (the anthers) from one flower, and transfer the pollen from the other flower to the stigma of the first one. This is delicate work, requiring good manual dexterity and often a small paint brush. To keep the plant from being further pollinized by any stray bee or gust of wind, the flower is usually tied up in paper or muslin until the seed ripens. The plants produced from this union are called F_1 hybrids. Most hybridizing starts at this point, by all sorts of experiments with these F_1 hybrids, but the principle used is the same.

It often takes years to stabilize new strains, since the course hybrids will take is very unpredictable at first. Because it is hand work and many hybrids are shy seeders, the seed often is expensive. Also, unless the hybrid is well established and had good stable parents, you cannot rely on the seed to come 100 per cent true to description. But the hybridizers have done wonders with almost every annual, as you will see all through this book.

When you consider the almost limitless choice of flowers we have today, and what has been accomplished by these patient workers, you know how grateful we should be for their skill and efforts. Maybe you would like to try your own hand at it. Many commercial varieties today have been bred by home gardeners and bought by the commercial seedsmen. I saw a beautiful new Shirley Poppy at one seed farm from one of their customers which they were considering buying. Although, for most gardeners, the real thrill would be in experimenting rather than in any potential sale.

The garden bed. Exposure and size are the two important elements in making a garden bed. Annuals are sun-loving plants, and while they will flower abundantly in a sunny position they are niggardly about flower production in a semi-shaded one, and full shade is hopeless. At least 5–6 hours a day of sun is needed, and full sun is usually even better.

The bed should be at least 3 feet wide so that you can plant enough flowers to make a showing. But unless you can cultivate from the back as well as the front, 5–6 feet should be the maximum width. As a matter of fact, 5–6 feet in width gives plenty of space for a well planned attractive bed, and in a larger annual bed the effect of the individual flowers tends to be lost. The length is usually regulated by the lay-out of the property. At this point I would like to give a well considered word of advice and that is do not bite off more than you can chew. Gardening is a lot of fun but it also takes time. Weeds are always with us and can only be kept down with constant vigilance. When there is so much garden to attend to that the whole undertaking becomes a burden, the real purpose of gardening is ruined. Try to plan your garden so that the beds are an easy size to manage, and then they will always look well and you will have time to enjoy them. You can always expand. But once you have dug beds and put them under cultivation, it takes much will power to reduce them in size.

A seasoned gardener can make lovely beds with a great variety of annual and perennial plant material. But having looked carefully at gardens for years, and having experimented quite a bit myself, I am now convinced that the best annuals beds are not a conglomeration of flowers in all the colors of the spectrum, but those with a definite color plan and only a few types of flowers in massed groups.

The important thing for the novice is not to try to grow

a large number of different plants, but rather to stay confined to a few and choose those with the greatest thought for color, variety and habit of growth.

What to plant. What shall you grow? What particular flowers shall you choose from the more than 150 annuals offered in seed catalogues? The pictures look appealing, the catalogue descriptions are beguiling, but with never a warning about possible pitfalls. According to what seedsmen say about their sales, and judging from the average garden, most people plant just three flowers—Zinnias, Marigolds, and Petunias. There are sound reasons why these three are far and away the most popular. They flower quickly if planted at the right time, are available in a large color range, and most important of all—flower gloriously even during the hottest and driest summers.

I love these three flowers, but object to the way they are generally used. Zinnia mixtures, unless carefully chosen, are full of clashing and unattractive colors. Petunias can be very beautiful; they are so popular that hybridists pay special attention to creating new Petunia varieties and the result is some exquisite colors and forms. But you would never know it judging from the flowers you usually see in beds: small white ones, magenta, and a horrid bright pink—far too often combined with orange Marigolds or red Salvias or Geraniums. Marigolds, fortunately, have no clashing colors, since the range is limited to yellow, orange, and blending shades of copper-red. Left by themselves, you cannot get into trouble. It isn't until you begin combining them with Petunias that you run into trouble. Beautiful beds are possible with these three basic flowers, but colors and varieties must be heeded.

Other popular flowers are Asters, Sweet Peas and Larkspurs. I was interested in the fact that Sweet Peas are high on the list of commercial seed sales. They are not easy to grow in most parts of the country, but are so well loved that gardeners try them in spite of the difficulties. The ROYAL and CUTHBERTSON FLORIBUNDA Sweet Peas (which withstand heat far better than do other types) should make it easier for more people to grow these lovely flowers.

Many more annuals are well worth growing. In discussing just what you want to plant, it seems to me three factors should be taken into consideration.

The first is purely practical. Select plants that do well in your vicinity. In the South, you need flowers that will stand the hot dry summers. In the North, you want annuals that bloom quickly because the late spring and early fall frosts result in relatively short summers.

The second consideration is color. If your flower beds are to be pleasing, there must be a planned color scheme. Miscellaneous plantings of packages of mixed seed result in a chaotic looking garden. Annuals are often very vivid and care is needed to avoid bad color combinations. It is easy enough to select varieties by color so that you will have a bed where colors blend. Do you want bright colorful beds, or soft restful ones? Red flowers for many years have been the most popular color, although the various shades of pinks and salmons are close. White is a strong second. Solid red beds are seldom effective but you can make beautiful ones with scarlet, orange, and bright yellow flowers. Pink and blue beds are usually better if enlivened by white, purple, or pale yellow flowers.

In choosing colors, consider first your own taste. The color of your house might influence your choice—pink Petunias against red brick could hardly be called pleasing. Also you will need flowers to cut which will look well in your house. If your living room is blue and rose you won't want it full of bright orange Marigolds.

It may seem that two conflicting ideas have been presented. One is a warning not to try too many different kinds of flowers at once, and the other is a plea to experiment with new plants; actually in your gardening experience these two should come in sequence.

The tendency of most beginner gardeners (and even of experienced ones) is to attempt far too much. Don't rush out and buy numerous packages of seeds of plants you have never grown. Unless you have a full-time gardener, or are an energetic worker yourself, you probably won't have the time or patience to plant the seed and bring the plants to successful flowering. Then too, many annuals have drawbacks such as a short blooming period, an aversion to some local climatic condition, or just plain unattractive flowers. It is much better for a beginner to stick to fool-proof flowers for a year or two because initial success is psychologically important.

Once you have found how easy it is to grow flowers from seed, the experimenting should begin. But again let me urge caution. Don't attempt too many, but try 4 or 5 new annuals every year. Read the cultural directions first. Some require an early start for which you may not have the facilities, or should be started very early outdoors and perhaps it is already May. Many will not stand hot weather, so are hopeless in some parts of the country. There is no sense trying to overcome almost impossible difficulties. Plenty of annuals can be grown early wherever you live. If you like gardening, you will find this experimental work completely fascinating. Probably you will find some plants you don't like, but you will also make some exciting discoveries.

Seed buying. Before you buy any seed, you should decide which colors you want in your garden, and which flowers will supply them. In a few instances mixtures of seeds are the best buy, but in general you should purchase seeds in separate varieties. Then you will get the colors you want.

From the information in seed catalogues, it is very difficult to know which varieties are best. Often the differences seem infinitesimal and are, but sometimes one variety is very superior to another. I have tried to recommend reliable varieties in the sections on the individual flowers, and as your interest in flowers grows you will find yourself increasingly more variety conscious. Acquire the habit of asking the name of any flower you admire in someone's garden. Many towns and cities have ambitious nurserymen who grow annual plants and they are usually most willing to be helpful. Flower Shows are often a good way to see new plants, also.

The next consideration is: Where are you going to purchase the seeds? The best planned garden in the world isn't going to amount to much if you do not plant viable seeds which are true to name. Stale seed often germinates poorly or not at all, and cheap seed often comes from plants which have not been carefully bred so that color and habit of growth may be poor.

Probably the safest practice is to buy your seeds from seedsmen with established reputations who select seeds from various sources. When I first started gardening I thought that all the firms who sold seeds and issued catalogues grew their own seeds. In time I found out that this was not the case. Actually very few retail seedsmen grow all their own seeds. For domestic seeds there are a number of large commercial seed growers, mostly in California, who have hundreds of acres under cultivation growing standard strains. Some of the retail seedsmen in turn run comparative trials to select the best growers. These seedsmen also have growers under contract to grow seeds supplied by them. This is the domestic situation. Seed production also takes place almost all over the world in regions which are good for climate and soil as well as being economically feasible—Europe, Asia, Central and South

America, and the Near and Far East. For example, about 90% of the Petunias sold here are produced in Central America and the balance in Japan. This is true of many other crops.

I visited some of the large California seed farms and found them most impressive, not only for size, but for the pride that is taken in growing good plants. The planting is well timed, the ground is fertilized, and the plants are thinned to allow them sufficient space. Often seed is started early in greenhouses. The fields are kept culti-vated—it is rare to see a weed. When the plants start to flower they are rogued by experts. The word "rogue" is a technical one and it means to pull up, but the plants pulled are always undesirable ones. Roguing is done for various reasons—the color may not be true, the flowers may be single instead of double, or the plants may be too small—it all depends upon what is considered the best traits for that particular plant.

Seedsmen not only try to grow the best possible strains of existing flowers, but also have hybridists constantly working on new varieties. When you first read seed cata-logues it seems unlikely that any more items are necessary, yet there are some gaps in flower form, color, and some-times adaptability to climatic conditions. Hybridists work on such problems as heat-resistant Sweet Peas, doubling Petunias, and adding new colors. If you read seed cata-logues of many years ago and compare with those of the present day, you will get some conception of the huge task that has been performed.

Some of these new flowers are excellent, but sometimes the seed is not fixed and the resulting plants not true to description. I think that in doubling some flowers they have spoiled the true charm of the form. And sometimes new varieties are very similar to older ones. As a sort of testing ground, in 1932 a committee of the American Seed

Trade Association instigated the All-American Selections Awards. Any grower who has a new plant and wishes to enter the competition sends seeds to the committee. They in turn send them to trial gardens which are located all over the country, thirty for flowers and twenty-five for vegetables. The name of the grower is not disclosed, and the seeds are given an impartial trial. They are tested for growth, flowering habit and health and, to win an award, must be different from, or an improvement over, existing varieties. At the end of the season each entry is judged by competent authorities, and the awards are given: Gold Medal, Silver Medal, Bronze Medal or Honorable Mention.

If any variety mentioned in this book has won an award, this is stated. All seedsmen attach a great deal of importance to these awards, and there is little doubt in my mind that some first-class annuals have won them.

There are two types of retail seed catalogues—those that list almost every available plant and variety, and those that have a limited selective list. There is no particular advantage other than convenience in buying seeds from a local seedsman. This is not true of nursery stock such as plants, trees and shrubs which often should be bought locally, since local plants are adapted to the growing conditions. But it is a good idea to look at local catalogues (I am using local in a very wide sense) because the plants these catalogues list are usually ones that do well in that particular locality. This is especially important in the South and West.

Seed catalogues are fun to read, not only for the flowers and vegetables but also for all sorts of other planting material and useful information. So I would suggest getting several, especially since I usually find that you need more than one to locate the different varieties you want. Catalogues may be obtained free by writing for them. They are advertised in garden magazines such as *Horticulture*. Or select some from the following list.

The seven I have used for this book are on page iv with their addresses. They are all actually quite different. The ones with the widest selections are Park's and Stokes. Park's is the place to look for unusual and hard to find seeds as well as all the standard ones. It is a most attractive catalogue with every page loaded with colored illustrations. Burpee is well known, as I guess "the biggest mail order seed company in the world" should be. They also have a wide choice, with both colored and black and white illustrations. I am quite partial to Harris, which has a more selective list; many of the plants are Harris' own introductions. Their good-looking catalogue has large illustrations, many in color. Burnett also has a selective list, but within their range they have an exceedingly wide choice of separate colors, often ones not found elsewhere. Stokes has a real no-nonsense catalogue, not visually appealing, but very useful. Their main business is with market and greenhouse growers, and the catalogue is packed with valuable information about when to plant, suitable growing conditions, when the plants will flower and so on. In some ways their selection is as wide as Park's, in fact wider on items that are popular with their special clientele. Olds and Comstock, Ferre are both long established sound seedsmen, with smaller selective listings. There are, of course, other good seed sources besides the ones I have used.

Every annual listed in the rest of this book can be found in at least one of these catalogues. When it is listed by most of them, no source is given. For the harder to find seeds, the source is mentioned.

I have a few admonitions about seed buying. I advise against fussing with any free seed offered as a come-on on a radio program; it may be a waste of time. I wouldn't buy seed from anyone but a seedsman, because his reputation depends on selling good seed and this is not necessarily true of a hardware or chain store. It does not pay to buy by price, trying to save a nickel or a dime, because the best seed is very inexpensive in terms of return. I caution you, however, that when you buy seeds of rarely grown plants you risk getting stale seed, because apparently the commercial seedsmen sell so little of some of these items that it does not pay them to grow fresh seed every year. Not all seed is stale however just because it is 2–3 years old; it depends upon the viability of the particular seed.

Finally, place your seed orders early. They will be filled quickly then, but even more important, you will have the seed on hand when you want it. This is especially true of hardy annuals which should be planted early. Often in Zone E around the middle of March there are a few warm days when you can plant Sweet Peas, Larkspurs and other hardy annuals—if you have the seed. Another advantage is that you can get what you want, before it is sold out. Seedsmen take great care to have sufficient stocks, but the sales of both flower and vegetable seeds have skyrocketed, catching seedsmen unaware and resulting in inevitable shortages. So play safe.

Starting seeds early. The dull cold days of February make most of us long to see something green and growing, and this longing is usually accelerated by Flower Shows held in the early spring. Many gardeners, at this season, begin indoor seed planting. The practical advantages are: you can grow plants that require a long season and are expensive to buy at a local nursery; you can extend the growing season of long blooming annuals; you can give a head start to plants which must be well established before the weather becomes too hot; and by getting your own seed you can be sure of having just the colors and varieties you want. This last factor is highly important, because the average local nurseries grow only a limited number of varieties, and not always the best ones.

I am in entire sympathy with this desire to grow plants indoors, but my advice is a bit more cautious than usual. I've had so many pans and seed flats full of dirt and seed cluttering up bedrooms and bathrooms that my first wild enthusiasm has been tempered. There are several serious drawbacks about indoor seed planting which really *must* be taken into consideration.

One is the all-important matter of light. Young plants will not grow sturdy and strong if they do not get proper sunlight. From the inside of a window sill, the plants have to reach at an angle toward the sun; this is all right just after seed germination when the seedlings are very young, but it soon makes older plants leggy and spindly. Unless you have a greenhouse, where light conditions are more even, seeds should not be started indoors more than 4 weeks before the outdoor planting date, and often 3 weeks is long enough for fast growing plants.

Another practical difficulty is that of space. The plants require several hours a day of sunlight which limits the window space available in most homes. You can start a large number of seeds indoors in a few bulb pans or flower pots, or in one large seed flat, if you are going to transfer the seedlings directly into the garden. But if you start them so early that they must be transplanted indoors, then you may have a problem. It is possible to start fifty or more Petunia seedlings, for example, in one 6-inch bulb pan which takes up very little space, but you must move them from these crowded quarters as soon as the plants have their first or second set of true leaves when each seedling needs at least 1½ square inches of room. Multiply that area by 50 and you begin to realize that transplanting doubles the space you will need. Unless your house has a large number of sunny windows and you are willing to use all of them, it is inadvisable to start a large number of annuals indoors so early that they will have to be transplanted indoors.

Therefore when you begin to make plans about indoor seed planting you should bear these factors in mind. You will probably conclude that you should not start operations until about a month before the date for outdoor work, so that the majority of plants can go directly from flats or pots into the garden with no intermediate transplanting. Actually this "indoor month" sometimes advances the blooming season about 6 weeks because the plants get a good start under warm conditions with plenty of water. Plants that are slow to germinate, like fancy Petunias, Stocks and Lobelias can be started 6 weeks ahead of time.

Another reason why you should not try to beat the season by too early a start is that sunlight is wan and meager at the end of winter. Gardeners who live in the long frost areas should really do winter gardening in an armchair with seed catalogues and garden books, and wait until March or early April for practical indoor gardening allowing a month or six weeks before the outdoor date. But remember, if you are trying indoor planting for the first time, it is better to be successful with two annuals than to fail with ten.

Here is a summary of the procedure for indoor planting. There are two essentials for seed planting—containers and a potting medium. The containers formerly were clay pots, clay bulb pans and wooden flats. They are all still around but have been largely superseded by newer and more efficient containers. Flats in a variety of sizes are now made from plastics which are much lighter than wood, but are still strong and do not develop green algae or fungus growths. Plastic pots are also now available, and there is a wide choice of sizes. Park's has 7 sizes, all round: 2½-inch, 3-inch, 4-inch, 5-inch, 6-inch, 8-inch and 10-inch. They are made from styrofoam and breathe like clay. There are saucers to match for all but the smallest two sizes. Olds also has plastic pots and a 6-inch plastic bulb pan as well. They are commonly available.

In addition, excellent "peat pots" have appeared on the market. They are imported from Norway and Denmark and are molded from a mixture of peat moss and wood fibre to which soluble fertilizers have been added. After they are thoroughly soaked they need much less watering than clay pots. The roots grow right through the pots and, when it is time for the garden, they are planted pot and all, so there is no transplanting adjustment. The common sizes are 1½-inch, 3-inch and 4-inch, either round or square. In the Stokes catalogue suggestions are made for the right size for some plants and vegetables. These peat pots also come in Jiffy-Strips, made up of square pots molded together for ease in handling. There are 12 in the 1¾- and 2½-inch size pots, and 6 in the 3-inch pots. These peat pots have to be filled with a potting medium.

There is a new contraption that comprises container, potting medium and a little fertilizer called the Jiffy-7. They are compressed into a ⅓ by 1¾-inch pellet that looks rather like a Hydrox. When watered they quickly swell to about seven times their original size and the seeds can then be planted. They are enclosed in a plastic net which holds everything together. The roots grow right through the net and the entire works can either be put into a larger pot or right into the garden—pot and all.

Seed starter kits are offered by most seedsmen with everything you need, usually at a special price. The Harris kit, for example, has 3 sturdy plastic trays (each capable of holding 24 Jiffy-7 pellets), 75 pellets, 15 labels, a marking pen which is sun-, weather- and water-proof, a package of starter solution for transplanting, and 3 clear plastic bags to enclose the trays, keeping moisture and temperature more even. Other seedsmen have similar kits.

I would suggest using peat pots or Jiffy-7 pellets for the majority of your seeds. Use the pellets or small pots for tiny seeds, and larger pots for big seeds such as Morning-glories and Nasturtiums. One added advantage of these peat pots is that you can start seeds early which normally should not be transplanted. Put 3 or 4 seeds in each pot and thin to one plant as soon as the true leaves appear. If you want many seedlings of any one annual, then use a large pot, bulb pan or flat and transplant directly into the garden.

My potting medium is either vermiculite or, better still, a mixture which is basically vermiculite but with added peat moss and nutrients. When I originally wrote this book I said: "This satisfactory product, I am sure, has added years to my life." That was because before vermiculite became available I had used ordinary soil, which either caused trouble such as damping-off (a fast spreading fungus that attacks young plants and can topple a whole flat of seedlings and kill them overnight) or required sterilization by heating. Vermiculite is exfoliated mica which has been roasted at 2000°F. until, apparently, it pops. It is essentially sterile and is weed-free. This is also true of the mixtures which are marketed under various trade names, and sold by most seedsmen. Both vermiculite and the mixtures hold moisture extremely well, and unlike soil are so light that the delicate roots of seedlings can easily penetrate them; in fact the root systems of plants grown in them are often quite fantastic. When it is time to transplant the seedlings, they slip out so easily that you have no trouble removing even the tiniest root. These potting mediums are clean, easy to handle, and available when you want them. Most gardeners are not farsighted enough to get ordinary soil ready in the fall for early spring indoor planting and when the ground is frozen hard this is not the time to dig some up. But vermiculite and the mixtures are all ready to use. Vermiculite itself contains no nutrients, so when used alone these must be added. Until the seeds have germinated, water is sufficient; when the seedlings are up, you can feed them with a plant food such as Rapid-Gro or Hyponex (following the manufacturer's directions). Since the mixtures have nutrients already added, they are a little easier to use so are recommended. I suggest using Stokes' Jiffy-Mix, Harris' Jiffy-Mix or Seed Starter Mix, or Burpee's Special Growing Formula. I shall just call the mixtures Jiffy-Mix from now on, since there seems to be no standard term.

So now you have your flats, peat pots, pellets, large plastic pots or bulb pans ready to use. Any container that is to be filled with Jiffy-Mix should have its drainage holes covered over or the mixture will run right out. Pieces of glass or coarse stones are good for this. Fill the container with Jiffy-Mix, which should be thoroughly moistened before planting your seeds. Seeds are usually sown in rows about 2 inches apart in a flat, and broadcast in a bulb pan or pot. In peat pots sow 3 or 4 seeds and thin to one seedling when the first true leaves appear. Mark each separate variety with a label and also date the label. Fine seeds just need to be pressed into the surface. Large seeds should be covered with about 1/8 inch of the mix. Don't bury them—this is often the reason why seeds do not sprout. Then either put the container in a plastic bag or cover the top with a piece of brown paper and a piece of glass. The seeds should be kept covered until they germinate to prevent too much evaporation of moisture. They also should be kept out of the sun until they sprout, and the temperature should not be too warm—65° to 70° F. is perfect. The seeds should be kept moist but not soaking wet. Jiffy-Mix holds water so well that sometimes no additional watering is needed until the seeds have germinated, but you should touch the top every day to make sure it is moist. Seeds just will not germinate without moisture.

When the seeds have germinated, remove the cover and put the container in the sun. Then turn the container around every day so that all sides get equal sun. If you have not done this planting until a month or so before the outdoor planting date, the only attention the seedlings will need is watering until it is time for them to be transplanted outdoors. Even when the plants are very crowded no harm is done if they are small. I have had 240–250 Marigold seedlings in one flat and they all flourished.

The annuals in the basic group of 25 which benefit from an early start are Ageratum, Asters, Dahlias, Marigolds, Snapdragons, Verbenas and Morning-glories. The ones which definitely require it are the ruffled, fringed and double Petunias. If you are reasonably new at this game I would suggest trying two or three of the fancy Petunias such as SUNBURST, CALYPSO, STARFIRE, POLARIS, or any of the others that are listed on pages 162-165. They are all beautiful plants, and it is quite a thrill to raise your own. Start them in separate peat pots, two months before the latest spring frost date. By the time they are ready to be put into the garden they will be almost flowering—these Petunias start to flower when the plant is very small.

Some good annuals in the list starting on page which require an early start are Begonias, Delphinium, Digitalis, Geraniums, Hibiscus, Impatiens, *Lobelia, Salpiglossis, Statice,* Stocks, and Vinca.

I have a contraption which works out very well as a small greenhouse. It consists of 4 window sashes, constructed like this. It is put up in the spring outside a southern window, and with the window left open is heated by the heat in the room. It holds 3 large flats and some individual pots (for my Morning-glories), and can be used to start dozens of plants. It is then taken down and put away for the next year.

Coldframes are also very useful for starting seeds early. In fact, coldframes have many uses. Special seed can be planted in them all spring and summer, and plants which cannot stand outside winter conditions can often safely be carried over in a coldframe. A coldframe is nothing but a bottomless box which has a sash on the top; one end should be 6–8 inches higher than the other so that the rain can drain off. Coldframes should be placed to slant to the south or southeast. The sash protects seeds and plants from rain, and helps maintain a temperature slightly higher than that outside. When coldframes are heated, either with manure or electricity, they become hotbeds.

The materials used to be plain wood with glass sashes. Now there are better materials on the market. One is aluminum with fiberglass windows. Burpee has one that is 3 x 3½ feet for around $35.00—no rot, no rust, no painting, and no glass to break. They claim it is easy to assemble. For about $50.00 there is a coldframe which is sun-powered to open the cover automatically at 72° F. and close it at 68° F. It measures 3 x 4 feet, all heart redwood, has a tough acrylic cover and is portable. I saw it advertised in *Horticulture* and to order one write to: Dalen Products, Inc., 201 Sherlake Drive, Knoxville, Tenn. 37922. Even a small coldframe can be very useful since the seed rows can be placed 4 inches apart and you can start a minimum of 2 dozen plants in a row one foot long.

Coldframes are for half-hardy annuals rather than tender ones, since obviously they do not maintain very warm conditions. Marigolds, Ageratum, Snapdragons, Dianthus, Pansies, Violas and bedding Petunias are all good plants for the coldframe. The seeds can be planted 2–4 weeks earlier than the outdoor planting date, and give you a good head start on the season. These plants will be hardier than ones sown indoors in more heat. Treat the seed with Benomyl as a precaution against damping-off, and open the sash on a sunny day for the same reason. Keep it closed on rainy days, and always shut it at sundown. Sometimes seed is planted in flats and the flats put in coldframes. It is a good way to keep varieties separated, and the flats are handy to carry around when it is time to transplant the seedlings.

When a coldframe is heated it is a hotbed. Those heated by electricity with thermostatic control work very well, but the drawback is that you need an electric outlet close by. For most reasonably small-scale gardeners, a coldframe and some flats and bulb pans indoors serve the early seed starting needs.

Outdoor seed planting. At the first sign of spring you can usually start planting hardy annuals outdoors. Even before the frost is out of the ground, seeds of some annuals such as Sweet Peas, Calendula and Eschscholzia can be put in the ground. The half-hardy and tender annuals follow at various times after the last spring frost date. The actual planting is simple. Fine seed should be placed on the surface and not covered, and no annual seeds need more than ¼ inch covering; the delicate seedlings cannot break through too much soil overhead, and it is better to have the depth of planting too shallow rather than too deep. The soil should be firmed around the seeds, either with your foot or the back of a hoe, to insure a quick exchange of moisture from the soil to the seed. If seeds are planted in the spring when the soil is dry, make a very shallow trench with the handle of a hoe and soak the soil in it. Then plant your seed, cover lightly with dry soil and tamp down well; the seeds will then have enough moisture for germination.

When you first start gardening, you do not know how to differentiate flower seedlings from weeds which often sprout about the same time. An easy way to face this situation is to plant seeds in rows, and label them, so that when a number of identical seedlings sprout you cannot help but know that these are your flowers. The seedlings can be thinned and some can be transplanted when they have their first or second set of true leaves. It is important to do any necessary thinning or transplanting as soon as possible after the true leaves appear.

It is less of a shock to plants to be transplanted when they are little, and early thinning means less root disturbance to the plants that remain in the ground.

Destroying plants always seems like a form of murder to me. It has taken years of firm schooling to bring myself to thin ruthlessly and do it early. If you do not give each plant the space it needs, you will find yourself with spindly plants and far fewer flowers than you should have. Seeds should be sown quite thickly, since 60% germination is all you can normally count on; seed is cheap and most packages have far more seeds than you need, so it is safer to plant with a lavish hand, and thin later.

Transplanting is easily accomplished when seedlings are small. Some annuals should not be transplanted, usually those with a long tap root which is inevitably broken when you dig up the plant. But most of them stand transplanting well, and often it even benefits the plant. Moisten the soil first so that the roots will slip out easily, and then lift the seedlings out carefully, using a wooden label for small ones and a trowel for larger ones. Make a hole in the place where you wish to put the plant, having it as deep as the roots are long, and here again wooden labels are very handy for small plants. Pour some water into the bottom of the hole, and set the plant in the hole making sure that the roots aren't crowded. Firm the soil around the plant. No further watering is needed for the next day or so. Then they should be well soaked once a day for about a week. If possible do transplanting on a cloudy day. The sun evaporates water from the leaves, and makes it more difficult for the plant to get established. However, if the seedlings are small they usually stand transplanting under any conditions. Large plants should be kept well watered, and it helps them along if you protect them with some covering like a hot-cap.

One additional point should be mentioned about transplanting seedlings. The tendency is to pick only the largest, healthiest looking plants, but this is an error. These may be just the plants that revert to the wild type, and the tiniest seedlings may be the choicest. So it is best to take some of both.

When to plant. Climatic conditions are very diverse in this country, and any general rules for planting seeds obviously will not apply everywhere. In some regions there is no frost at all and flowers will grow all through the year, while in the most northern and some mountainous sections, the frost free season is confined to a few months, so that only the quick blooming or very hardy annuals can be grown.

For the rest of the country the main considerations are the average dates of the last spring frost and the first fall frost. In the eastern and middle states there is a reasonably uniform progression in the last spring frost dates and the first fall frost dates from the south to the north that makes division into zones possible. In the accompanying maps on pages 282 and 283 there are seven zones shown, marked A to G. Below are tables summarizing the average dates of spring and fall frosts.

Average dates of Latest Spring Frosts

Zone A	Feb. 15 –March 1
Zone B	March 1 –March 15
Zone C	March 15–April 1
Zone D	April 1 –April 15
Zone E	April 15 –May 1
Zone F	May 1 –May 15
Zone G	May 15 –June 1

Average Dates of Earliest Fall Frosts

Zone A	No fall frost

Zone B	Nov. 25–Dec. 10
Zone C	Nov. 10–Nov. 25
Zone D	Oct. 25 –Nov. 10
Zone E	Oct. 15 –Oct. 25
Zone F	Oct. 1 –Oct. 15
Zone G	Sept. 15–Oct. 1

It is impossible to be entirely accurate about these dates, because the weather obviously is unpredictable. However, the dates are close enough to be very useful. I live in Zone E, for instance, and only 1 year in the past seven have we had a spring frost later than May 1. If your location is borderline, split the difference between the dates for the adjacent zones.

In the western states there is no uniformity in the frost dates, owing to the effect of the Rockies and the Sierra Nevada on climatic conditions. Sample dates are given in the two maps illustrating some of the extreme variations. Planting dates must therefore depend upon local conditions in these regions; from the sample dates or personal experience decide which zone you would be in if you lived in the Middle West or East, and use the corresponding planting dates for this zone.

It is very important to keep these frost dates in mind when you plan your garden work, if you wish your annuals to grow to their maximum capacity.

In the spring, hardy annuals can be sown two weeks before the first date in the spring chart (for example about April 1 in Zone E although up to April 15th is usually all right). Half-hardy annuals must not be frostbitten, so delay sowing them until the second of the two dates (May 1st in Zone E). Tender annuals need warm weather, which as a rule is about two weeks after the second date (May 15th in Zone E).

The average dates of the earliest fall frost are important

to bear in mind if you live in a section of the country where the summers are short. If you can expect a fall frost before the first of October, there is no point in planting tender annuals like .late Asters and Cosmos (unless you start them indoors or in the coldframe)—they either will not have time to bloom at all, or the blooming period will be too short to bother with. The fall frost dates should also be consulted for hardy annuals that are to be fall planted; these should not be actually sown until just before the first fall frost date so that they will remain dormant and not germinate until spring.

Some catalogues and books advise guiding your planting by other methods, such as by watching maple trees and when they first start to leaf, plant hardy annuals and so forth. In my experience no two maple trees are entirely uniform in their leafing habits. There is some talk too about using the moon as a guide. I was going to say some monkeyshines but maybe that is a little strong; nobody can say for sure just what the effect of the moon is on the weather, and I'd be the last one to pose as an authority on such a dubious question. But I do know that after extensive experiments, there does not seem to be much evidence to support planting by moon cycles. Anyway, you are reasonably safe with zone maps, and there is no hocus-pocus about them.

All annuals are not equally particular about when they are planted. Some hardy annuals *must* be planted early, especially in sections of the country where the summers are hot, for example, Sweet Peas and Calendulas. Other hardy annuals can be planted later, though the plants will not be as large as from early sown seeds, and the flowers not as numerous.

However, if in any year for some reason you cannot garden at all until late May or early June, then the trick is to plant quick blooming annuals which will germinate and grow even in hot weather. Soak the seed bed before planting, and if possible cover it with burlap to retain the moisture until the seeds are up. The flowers that will bloom at all will bloom very quickly then—Portulaca and annual Gypsophila in 3–4 weeks; Candytuft, Phlox, dwarf Zinnias, Alyssum, *Centaurea cyanus*, Hunnemannia and dwarf Marigolds in 5–6 weeks.

Care of the garden. At planting time and for a while afterwards, there is no point in deluding oneself into thinking that gardens do not require care. "Such gardens are not made, by singing: 'Oh, how beautiful!' and sitting in the shade." The main trouble with annuals will be weeds, which during the lush spring growing season will outrun the flowers if not checked. They not only look bad, but they use plant material and water which the plants should rightfully have. There are various so-called weed killers available—all you have to do theoretically is sprinkle them around and the weeds will be killed as they germinate—but I cannot vouch for them. There is also an instrument called a Killer Kane which kills dandelions and broad leaf weeds on contact. But for the average flower gardener you face the facts of life and remove your weeds by hand.

If you are conscientious and go over the garden weekly with a cultivator, weeds are not too much of a problem since they do not have a chance to get obstreperous. Annuals are shallow rooted and the cultivation should not be more than an inch deep. There are theories which tend toward the belief that you cultivate only for weed control and not also to form a surface dust mulch, so obviously no weeds (which may happen during a dry summer spell) means no cultivating.

If you want to save yourself the trouble of cultivating, you can mulch your garden when the plants are all set and the soil moist. Mulching, which consists in placing a layer of some material such as straw around the plants, is an excellent practice with only one drawback—most mulches do not enhance the appearance of the garden. Grass clippings quickly dry out and look strawy, and hay and straw show up too prominently. I have tried buckwheat hulls; they are tiny, clean, weed free, easy to handle, and a dark brown color that looks even better than plain soil. They are fine for a small bed but somewhat expensive for a large area. Peat is also good because it has a high water-holding capacity, and cocoa shells are also good. However one way to avoid both mulching and weeding is to place annuals closely enough together so that when they are well grown they will shade the ground and only a few die-hard weeds will appear.

Although many annuals will normally flower without being watered, if there is a prolonged period of drought or the soil is very dry, it is best to water them to obtain proper growth. There is a common misconception that watering means sprinkling the flowers lightly once or twice a day. In reality, this is almost worse than no water at all, because it brings the roots to the surface, and the plants may topple over or the roots get destroyed when you cultivate.

In proper watering, the soil should be soaked so that the water penetrates about 6 inches deep.

Although annuals do not require fertilizing, most of them will benefit from an application or two of any standard commercial fertilizer. Use a pound for 15–20 feet of row, sprinkling the fertilizer around the plants. You can also apply manure water, made from a dried packaged manure; although fresh manure is often recommended, it is so full of weed seeds that it is an absolute menace.

Annuals are so seldom bothered by insects or diseases that no general discussion is needed; in the few cases where there is a problem it is mentioned in the section dealing with the individual flower.

Fall work. There are many advantages to fall gardening. The summer heat is over, weeds grow slowly if at all, and the winter resting period is ahead for many of us when we cannot do any gardening at all. The two phases of fall gardening are soil preparation and seed sowing.

SOIL. The first step in preparing the ground for the winter is thorough weeding. If you have been an assiduous gardener all summer, you will not have any weeds to remove. But intense summer heat and vacations often mean neglected gardens, and in that case the weeds should be pulled out before frost. Leaving them in delays spring planting, since you will not be able to get rid of the weeds until the frost is all out of the ground, but you can plant some hardy seeds before then. The weeds also will be able to ripen and drop their seeds, and there is a harsh but true saying which goes: "One year's seeding, nine years weeding." There is also a special sort of pleasure in fall weeding, because once you have cleared a place it stays clear, unlike in spring and summer when weeds literally spring up overnight.

After the weeding is done you can fold your hands until the first frost kills most of your flowers, and then the ground should be turned over to a depth of 6–8 inches. Deep digging is not needed, but some digging exposes many diseases and insects to freezing and thus eliminates them. The parts of the garden that you are planning to use for annuals that have to be sown early in the spring can be raked and left smooth for the spring.

SEED SOWING. In parts of the country where severe winters are the rule, many people do not realize that annual seeds can be fall planted. Actually, hardy annuals when planted in the fall often produce earlier and stronger plants than spring sown seed; Larkspur and Cornflowers are instances. In temperate climates, many annuals are fall sown for winter and early spring flowering. By fall sowing, just what time during the fall do we mean? As a rule the time to plant is after the ground is frozen. The seeds are broadcast on the surface, and will not germinate until spring. For some reason I do not understand, these seeds which winter over outdoors will germinate earlier and produce better plants than even the earliest sown spring seeds. This spring, for example, I planted Larkspur seed outdoors just as soon as the snow had gone and at least two weeks before the last frost date—about April 1st in Zone E—in the bed in which I had had Larkspur the year before. In June, the plants from the self-sown seeds were 5 feet tall with 7 and 8 flowering branches—the newly planted seedlings were still only 8 inches tall.

Many of the very hardy annuals, which are cold weather plants, require fall sowing in warm sections of the country, and do best when fall planted anywhere. The seed should be planted thickly because some of it will rot or wash away. Some of the annuals which give excellent results when fall sown are: Larkspur, Shirley Poppies, Eschscholzia, *Centaurea cyanus,* Calendula, Calliopsis, Phlox, Candytuft, Godetia and Nemophila. Other annuals which are successful in most parts of the country are: annual Chrysanthemums, Clarkia, Alyssum, Anchusa, Cynoglossum, Didiscus, *Euphorbia variegata,* Kochia, Nicotiana, and Nigella.

Tools. It is impossible to be arbitrary about tools. Every seasoned gardener has a favorite for certain jobs, and you have to find out which tools suit you best. Tool buying is a fascinating business and all gardeners constantly fall for some new gadget supposed to take all the work out of gardening, and which usually is tried once and then left to collect rust in a forgotten corner of the shed. Gardening results are achieved by honest sweat and an occasional backache; the most important tools are a pair of hands which will not hesitate over earthy fingernails. Home gardening will never be mechanized.

However, for basic garden activities, a suitable tool is needed for each. In some instances there is not much choice. You can only water the garden with a hose or a watering can. In other cases, such as cultivating, there are a number of possibilities, and I can only tell you what I have found most satisfactory and state the other choices. Fundamentally, the same tools are needed for a small garden as for a large one. Also, I do not believe there is much difference between tools that men would use, and those for women, in spite of the somewhat condescending way some are labelled "ladies size." *Better Homes and Gardens* had an article on "Favorite Garden Tools," written by twelve men gardeners who know the field, such as the president of the Men's Garden Clubs of America. While there was a considerable diversity of opinion, only one specified a tool that would be fairly heavy for a woman to use for any length of time. So don't let the term "ladies size" put you off; the chances are the lighter tool is just as effective and a lot easier to use.

The following is my list of tools for essential operations in the flower garden. You will obviously need a mower for your lawn and various cutting and pruning tools for trees and shrubs. At the back of any good catalogue from a seed or hardware store, you can find all the other miscellaneous tools—good, bad and indifferent—you can and undoubtedly will spend your money on.

DIGGING. The soil in a garden (unless it is a perennial border) is usually turned over in the spring and fall. For this job, you can use a spade or a spading fork, and opinion is divided as to which is better. I prefer a spading fork with the standard four flat tines; it does a good job of penetrating the ground and is easier to use in breaking up clumps of earth.

CULTIVATING AND WEEDING. For large cutting gardens, planted in straight rows, many gardeners swear by a wheel hoe which can be pushed along at a steady walk. Others use a scuffle hoe, which has a very sharp blade about 6 inches wide; it is pushed along just below the surface of the soil and decapitates the weeds. Using a scuffle hoe is a good way to do a speedy job, if your weeds have got ahead of you, but the trouble is that the weed roots are left in the ground, to send up new tops. The only way to weed successfully is to get the whole weed out. I use a tool which is sometimes called a cultivator hoe and sometimes a potato hook. I have two sizes, one small with three prongs, one large with five prongs, and do practically all of my cultivating and weeding with one or the other, depending on how close the work is. They loosen the soil and pull weeds out by the roots, all without disturbing the soil too deeply.

RAKING. Two kinds of rakes are needed. For general light cleaning up and cleaning out leaves and trash, a steel Brume rake is best and lasts far longer than the formerly popular bamboo rakes. For heavy raking to remove stones from the soil, for smoothing the ground in the spring, and for putting the garden to bed in the late fall, a steel garden rake is necessary. The regular size has 14 or 16 teeth. The small or "ladies size" with fewer teeth is useful for odd corners.

TRANSPLANTING. For transplanting and setting out plants and bulbs, a trowel is needed. It is best to have two, with wide and narrow blades. However, one will do. There are cheap trowels but they soon twist out of shape. A

$2.00–$3.00 forged steel trowel which will last for years is more economical. There are various dibbles on the market for making holes. One's finger or a stick works just as well.

CLIPPING AND CUTTING. No annuals need pruning, but the garden needs constant snipping here and there to keep it neat. I find that a pair of hedge shears and a pair of pruning shears are ample for trimming the edges of beds and for cutting off dead flowers and stems.

TRASH COLLECTING. A great deal of material has to be taken out each year from the garden for disposal. A wheelbarrow is usually needed for early spring and late fall work. During the summer I much prefer a light two-wheeled cart with rubber tires. Grocers' bushel baskets are useful and easy to carry around.

GARDEN BASKET. To carry small tools and various supplies, a garden basket with a handle is essential. Otherwise you will spend a great deal of time looking around for what you have mislaid. In mine, I always keep pruning shears, a small three-prong hand cultivator, trowels, labels, cord, scissors, and pencil and paper for notes. And, of course, seed packages at planting time.

WATERING. In all sections of the country where the summers are hot and dry, watering is essential if you want your flowers to flourish. If you have only a few beds, you can do this with a watering can. A large garden will need a hose, with an adjustable nozzle. Actually, the best way to water flower beds is to use "oozer hose," which is made of canvas, 2 inches in diameter, and comes in 18', 30' and 50' lengths. Lay this hose among the flowers, and the water seeps out, thoroughly soaking the soil without any possible damage to the flowers. For general use, plastic hose is highly satisfactory and is much lighter than rubber hose, although not quite as flexible.

SPRAYING. This is not much of a problem with annuals. A small bellows blower for dust insecticides and a hand sprayer for solutions will be sufficient. A flit gun is quite adequate as a hand sprayer for annuals.

CARE OF TOOLS. Many garden books recommend oiling tools after each use, and other good practices for which the average gardener never has the time or the willpower. Frankly, I oil my tools once a year. During the gardening season I keep them under cover and reasonably dry, and just rub off any soil that accumulates. One day in January or February when we have a thaw and I long to work in the garden and can't, I rub the tools with oil and put a coat of fresh red paint on the handles. The red paint is a good stunt—it protects the wood, and makes it easy to find tools you will probably leave around the garden.

Removing rust can be something of a task. People who suggest sand paper and kerosene, I am sure have never tried actually doing this themselves. It takes forever and doesn't work any too well. There are various rust removers on the market. Just follow the manufacturer's directions. Then dry, cover with oil, and you're all set.

AGERATUM

Ageratum [a-jur-ray′-tum]. *Ageratum houstonianum (A. mexicanum). Compositae* family. This plant originated in tropical America, and about 30 species are known.

History. The name comes from the Greek meaning "not old age," referring to the great length of time that the plant continues to flower without changing. Common names are Tassel-flower, Floss-flower, and Painter's Brush. A native of Mexico, the seeds were taken to England in 1822 by a Mr. Bullock, the proprietor of a London museum, who, with considerable temerity for those days, took a trip through Mexico. The first cultivated plants were raised in a London botanical garden, and are described as being 1½–2 feet tall, much branched, with light blue flowers.

Description

HEIGHT: Dwarf varieties 4–9 inches
            Tall varieties 18–24 inches

PLANTING DISTANCE: Dwarf varieties 6 inches apart
      Tall varieties 12 inches apart
COLOR: Blue, white and pink
TYPE: Tender
GERMINATION TIME: 6–10 days
SEED TO BLOOM: 9–12 weeks
BLOOMING PERIOD: Continuous from the first flowering until
  frost
IS INDOOR OR COLDFRAME START REQUIRED? Coldframe planting
  is advisable because Ageratum takes a relatively long time
  to bloom, but it is not necessary
CAN BE TRANSPLANTED: Yes
SELF-SOW: Yes
FALL SOW: No, except in the South

There are two types of Ageratum. One is of medium height, well-branched, with long-stemmed flowers which are good for cutting. The other is a dwarf plant with a very neat, erect, upright habit of growth, and this is the one most generally grown. In fact, of the dozen or so varieties listed in seed catalogues, only two are tall—a tall blue and a tall white. Ageratum flowers have fluffy, tassellike, ball-shaped heads 1–2 inches in diameter which grow in clusters well above the foliage. They have a very mild fragrance. The dwarf varieties are compact and have many flowers on short stems. The tall varieties have a more scattered bloom. The leaves are opposite, small, heart-shaped, and have a good deep green color.

The characteristic color of the flowers is a so-called blue, which is actually a violet-blue with a strong lavender tinge, and in different varieties ranges from a pale to a very deep color. There are also white and pink varieties. The white is misty, rather than clear and bright. The tall whites are rather nice for cutting; the new dwarf hybrids are good for edging instead of the more usual white Alyssum. The pink is a deep rose-pink—not a light salmon as some catalogues state. In my garden pink Ageratum is much slower to bloom than the blue, and does not flower nearly as freely; here again there are far more effective pink annuals. There are two yellow-flowering plants which are sometimes mis-named Ageratum. One is *Eupatorium Lasseauxii,* which is similar in plant habit to the tall Ageratum and has pale buff, rather dirty looking flowers. What is called Golden Ageratum is in reality *Lonas indora,* and has small mustard-colored flowers. Neither of these yellow, so-called Agera-tums seem to me worth bothering with. Blue Ageratum, however, has a very definite place in the garden because there are so few long-flowering blue annuals (or perennials either for that matter); and the plants flower so freely and continuously that they give a lovely solid blue effect for months.

Classification and recommended varieties. The two types, already described, are the dwarf and the tall.

DWARF: Many people who have purchased Ageratum seeds or plants for edging without knowing much about varieties have been disappointed because the plants grow too tall. The dwarf varieties, unless carefully chosen, have a tend-ency to get out of hand and exceed the stated catalogue height. Varieties must be chosen carefully for color also, to get a good deep blue rather than a pale anemic one.

BLUE BLAZER. F_1 hybrid, very early blooming. Uniform plants 4–6 inches tall. Quantities of flowers cover compact domes. Makes a lovely border.

MIDGET BLUE. All-American. True dwarf plants 4–5 inches high, smothered with flowers of a good color.

BLUE MINK. Larger flowers and plants than the preceding two varieties. Free blooming and strong upright plants.

ROYAL BLAZER. Stunning new real royal purple flowers on dwarf 5-inch plants. Park's.

PINKIE. The only available pink variety, dwarf light pink, holds color best in light shade. Park's.

SUMMER SNOW. Dwarf white F_1 hybrid with the same size, vigor, earliness, and uniformity as BLUE BLAZER.

TALL: There is not much selection here.
BLUE CHIP. F_1 hybrid, tallest (1 foot) and most vigorous of the hybrid Ageratums. Same profusion of bloom as BLUE BLAZER but the flowers are larger.
TALL WHITE. Not often listed. Burnett has it called MEXICANUM ALBUM and Park's has blue and white mixed.

Culture. Ageratum is very easy to grow. It will flower in almost any kind of soil, and in a wide range of climate. However, since it is a tender annual—which means late planting and 9–10 weeks before flowering—if you plant it right in the garden (May 1st–May 15th in Zone E for example) you cannot expect full flowering until fairly late in the season. So the best procedure is to plant seeds in the coldframe 6 weeks before the outdoor planting date, or buy a flat or two of seedlings from a nurseryman. I would advise the coldframe so that you can be sure of getting the variety you want. Ageratum reseeds prolifically and after the first year you will have self-sown plants of your own. The only difficulty is that Ageratum plants when young look so much like the equally prolific weed Galinsoga (which germinates about the same time) that it is almost impossible to tell them apart. If you are ambitiously trying to keep all your weeds down, the chances are that you may dig up most of your self-sown Ageratum seedlings.

In the autumn, young plants started late in the season can be put in pots indoors and will flower for several weeks.

When to plant. These are the earliest safe dates for sowing seeds in the garden or setting out plants. (See page 282 for

Spring Frost Zone Map.)

Zone A	March 1 –March 15
Zone B	March 15–April 1
Zone C	April 1 –April 15
Zone D	April 15 –May 1
Zone E	May 1 –May 15
Zone F	May 15 –June 1
Zone G	June 1 –June 15

Seeds should be planted in the coldframe or indoors 6 weeks earlier than the above dates.

How to plant. In the coldframe, sow the seed in a straight row and cover with $\frac{1}{8}$ inch of soil. Do this about 6 weeks before the dates given above, and leave alone until time to transplant into the garden. The seedlings are very sturdy and do not grow quickly, so crowding will not bother them. You can get literally dozens of plants from a 2–3 foot row in the coldframe. If sown right in the garden, thin or transplant about 6 weeks after sowing.

Care and cultivation. Ageratum is not a bit fussy, and requires only good routine garden care. If planted closely together, the plants soon branch enough to cover the ground and need little weeding. It is a good idea to cut off faded flowers so that the solid blue effect will not be marred.

Uses and planting combinations. Ageratum is used principally for edging and bedding; also for window boxes and pot culture.

EDGING. Blue ageratum can be used alone, or the total blue effect can be broken by patches of pink or white flowers, such as pink Ageratum, Alyssum CARPET OF SNOW, Verbena CHRYSTAL or DELIGHT.

It makes a suitable edging for beds with white, lavender, purple, pink and rose flowers and these beds are especially attractive if a few light yellow flowers are used for contrast such as canary yellow Snapdragons, yellow Zinnias, or lemon-yellow Marigolds. The violet-blue of Ageratum does not blend well with bright reds, and although it is often used with orange Marigolds, to me it is not a pleasing color scheme.

Possible bedding flowers to edge with Ageratum Dwarf Blue Blazer or Midget Blue are:
Asters. Any colors.
Cosmos. White and pink.
Dianthus. Salmon and white.
Larkspurs. All colors.
Nasturtiums. CHERRY-ROSE with background of white Zinnias.
Pansies and/or Violas. Blue, white, purple and yellow.
Petunias. WHITE JOY, PINK JOY, and MOON GLOW.
Petunias. CASCADE series WHITE, CORAL, ROYAL and BICOLOR.
Phlox. Tall chamois, rose, yellow and white.
Scabiosa. BLUE CORAL and SILVER MOON, or mixed colors.
Snapdragons. White, light pink, canary yellow, and ROCKET
     red.
Verbenas. Salmon-pink, white, lavender, royal blue.
Zinnias. LILLIPUT—flesh-pink, white, salmon-rose, canary-yel-
     low.

BEDDING. Ageratum BLUE BLAZER is excellent for solid beds, especially if there is a green background or wall behind the bed. Space the plants about 10 inches each way, and your bed will be a mass of misty blue all summer. If the bed is not too large, cover it with burlap or an old sheet if a light frost is expected on early fall nights, and you can extend the blooming period until hard frost.

Possible bedding combinations are:

Ageratum BLUE BLAZER, SUMMER SNOW and PINKIE, middle
Petunias SUNBURST, background ORCHID Snapdragons.

Ageratum BLUE BLAZER, SUMMER SNOW and PINKIE, middle
Petunias SUNBURST, background orchid ROCKET Snapdragons.

Ageratum ROYAL BLAZER, middle Petunias GLACIER, background Zinnias ELDORADO.

ALYSSUM

Alyssum [a-liss'some]. *Cruciferae* family. As many as 100 species are known in middle Europe, the Mediterranean region, and the Caucasus.

History. The name comes from the Greek meaning "not rage," and common names for the plant are Madwort, Sweet Alice, Heal-dog, and Heal-bite. The rage or madness they were supposed to cure was not insanity but the rage brought on by a dog's bite, and Gerarde calls them: "A present remedie for them that are bitten of a mad dogge." Vernon Quinn says that although it was believed that Alyssum would cure hydrophobia, the ancients used it merely to cure hiccoughs, and in Southern Italy a spray of Alyssum was kept in the house to prevent devils from entering, and as a charm against the Evil Eye.

Description
HEIGHT: Dwarf varieties 3–5 inches
     Tall varieties 10–12 inches
PLANTING DISTANCE: 6–8 inches apart

COLOR: White, purple and pink
TYPE: Very hardy
GERMINATION TIME: 5–10 days
SEED TO BLOOM: 5–6 weeks
BLOOMING PERIOD: Usually from the first flowering until frost
IS INDOOR OR COLDFRAME START REQUIRED? No
CAN BE TRANSPLANTED: Yes
SELF-SOW: The white varieties do self-sow, but the seeds of the purple varieties do not live over the winter and therefore do not reseed themselves
FALL-SOW: The white varieties can be fall-sown

Alyssum is a low-growing, spreading, branching plant with numerous small terminal-clustered white or purple flowers which grow above the foliage and give the effect of a solid mass of color. The small leaves are about 1½ inches long, light green, and lance shaped. Annual Alyssum is generally called Sweet Alyssum, yet it is the tall variety, *Alyssum maritimum,* which is the most fragrant or "sweet" Alyssum. Gertrude Jekyll calls it "a pleasant scent, though it is nothing remarkable," and it is true that the scent is mild and unobtrusive.

Classification and recommended varieties. White Alyssum is available in two types of plant. The dwarf, low-growing 3- to 5-inch type is the best for edgings. The original tall *Alyssum maritimum,* which is about a foot high, is fragrant, and good for general border use.

CARPET OF SNOW is the popular standard dwarf variety, 3–5 inches tall and about a foot across, completely covered with tiny white flowers. NEW CARPET OF SNOW is supposed to be a superior strain which is only 3 inches high and stays extra dwarf all summer. TINY TIM is earlier and spreads less, 3 inches and compact.
VIOLET QUEEN. Dwarf violet, 5 inches, compact plants that are free-flowering.

ROYAL CARPET. All-American Selection. Purple with light centers. 3 inches tall and 10–12 inches across. Best sown where expected to bloom.

ROSIE O'GRADY. All-American Selection. Masses of deep rose-pink flowers which do not fade in the summer. 3 inches tall and a good companion for ROYAL CARPET and CARPET OF SNOW.

Culture. Alyssum is of the easiest possible culture. It germinates and flourishes under almost any conditions, tolerating both cold weather and hot, dry summers. It is very hardy and can be planted very early in the spring; one year I sowed seeds on March 23rd to edge a border of Sweet Peas which were sown at the same time, and the Alyssum was blooming by May 30th. Alyssum can also be sown any time during the spring and summer. It flowers in 5–6 weeks, starting to bloom when the plants are very small. In some climates even the early-sown plants will continue to bloom until frost. In the South early spring-sown plants may bloom out in the hot summer, and a later planting is needed to keep a continuous flowering.

When to plant. Where winters are severe, Alyssum can be planted outdoors as soon as the ground can be worked, which is usually about two weeks before the last frost date. It can also be sown any time during spring and early summer, or in fall for very early spring flowering. I usually have self-sown seedlings blooming in the garden by the middle of May which shows how very early the seeds germinate in spring. In temperate climates, Alyssum can be planted any time during the year.

These are the earliest dates for planting seed in the garden: (see page 282 for Spring Frost Zone Map)

Zone A   Feb. 1   –Feb. 15
Zone B   Feb. 15 –March 1

Zone C	March 1 –March 15
Zone D	March 15–April 1
Zone E	April 1 –April 15
Zone F	April 15 –May 1
Zone G	May 1 –May 15

How to plant. Just broadcast the seed rather thickly on the surface of the ground; Alyssum should usually be planted in masses. It does not need to be covered. It can be thinned if you wish, but I seldom bother. The plants spread, so if you do thin them, allow about 6 inches each way.

Cultivation and care. If the seed is sown quite thickly, the small plants quickly cover the surface and no cultivation is needed; even the weeds are crowded out. Some hand weeding will be needed for the first three or four weeks, but after that they require very little care. If they have been flowering for a long time, and begin to bloom themselves out, cut them back with scissors to encourage fresh branching and new flowering.

Uses and planting combinations. Alyssum is used for edging, bedding, to cover sunny banks, for pots, terraces, and as a quick filler for rock gardens. For terraces, just plant a few seeds between whatever stones you have, and the plants will bloom even in sand; to prove just how lusty Alyssum is, I have even seen it growing out of rocks! A further use is for indoor winter blooming. Just sow some seeds in a flower pot in the fall and keep it in a sunny window. I have seen such a pot used for decorating a dining-room table in March; there was an 8-inch spread of flowers and it looked so springlike that I recommend this to anyone who longs for garden flowers in winter, and gets no satisfaction from an expensive bunch of florist's fare.

EDGING. This is by far the most popular use of Alyssum, and white Alyssum can be used with almost any other flowers. The following list is only partial, since possible planting combinations are almost endless. The purple must be used with more discretion. It is a bright, harsh purple but since the flowers are small, the general effect is not as harsh as the individual flowers would indicate. One seed catalogue shows a pleasing colored photograph of purple Alyssum bordering white Petunias (SNOW-STORM). I do not like purple Alyssum used alone, but it has its definite uses combined with white Alyssum (CARPET OF SNOW), to edge a bed containing white, pink, rose, blue, purple or yellow flowers. Either the two kinds of seed can be mixed together before planting, in a ratio of about 4 parts white seed to one part purple. Or you can alternate the two, with 5 or 6 feet of the white and about a foot of the purple as I first saw it growing in the gardens of the Agricultural Experiment Station in Bermuda; i edged a bed of mixed Larkspur, and was most attractive.

Possible beds to edge with Alyssum Carpet of Snow are:
Ageratum BLUE BLAZER, background Cleome PINK QUEEN.
Bush Balsam ROSE (actually shell-pink).
Background—Cleome PINK QUEEN; middle ground—Nasturtium CHERRY ROSE.
Calendula FLAME, LEMON and CREAM BEAUTY, Cynoglossum FIRMAMENT.
Background—Morning-glories HEAVENLY BLUE; middle ground —Petunias white, salmon pink, crimson and bicolor.
Background—Tall yellow African or Cactus Flowered Zinnias; middle ground—mixed Dahlias double UWNIN'S HYBRIDS or single COLTNESS.

BEDDING. *Alyssum maritimum* is a nice plant for bedding, especially if it is used along a walk or around shrubs. It is fragrant and looks cool even on the hottest days.

Possible bedding combinations with this Alyssum are:
Bed of *Alyssum maritimum* edged with Snapdragons FLORAL
CARPET, or Marigolds SUNNY, or *Lobelia* CAMBRIDGE BLUE,
or Ageratum ROYAL BLAZER or Pansies BUTTERFLY
HYBRIDS.

Asters. Genus *Callistephus* [kal-lis'-tee-fuss]. *Compositae* family. There is only 1 species, originating in China.

History. The word Aster means star, while *Callistephus* means beautiful crown. Annual Asters often are called China Asters to distinguish them from the fall-blooming perennial asters which are quite different in flower form and growing habit. In 1731 a Jesuit missionary to China, Father d'Incarville, sent the first Aster seeds to the Royal Garden in Paris. The flowers were single, pale lavender or white, about 3 inches across and the plant was about a foot tall. Asters were well known in American gardens by about 1800, but it was not until around 1837 that numerous varieties having definite colors were available. The modern double Asters are about 50 years old, and since then hundreds of varieties have been developed; in fact there are so many types and varieties of Asters today that they are one of the most complicated of all annuals to classify; one wholesale seed house actually grows and sells 193 varieties and all seed catalogues list dozens of them. Twenty years ago China Aster seed had the largest commercial value of any flower, and it was the most important cut flower. Various diseases and insects trouble Asters so much now that their commercial value has lessened, but they are still among the top six most popular garden and florist's flowers.

Description

HEIGHT: **1–3 feet**

PLANTING DISTANCE: Early varieties 9–12 inches apart; late (tall) varieties 15 inches apart

COLOR: White, all shades of lavender (called blue in the catalogues) and purple, light pink to deep rose, red, yellow

TYPE: Tender

GERMINATION TIME: 6–10 days

SEED TO BLOOM: 12 weeks to 5 months

BLOOMING PERIOD: Mid-summer to frost, but only if two or more types are planted. Individual types bloom for about a month

IS INDOOR OR COLDFRAME START REQUIRED? Preferable in sections of the country where the summers are short since Asters take so long to produce flowers from seed

CAN BE TRANSPLANTED: Yes
SELF-SOW: No
FALL-SOW: No

Asters are so beautiful and are available in so many lovely colors and flower forms that everyone would like to grow them. However, as a New York State Agricultural Experiment Station Bulletin on Asters says: "The popularity often has been seriously challenged by the prevalence of plant diseases. The past history of the China Aster is composed of cycles in which its popularity has waxed and waned in accordance with the prevalence of some plant disease, although it was not always the same organism that was the limiting factor." The difficulties today in growing them are discussed in the culture section. Readers should be warned at the outset that it is not easy to grow good Asters in every part of the country. The thing to do is try them. I, for instance, never have any trouble with them in our particular soil, in Connecticut. If you encounter any of the Aster troubles, stop growing them for a year or two and then start again.

There are many types of Asters, all lovely, and varying in habit of growth, period of bloom, and flower structure. The plants are upright, with an attractive medium green foliage, and plenty of flowers which are borne at the end of the branches. Some of the plants have branches from the main stem, other varieties have several stems which are base-branching without laterals. The flowers are double and single, with a variety of petal form in the double group. Most of the standard varieties of double Asters have one of two flower forms: (A) the CREGO type has long, broad, flat-tipped, ribbonlike petals which curl and (B) has shorter, bushier pointed petals which are incurved with a slight swirl at the center. (Although a prevalent flower form, Type B has no special name.) The following illustrations show the difference between the two types.

ASTER - TYPE A or CREGO   ASTER - TYPE B

Both are attractive so the choice is a personal one. In addition to these two main double forms and the single one, there are some deviations which I call novelties and describe in the next section.

The color range is extensive and every color is attractive and blends well with other colors: white, palest pink through rose to a deep crimson, pale lavender (called blue) **to deep purple, one red variety, and yellow.**

It is sometimes difficult to buy the colors you want, and Gertrude Jekyll explains that for years she was hindered because of the inaccurate way they are described in seed lists since the descriptions are fanciful instead of correct. The customer has to learn a code in order to get the desired colors. The beautiful, pale silvery lavender China Aster is called "azure blue." A full lilac color is called "blue," and a full purple, "dark blue." The word blue should not be used in describing these flowers since there are no blue China Asters.

There are early, mid-season and late Asters. The early varieties bloom in about 12 weeks from seed, have shorter stems, fewer flowers and smaller plants than the late Asters which take 4–5 months to flower. The late varieties have beautiful large flowers but are not of much garden value in parts of the country where summers are short.

Classification and recommended varieties. Classifying Asters is a headache not only for the amateur gardener but also for the professional seed growers. In an attempt to do an adequate job of it myself, I have consulted at least half a dozen type-charts devised by people who specialize in Aster culture; yet none of these charts seemed completely clear to me. An Indiana Agricultural Experiment Bulletin says: "Many attempts have been made to organize all Aster varieties into definite classes. However, changes have and are still coming about with such rapidity that it is impossible to construct a satisfactory classification, especially if an attempt is made to include all the recognized groups of the trade."

In my collection of seed catalogues there are 23 types of Asters and over 100 varieties. Not all catalogues list all types, but each one still has an appallingly large number of varieties. In an attempt to get some order out of chaos it is obviously essential to do some eliminating. On the other hand, it is also interesting to know something about the most commonly grown types. The chart which follows lists more Asters than most amateur gardeners would ever grow, but I hope it is clear enough to guide the reader into making a wise choice. At the end of the chart are some suggested lists for purchasing seeds.

In buying Aster seeds there are two main considerations. The first is the problem of wilt. In some localities wilt is so prevalent that it is foolish to buy anything but wilt-resistant seed; and unless you know you are going to be safe (a gardening neighbor can usually give you first-hand experience on this) you had better stick to wilt-resistant varieties.

The second consideration is blooming dates. Early

Asters, which usually start to bloom the beginning of July, will only flower for a few weeks and cannot be counted on to last until frost. But the late ones, although they have larger flowers on longer stems, often bloom too late to be of much use to anyone living in a locality where the first frosts come early in fall. Approximate blooming dates are given in the chart, and a Fall Frost Zone Map is on page 283. If you can expect only two or three weeks' bloom for the late types, better skip them and concentrate on the early and mid-season ones. Ideally, for a continuous season of Asters, you should plant early, mid-season and late varieties. In short summer localities, however, what I would suggest is this; choose one early and one mid-season type (EARLY DWARF QUEEN and AMERICAN BRANCHING or CREGO are good reliable ones), and each year try one or two of the novelties.

A word about the colors. The standard types of Asters are available in separate colors, and they are mostly the same ones; white, pink, rose, crimson, lavender, purple. They all blend well together and are good with the exception of the color called peach blossom which is almost white and completely without character. Some of the rose shades lean toward mauve-pinks, while others are more on the salmon side, so select your variety according to the color you prefer. Packages of mixed Aster seed are more satisfactory than those of most other annuals, but you will get better results buying by separate colors. The novelty Asters, as a rule, can only be procured in a very limited number of varieties or in mixtures.

The following chart is divided into two parts. The first group includes the standard types of Asters, arranged according to blooming dates. The second group I have called novelty Asters because their petal form differs from the usual CREGO and Type B formations.

Standard Asters

1. EARLY CHARM. Wilt-resistant. Early July.

The earliest flowering of all Asters, starting to bloom about the first week in July from seed planted outside the last week in April. Ostrich Feather type 3–4-inch blooms on 12–18-inch plants. Although the plant is short, the stems are long enough for cutting. Only in mixtures from Olds, Burnett and Stokes.

2. DWARF QUEEN. Wilt-resistant. Early July.

Another early Aster with uniform plants about 10 inches tall and 10 to 12 inches across, covered with fully double 3-inch Type B flowers. Useful for pots and window boxes, as well as for bedding. Park's and Harris have mixtures. Stokes has 7 colors: blood red, bright red, rose pink, dark blue, light blue, white, and yellow. Olds has 3: carmine, deep blue, and white.

3. PERFECTION. Wilt-resistant. Mid-August.

Some seedsmen consider this the best mid-season Aster. The large fully double flowers are up to 4 inches across and have broad overlapping petals which completely cover the centers. The plants are 3 feet tall with very long strong stems which make them excellent for both garden display and cutting. This is generally available in separate colors and Comstock, Ferre and Burnett have equally large selections. Crimson, mid-blue, purple, peach blossom, pink, rose, white.

4. CREGO (Ostrich Feather). Wilt-resistant. Mid-late August.

The CREGO type Asters differ from the others in petal structure, as described on page 54. The flowers are 4 to 5 inches across, the plants 2½ feet and branching. A very popular mid-season variety. For colors Park's has crimson, royal blue, shell pink, and white. Stokes has these and azure blue, dark blue, and rose-pink.

5. AMERICAN BRANCHING. Also called LATE BRANCHING, SEMPLE's or VICK's BRANCHING. Wilt-resistant. Late August or early September.

A very popular late Aster. The 2–2½-foot plants are branched with good long stems. The flowers are 3 to 4 inches across and Type B in form. The colors in the mixtures are white, pink, rose, azure blue and purple. Stokes' separate colors are azure blue, crimson, rose, purple and white. Olds' are white, blue, purple and shell pink.

6. AMERICAN BEAUTY. Wilt-resistant. Early September.

This Aster is much like the AMERICAN BRANCHING, with 3–4-inch flowers of the same form. Burpee has 3 colors: blue, scarlet, and white. Burnett has 2: MOONBEAM (lovely pure yellow) and SALMON QUEEN.

7. SUPER GIANTS. Wilt-resistant. Early-mid September.

A beautiful mid-late type with the largest and most fully double flowers, 5 to 6 inches across on 3-foot plants. The flowers are the Ostrich Feather CREGO form. Park's has 6 separate colors: azure blue, pure white, peach blossom, crimson, deep rose, and dark purple. Burnett also has six colors, one of them, LOS ANGELES (shell pink), which Park's does not have.

Novelty Asters

8. SINGLE GIANTS OF CALIFORNIA. Not wilt-resistant. September.

This type actually should not be called a novelty since it is an improved form of the original single Asters. But the double ones are so much more usual now that we are prone to forget these single ones, which are most attractive. The flowers are 3 to 4 inches across with broad daisylike petals surrounding a raised quilled yellow center. The 2-foot plants are branching. Sold only in mixtures which include salmon, crimson, light pink, lavender and purple flowers.

9. POWDERPUFFS (bouquet type). Wilt-resistant. Mid-season, usually August.

This is a new strain called bouquet type because the upright stems branch from the base so the whole plant can be cut to form a large bouquet with as many as 20 long-stemmed flowers. The plants are 2 feet tall. The medium size 3–3½-inch flowers are fully double with quilled high-crested centers surrounded by several rows of broad petals. Generally sold as mixtures, Stokes and Burnett have separate colors. Stokes: coppery rose, crimson, rose, scarlet, white, mid-blue and rose-pink. Burnett: azure blue, peach blossom, purple, rose, white and scarlet.

10. POMPON. Not wilt-resistant. Mid-season.

This is another bouquet type Aster. The well-rounded 2-inch flowers have quilled centers surrounded by a few rows of short, broad petals. The plants are about 2 feet tall. Stokes has 6 colors: purple, violet blue, white, red, SCARLET PIMPERNEL (scarlet with yellow centers) and LADY PIMPERNEL (crimson with white centers).

11. LADY SERIES. Wilt-resistant. Mid-late season.

PINK LADY was the first in this series and was called the most attractive new variety in recent years. Fine for cutting, the base-branching plants have very heavy 30-inch stems and beautiful extra-long incurved blooms. Stokes has 7 colors.

12. PRINCESS. Wilt-resistant. Late August.

Introduced in 1941, this form is decidedly well worth growing. The 3-inch flowers have a crested, quilled center surrounded by several rows of guard petals. The 2-foot plants are branching. Stokes has 9 varieties: PRINCESS ANNE (peach blossom), PRINCESS BARBARA (orchid), PRINCESS BONNIE (soft salmon rose, and a beautiful flower), PRINCESS LINDA (clear rose), PRINCESS MARSHA (cinnabar scarlet), GOLDILOCKS (pale yellow), PRINCESS MARGARET (rose), PRINCESS ELIZABETH (white) and PRINCESS PAT (brilliant crimson).

13. HEART OF FRANCE. Wilt-resistant. Late August.

Fully double large ruby-red flowers on long-stemmed 2-foot plants. This is a most popular Aster and the best red one ever introduced.

14. CALIFORNIA SUNSHINE. Wilt-resistant. Mid-September.

Many people consider this the loveliest Aster. The flowers

are very unusual looking with large, creamy-white quilled centers surrounded by a single row of ray petals of lavender or rose. The flowers are 4 to 6 inches across, and the plant 2–3 feet tall and well-branched. They bloom profusely, rather late.

Suggested Seed Orders

1. SIMPLE BASIC ORDER FOR ASTERS WITH TYPE B FLOWER FORM.
   1 package DWARF QUEEN, mixed
   1 package PERFECTION, mixed
   1 package CALIFORNIA SUNSHINE
2. SIMPLE BASIC ORDER FOR ASTERS OF CREGO TYPE.
   1 package EARLY CHARM, mixed
   1 package CREGO, mixed
   1 package SUPER GIANTS, mixed
3. FOR ALL SEASON ASTERS IN EARLY FALL FROST AREAS.
   1 package EARLY CHARM, mixed
   1 package each DWARF QUEEN bright red, light blue and yellow
   1 package each PERFECTION purple, pink and white
   1 package each CREGO shell pink and azure blue
   1 package each POWDERPUFFS scarlet, mid-blue and white
   1 package each PRINCESS BARBARA, BONNIE, ELIZABETH and GOLDILOCKS
4. FOR ALL SEASON ASTERS IN LATE FALL FROST AREAS.
   1 package EARLY CHARM, mixed
   1 package each DWARF QUEEN bright red, light blue and yellow
   1 package each PERFECTION purple, pink and white
   1 package each CREGO shell pink and azure blue
   1 package each POWDERPUFFS scarlet, mid-blue and white
   1 package PINK LADY
   1 package CALIFORNIA SUNSHINE
   1 package HEART OF FRANCE

Culture. When I said before that Asters are not easy to grow, it is not because of any difficulty in the actual culture —in fact Asters are easy to manage. The trouble lies in two diseases which attack Asters in many parts of the country and make it almost impossible to raise them. They are Fusarium Wilt and Aster Yellows.

FUSARIUM WILT. Caused by a soil-inhabiting fungus the spores of which can live in the soil for a considerable time. The fungus gains entrance through the roots and causes the plant to wilt, usually only on one side. The stem blackens, the diseased area turns dark, and the leaves curl up; ordinarily the entire plant finally dies. There is no known cure. If a dark streak appears on one side of your Aster stems, pull the whole plant up immediately and burn it. Wilt seems prevalent in some parts of the country and non-existent in others.

ASTER YELLOWS. This is a virus disease transmitted by leaf hoppers, those small yellowish green insects which suck the sap from the under side of the leaves. First the leaf veins turn yellow, then the new leaves look yellow and the plant is stunted and spindly with a rosetted appearance. Only half the plant is affected, but if flowers appear they are greenish and open unevenly. Here again only certain sections of the country are affected. Commercial growers grow Asters in cloth houses to keep the leaf hoppers off the plants but obviously that is no solution for the home gardener. Fortunately the new DDT sprays are said to be outstanding in their effects on leaf hoppers and should be tried. Pull up and burn any diseased plants. And as a safeguard against both these troubles, do not plant Asters in the same place more than once in three years.

Don't let this talk of diseases put you off trying Asters. Many people never have any trouble at all.

Asters take a relatively long time to bloom, but the period can be extended by starting seeds indoors six weeks before the outdoor planting dates. However, they do not actually need this early start.

When to plant. Outdoor planting requires careful timing with Asters. Trying to rush the season by early planting gets you nowhere because both the seeds and small plants stand still if the weather is cold or wet. There was a record-breaking wet May in 1948 and some Asters which I had started indoors and transplanted into the garden didn't do a thing for over a month. On the other hand, seeding should not be delayed because Asters take a long enough time to bloom anyway, and while late-planted seeds will produce flowers, both the plants and flowers will be dwarfed. In general, unless the season is late, 1–2 weeks after the last frost date should be a safe planting date. In California, the Burpee people plant April 1–April 15th. If early, mid-season and late varieties are all planted at the same time you should have continuous blooms from early August until frost.

Indoor planting should be done six weeks before the latest outdoor planting dates.

The earliest safe dates for planting seeds in the garden are: (see page 282 for Spring Frost Zone Map)

Zone A	March 1 –March 15
Zone B	March 15–April 1
Zone C	April 1 –April 15
Zone D	April 15 –May 1
Zone E	May 1 –May 15
Zone F	May 15 –June 1
Zone G	June 1 –June 15

How to plant. To plant seeds outdoors, cover with about ⅛ inch of soil, and thin or transplant when the first or second set of true leaves appear which should be in 2–3 weeks. Keep transplanted seedlings well watered for a few days because it is important that Asters should continue growing right along. For indoor planting see the general directions on page 17. The seeds germinate readily and the little plants are quite stocky, so do not plant too thickly.

Care and cultivation. Feed Asters once or twice during the growing season with a complete fertilizer to keep them growing at a good pace. Do not pinch them out since the central bud will have both the largest and the earliest flower. If any of the plants look sick, do not try to doctor them but pull up and BURN.

Uses and planting combinations. Because Asters bloom rather late, and no one type blooms for too long a time, the best use is in a cutting garden. Plant an early and a mid-season type, in the colors you like best, and one or more of the novelties, and you should have flowers for the house from early August until frost. PRINCESS PAT, PRINCESS BONNIE, SINGLE GIANTS OF CALIFORNIA and CALIFORNIA SUNSHINE are all unusual and lovely cut flowers.

Although the short blooming period rules asters out for solid bedding, they can be used in combination with other flowers.

Some suggested bedding combinations are:
Background—white, pink, and purple Larkspurs; middle ground—mixed CREGO and CALIFORNIA GIANTS ASTERS; edging—Ageratum Dwarf ROYAL BLAZER and Alyssum CARPET OF SNOW.
Background—Cleome PINK QUEEN; middle ground—white, pink, and lavender Asters (choosing varieties from the classification list); edging—Alyssum CARPET OF SNOW.
Background—Cosmos EXTRA-EARLY SENSATION PURITY; middle ground—white, lavender and purple Asters; edging— Alyssum CARPET OF SNOW and VIOLET QUEEN.
Mixed bed—Asters EARLY CHARM or DWARF QUEEN or PER-

FECTION mixed; tall blue, rose and white Scabiosa; blue Cornflowers; pale yellow Snapdragons; edging—white, yellow, and purple Violas.

Mixed bed—Asters CREGO, LADY series and CALIFORNIA SUN-SHINE; Petunias APPLE BLOSSOM, SNOW MAGIC, MERCURY and CALYPSO; edging—Alyssum CARPET OF SNOW; dwarf Phlox TWINKLES.

Calendula [ka-len′-dew-la] *officinalis. Compositae* family. About 15 species are known, coming chiefly from the Mediterranean area.

History. The name comes from the Latin and means "the first day of the month" referring to its early vigorous blooming. It is also called Pot Marigold and Scotch Marigold. Calendulas have been grown for centuries. Called the goldflower in Chaucer's time, it was a pot-herb used as a remedy for sore teeth and "as a comforter of the heart and spirits." The name became Mary's-gold slurred into Marigold during medieval days when as Vernon Quinn says: "Belief was strong in devils and demons and it was most convenient to associate plants with the Virgin Mary, to have them handy as a charm against the power of darkness." Marigold was also put to practical use and eaten; apparently a haunch of venison seasoned with it and mint, garnished with a chopped salad of wild onions and violets, was often served with a stew of roses and primroses at Knightly feasts—when Knights were bold.

Description

HEIGHT: Tall 18–24 inches, dwarf 6–12 inches

PLANTING DISTANCE: 12 inches each way

COLORS: Orange, yellow and a so-called apricot which is actually a light straw color

TYPE: Very hardy

GERMINATION TIME: 6–10 days

SEED TO BLOOM: 2–3 months

BLOOMING PERIOD: All summer until frost

IS INDOOR OR COLDFRAME START REQUIRED? No

CAN BE TRANSPLANTED: Yes

SELF-SOW: Yes, but not very freely, at least in my garden, and may revert to single flower

FALL-SOW: Yes

Calendulas produce sturdy plants 18–24 inches tall and a foot in width which remain upright and not straggly all summer. The leaves are oblong and a nice grayish green. The 3–4-inch flowers are borne singly on strong stems; since the plant branches freely there are plenty of flowers. The original Calendula was a 2-foot tall plant with single orange flowers. Today all varieties are double in a wide range of orange and yellow shades, some with self-centers and some with dark brown ones. Although catalogues also list a color optimistically called apricot, all the ones I have ever seen were a lifeless pale straw color. Calendulas have a pronounced characteristic odor which Gertrude Jekyll says: "can hardly be called sweet, though the strong smell is of a wholesome quality."

Classification and recommended varieties. The real considerations in choosing Calendulas are whether you want orange or yellow flowers, or both, and the color of the centers. The orange flowers are truly beautiful but more difficult to fit into some color schemes. There is a little diversity of flower form. Some varieties have flat flowers with light or dark centers (and the contrast provided by the dark centers is most effective); while in other varieties the petals are loosely arranged and curve over the center. The difference seems comparatively unimportant to me, and Calendulas are not generally divided into classifications. Recommended varieties are:

TALL. PACIFIC BEAUTY is the leading strain, superior to the older ones; the flowers are uniformly large with fine bright colors on long stems. They have a commendable tolerance for heat. 1½ feet.

FLAME BEAUTY. Deep orange

LEMON BEAUTY. Pure lemon yellow

APRICOT BEAUTY. Buff and apricot yellow

CREAM BEAUTY. Most delicately colored, cream yellow

BALL'S MASTERPIECE. Deep orange with dark centers. Burnett and Park's have 3 unusual varieties they term "outstanding."

DWARF. BURPEE. Compact and free-flowering. Masses of well-doubled 3-inch flowers, 1 foot tall. Ideal for bedding and growing in pots.

GOLDEN GEM. Golden yellow

ORANGE GEM. Mid-orange

DWARF SUNNY BOY. 6-inch plants, 3-inch flowers, fully double, bright orange. Park's.

Culture. The one vital factor in successful Calendula growing is early sowing. They are one of the easiest and most successful annuals if sown early enough in spring to get a good start while the weather is cool. They hate heat during the early stages of growth, and if sown in hot weather will not grow at all, or are poor and stunted. If sown about two weeks before the last frost date (since frost does not bother them) they will bloom in any soil from early summer to frost providing good garden display and plenty of cut flowers. In the very hot parts of the country, they are best fall-sown for early spring bloom, since they will not survive the summer.

When to plant. The following are the earliest safe dates for sowing seeds in the garden: (see page 282 for Spring Frost Zone Map)

Zone A	Feb. 1 –Feb. 15
Zone B	Feb. 15 –March 1
Zone C	March 1 –March 15
Zone D	March 15–April 1
Zone E	April 1 –April 15
Zone F	April 15 –May 1
Zone G	May 1 –May 15

Unlike many hardy annuals which can be sown either early or later in the season, if Calendulas are not planted by the latter of the above two dates for the appropriate zone, or a few days later, you might just as well not sow them. Seed sown last year in my garden on April 8th (Zone E) were in bloom by July 10th and continued until frost; there was some petering out and smaller flowers in September but the plants were still in bloom. Seed sown later for experimental purposes did nothing. I would advise against the practice sometimes suggested of making a late May or June sowing for fall flowers.

How to plant. Cover the seeds with ¼ inch of soil. Since they are being planted while the soil is still cold, the growth at first will be slow, but plants should be ready for thinning or transplanting in about a month. Although they transplant readily, the young plants tend to wilt quickly when first transplanted, so be sure they are well watered and try to do the transplanting on a cloudy day or shade them for two or three days if it is sunny.

Care and cultivation. Calendulas require only ordinary good garden care, cultivation for weed removal, and watering during excessively dry spells. They will not stop blooming if flowers run to seed, but like any annual, the plants will be stronger if they do not have to expend energy in seed production.

Uses and planting combinations. Can be used in a mixed border or as bedding plants. They are attractive plants to grow in a border a foot or so wide in front of a low stone wall.

Good bedding combinations are·
Calendulas FLAME, LEMON, APRICOT and CREAM BEAUTY with edging of Alyssum CARPET OF SNOW.
Calendulas LEMON BEAUTY and CREAM BEAUTY with edging of Ageratum dwarf ROYAL BLAZER.
Calendula FLAME BEAUTY and Calendula LEMON BEAUTY and *Centaurea cyanus* BLUE BOY. This is a particularly good combination. Both should be planted early and at the same time and will bloom almost simultaneously, although the Cornflowers will not last quite as long.
Calendula LEMON BEAUTY, edged with Marigold yellow SUNNY, with a background of Zinnia CRIMSON MONARCH, makes a very colorful bed.
Middle ground—Calendula LEMON BEAUTY, Zinnias LILLIPUT CRIMSON and WHITE, Snapdragons TETRA yellow, Petunia CANDY APPLE; edging—Pansy MOON MOTH.

Celosia [sell-o'-si-a]. *Amaranthaceae* family. Some 35 species are known in the tropical and temperate regions of Africa, Asia and America.

History. The name Celosia comes from the Greek meaning burned, and could refer to the brilliant red color of
some of the flowers, or to the dry, burnt look of some
species. The hideous crested blood-red Celosia or cockscomb was used extensively for bedding in the past century
and is the plant many people think of with a shudder
when the name Celosia is mentioned. Seed catalogues of
60 years ago listed only two varieties of the lovely plumed,
feathery Celosias, crimson and yellow and both tall. Since
then, the color range has been extended, and dwarf varieties are now available as well as a new flower form.

Description
Celosia plumosa and *Celosia cristata*
HEIGHT: Dwarf varieties 12 inches; tall varieties 2–3 feet
PLANTING DISTANCE: 1 foot apart for dwarf varieties, 18 inches
    for tall varieties
COLORS: Red, crimson, golden yellow, pink, terra-cotta
TYPE: Tender
GERMINATION TIME: 6–10 days
SEED TO BLOOM: About 2 months
BLOOMING PERIOD: All summer until frost
IS INDOOR OR COLDFRAME START REQUIRED? No
CAN BE TRANSPLANTED: Yes
SELF-SOW: Yes
FALL-SOW: No

There are two types of Celosia, *plumosa* and *cristata*.
Plumosa is unusual with attractive looking plants and a
place in the garden if used with care. *Cristata,* or the well
known Cockscomb, is so stiff and ugly that as far as I am
concerned it should never be grown anywhere. The usual
form resembles the shape of a cockscomb, although the texture is like plush or chenille.
    The plants of *C. plumosa* are erect and pyramidal, with
many long tapering leaves which vary from light green if

the flowers are yellow through darker green and bronze in the red-flowered varieties. There is a central flower and many more growing on long stems from the leaf axils. In fact, Celosia is so floriferous and the colors so brilliant that the plants look like a solid blaze of color. The flowers are like beautiful, soft, wavy plumes, which accounts for their name. The colors are all very definite and bright. The yellow is a deep golden buttercup-yellow, the crimsons and reds a flaming fire-engine red. There is nothing namby-pamby about these Celosias; they are striking, dramatic plants to be used judiciously for exciting effects. They can also be dried for winter decoration.

Types and recommended varieties. *Celosia plumosa* has two forms, a tall 2- 3-foot one, and a dwarf 1-foot form which can be used for edging a tall bed. The dwarf form has a good upright habit of growth and is compact and neat enough to make a satisfactory edging where a colorful one is needed. All of the following recommended varieties are separate colors because the mixtures contain such loud and often clashing colors that they are impossible to use except perhaps in a row hidden behind the garage to be cut for dried bouquets.

There are so few varieties that the following list is complete except for the mixtures.

C. plumosa (plume type). Extra dwarf or Lilliput.
 FIERY FEATHER. Fiery red. 12 inches.
 GOLDEN FEATHER. Deep yellow. 12 inches.
 SILVER FEATHER. Silver-white. 16 inches (Park's).
C. plumosa. Semi-dwarf. First class for bedding.
 RED FOX. All-American Selection. New color, glossy coral red with bright green foliage. 18 inches.
 CRUSADER. Brilliant red plumes with bronze foliage. 18 inches.

GOLDEN TORCH. Ideal companion for CRUSADER with the
same numerous plumes. Golden yellow with fresh glossy
green foliage. 18 inches.

C. *plumosa*. Semi-tall.

FOREST FIRE IMPROVED. Brilliant scarlet-orange plumes,
striking contrast to bronzy red foliage. 2–2½ feet.

GOLDEN TRIUMPH. All-American Selection. Golden yellow
with bright green foliage. 2½ feet.

C. *plumosa*. Tall.

Generally available only in mixtures. Park's has GOLDEN
FLEECE, golden yellow. 3 feet.

C. *cristata* (Cockscomb type). Extra dwarf.

JEWEL MIXED. 6 inches. Scarlet, crimson, gold, yellow,
copper, and pink.

C. *cristata*. Dwarf. 11 inches.

EMPRESS. Deep crimson, dark foliage.

GLADIATOR. Golden yellow

C. *cristata*. Semi-dwarf.

FIREGLOW. All-American Selection. Giant combs of scarlet-
orange. 20 inches.

FLORADALE. Scarlet-cerise. 16 inches.

TOREADOR. All-American winner. Bright crimson red. 18
inches.

ROSE EMPRESS. Bright deep rose. 15 inches. Burnett.

Culture. Celosias are almost fool-proof. They are so adaptable and undemanding that even without any attention they
will push through the weeds and flower. Of course, the
plants will be taller and bushier and the flowers larger if
they are cared for. Plant the seed after the last frost date,
in any kind of soil and climate, and the plant will bloom
in about two months and continue until frost. It also often
self-sows and is back in the garden the following year, although in Connecticut it does not seed itself enough to
become a nuisance.

When to plant. Celosia is classified as a tender annual, although it will germinate and grow when the weather is still cool, and the seeds can be planted 1–2 weeks after the last frost date. However, it is not fussy about heat and can be planted late in spring; I have sown seed as late as mid-June and the plants were flowering in 6 weeks.

The earliest safe dates for planting seed in the garden are: (see page 282 for Spring Frost Zone Map)

Zone A	March 8 –March 15
Zone B	March 22–April 1
Zone C	April 8 –April 15
Zone D	April 22 –May 1
Zone E	May 8 –May 15
Zone F	May 22 –June 1
Zone G	June 8 –June 15

How to plant. Sow the seed in the garden, cover with ¼ inch of soil, and thin or transplant when the seedlings have four or six leaves. Plants are bushy, and need more than the customary amount of space; dwarf ones should be spaced a foot apart, and tall ones 18 inches. They do best in soil that is not too rich.

Cultivation and care. The one important phase in their care is to give the plants plenty of room if you wish them to branch properly, and this means early thinning. Otherwise only routine garden care is necessary, but water if the ground is very dry.

Uses and planting combinations. Dwarf Celosia may be used as an edging, or in window or porch boxes; the tall ones for solid beds or in the middle area of a mixed border. FLAME OF FIRE makes a good temporary hedge. Celosia is better looking and easier to raise than the omnipresent red Salvia, and could be used to replace that as a bedding plant.

Possible bedding combinations are:

C. plumosa, FIERY FEATHER, edged with Alyssum CARPET OF SNOW.

C. plumosa, ROSE EMPRESS, edged with Portulaca WHITE JEWEL.

C. plumosa, GOLDEN YELLOW, edged with Ageratum BLUE BLAZER and Alyssum CARPET OF SNOW.

C. plumosa, SILVER FEATHER, edged with Portulaca JEWEL.

C. plumosa RED FOX, edged with Phlox WHITE BEAUTY.

Mixed ZENITH Zinnias YELLOW, WILD CHERRY, and CARVED IVORY, edged with *C. plumosa* GOLDEN FEATHERS.

Centaurea [sen-taw-ree′-uh] *cyanus. Compositae* family. 600 species are known, and it is native to Southern Europe, where it grows as a weed.

History. An old Greek doctor, Dioscorides, named this plant Centaurea because it was supposed to have cured a poisoned arrow wound in the foot of the centaur Chiron. Hercules picked some blue cornflowers, crushed and held them to the wound and Chiron was immediately cured. *Centaurea cyanus* (cornflowers) grow wild in European grain fields where they bloom with the crimson poppies. They are also called Ragged Sailors, bluets, and Bachelor's Buttons (a name they share with other flowers; Louise Beebe Wilder says that nearly all neat, rather small round flowers have been called at some time or in some locality Bachelor's Buttons).

Description

HEIGHT: Dwarf varieties 12 inches; tall varieties 18–30 inches
PLANTING DISTANCE: Dwarf varieties 6 inches apart; tall varieties 12 inches apart
COLOR: Blue, pink, red, dark maroon, white
TYPE: Very hardy
GERMINATION TIME: 5–7 days
SEED TO BLOOM: 6–8 weeks
BLOOMING PERIOD: Spring-sown seeds usually bloom until frost. Self-sown seedlings, which bloom early in the spring, are so floriferous that they bloom themselves out in 1–2 months
IS INDOOR OR COLDFRAME START REQUIRED? No
SELF-SOW: Yes, the blue ones do
FALL-SOW: Yes

There are five species of Centaurea which are commonly grown in our gardens. *Centaurea cyanus* is far and away the most popular, and will be discussed in detail here. The other four species will be treated more briefly.

The plants of *Centaurea cyanus* are upright, with small but numerous gray-green leaves. Flowers are an inch or so in diameter and borne in great numbers. The type flower is the blue one, which has become naturalized in certain sections of the country. There are also pink, red, maroon and white varieties. The blue ones seed themselves, and fall or self-sown seeds give the largest plants. The seed germinates very early in spring and if given sufficient space, at least a foot all around, the tall plants will branch freely and have literally dozens of flowers in bloom at one time. They start flowering here in Connecticut the end of May or early June and continue until around the middle of July. Because they are so very prolific the plant exhausts itself. Spring-sown seed blooms in about 6 weeks; they are not as tall as the earlier plants, and do not branch as much or flower as violently, but will last until frost.

The original Bachelor's Button was a single flower, but now all flowers are double. This is one instance where double flowers are an improvement over the single ones.

Classification and recommended varieties. There are two types of *Centaurea cyanus,* and only a few varieties, just one for each of the different colors, so the following list is a complete one.

TALL CENTAUREA. 5 varieties are available. The blue is far the best, and my second choice would be pink. The other colors do not make effective garden plants but if all the colors are planted, mixed bouquets are quite attractive.

BLUE BOY. Typical cornflower blue
PINKIE. Light pink
RED BOY. Deep red
SNOW MAN. White
BLACK BOY. Dark maroon

DWARF CENTAUREA was first introduced in 1937. The plants are about a foot tall, with a tufted habit of growth with all the flowers at the top of the plant, which is distinct from the spreading, loosely-branched growth of the tall ones. Sometimes recommended for edging, they are really almost too tall, but are good plants for the middle of a flower border.

JUBILEE GEM. All-American Selection. Masses of cornflower-blue flowers. Bushy 12-inch plants.

SNOWBALL. All-American Selection. Plenty of pure white double 1-inch flowers above the foliage, rounded uniform 1-foot plants. Stands up to hot summers better than other Bachelor Buttons, staying cool and crisp through the hottest weather.

POLKA DOT MIXED. Dwarf 15-inch bushy plants that stay neat and covered with flowers. Full range of Bachelor Button colors including blue, maroon, red, rose-pink, lavender and white.

Culture. There are no problems in the culture of *Centaurea cyanus*. It is hardy so can be sown in fall or early spring, or any time until mid-summer. Plants are vigorous and will thrive in any soil, even poor sandy ground. It never is troubled by disease or pests.

When to plant. Seed can be sown in fall, or any time in spring. Just scatter the seeds on the surface of the ground two weeks before the last frost date and they will quickly germinate. It is not fussy about heat so can be sown any time until July. However, the earlier the seed is sown the taller the plants will be and the more flowers they will produce. Seed sown, for instance, about the first of April will have plants twice as large as from seed sown in June. Although successive plantings are often recommended for continuous flowering, I find that my spring-sown plants bloom until frost. However, since fall- or self-sown plants bloom out, you need an additional spring planting if you want cornflowers all summer.

The earliest safe dates for planting seed in the garden are: (see page 282 for Spring Frost Zone Map)

Zone A	Feb. 1	–Feb. 15
Zone B	Feb. 15	–March 1
Zone C	March 1	–March 15
Zone D	March 15	–April 1
Zone E	April 1	–April 15
Zone F	April 15	–May 1
Zone G	May 1	–May 15

How to plant. The seed can be scattered on the surface of the ground which is the way self-sown seeds get planted. It is better though to cover them with $1/4$ inch of soil. This anchors the roots and gives the tall plants better support. Seed should be sown where it is to bloom since these plants do not transplant well. Proper thinning will give each plant ample space to branch well and reach its maximum possible size.

Care and cultivation. Centaureas take care of themselves and are the least demanding of plants. Since they yield an abundance of flowers, and since seed production is hard work for a plant, it is best to remove wilted flowers. But this will not keep self-sown seedlings from a relatively quick death; and my spring-sown ones obligingly go on blooming even if I don't get around to snipping off dying blooms. If you want some of the plants to self-sow you naturally will have to let some of the flowers go to seed on the plant.

Uses and planting combinations. Centaureas are best grown in combinations with other flowers rather than in solid beds. A row of BLUE BOY, PINKIE, RED BOY and SNOW MAN can also be planted in a cutting garden for small bouquets.

Suggested beds using Centaurea

Centaurea BLUE BOY and yellow and orange Calendulas. This
color combination is a very happy one, and both plants
are hardy and can be fall-sown for very early bloom.

Centaurea BLUE BOY and Eschscholzia *or* pink and white Shirley Poppies. If these are fall-planted around bulbs,
the plants will be blooming by the end of May and provide a brilliant display of color to help cover up the wilt-
ing bulb foliage. This is not an all summer bed however.

Centaurea BLUE BOY and PINKIE; mixed Asters PERFECTION
and AMERICAN BRANCHING; tall blue, rose and white Scabiosas; pale yellow Snapdragons; edging of white, yellow
and purple Violas.

Marigolds MAMMOTH MUM, GLITTERS, FANTASTIC ORANGE;
Centaurea BLUE BOY.

Verbena SALMON PINK and SNOWY WHITE; Centaurea JUBILEE
GEM.

There are four species of Centaurea besides *Centaurea
cyanus*, none as extensively grown but all different and
interesting in their own way.

Centaurea imperalis. SWEET SULTAN. These plants have
similar foliage to *C. cyanus* but the flowers are not at all
alike. Sweet Sultans have fluffy, tassellike flowers with a
shiny silky texture and a pleasant fragrance. The plant is
strong, bushy and about 2 feet tall. The color range is wide,
with 6 colors offered in separate varieties: AMARANTH RED,
BRILLIANT ROSE, DEEP LAVENDER, DEEP PURPLE, WHITE,
and YELLOW *(Suaveolens)*. The yellow is a clear bright
butter-color and very lovely. The seed should be sown
after danger of frost is past, where it is to bloom. They
will bloom in 6–7 weeks and in cool climates will continue
until frost.

Centaurea americana. BASKET-FLOWER. This is the tallest
and largest flowered-form of Centaurea. It is native to

Mexico and central southern United States. Plants are 3–4 feet tall and flowers 3–4 inches across—very beautiful feathery ones, mostly fringe. The color is lavender or white in the two available varieties. Although the flowers are attractive and unusual (a not too common association) the seed is not often listed, probably because the plants are not supposed to be as easy to grow as the other Centaureas. It is hardy and can be sown early in the spring, preferably where it is to bloom. It will bloom during July and August, and the plants I have seen were in bloom in September in Pennsylvania and were exquisite.

Centaurea candidisimma (kan-did-diss'-im-a) and *C. gymnocarpa* (jim-no-karp'-a) are both foliage plants, perennial in temperate climates but treated as annuals in severe ones, although sometimes they live over in Connecticut in Zone E. They are commonly called DUSTY MILLER, and both have very light silvery white leaves which provide an effective contrast with the flowers. *C. Gymnocarpa* has finely cut fernlike leaves, is about 2 feet tall, and the flowers are purple. *C. candidissima* is not quite as tall, with large thick oval leaves and sulphur-yellow flowers. Dusty Millers flower well in mild climates; the residential sections of Beverly Hills use them in quantities for landscape work and the plants are full of long-stemmed flowers. However, when they have to be grown as annuals the bloom is very late or never does arrive. Although the flowers are nice, the primary use of the Dusty Millers is for foliage, so the lack of flowers is not a serious drawback. Sow early in spring for best results. These plants will stand transplanting.

Cleome [klee-oh'-me]. *Capparidaceae* family. 70 species are known, originating in tropical and sub-tropical regions.

History. This plant is a native of the South American jungles, and an article in the National Geographic Magazine says its "pungent foliage suggests just a little of the primal and earthy odors so characteristic of its jungle home." The common name Spider Plant is derived from the spidery look of its wide-spreading stamens. It is now found wild in the western states and from North Carolina to Louisiana, and is often known in the West as the "Rocky Mountain Bee Plant." The wild plant has muddy, purplish pink flowers, quite unlike the clear light pink of the cultivated *Cleome spinosa*.

Description

HEIGHT: 3–4 feet
PLANTING DISTANCE: 3 feet
COLOR: Pink, yellow, and white
TYPE: Very hardy
GERMINATION TIME: 7–10 days
SEED TO BLOOM: About 2 months
BLOOMING PERIOD: Until frost
IS INDOOR OR COLDFRAME START REQUIRED? No
CAN BE TRANSPLANTED: Yes
SELF-SOW: Yes   (almost a nuisance)
FALL-SOW: Yes

Cleome is a most unusual looking plant. It is tall and much branched with a flower at the end of each of the long stalks. The plant flowers when quite small, and new petals form on the top of the stems while the old ones fade and die and long narrow seed pods develop which look like spiders' legs, hence the name Spider Plant. The flowers in the one variety almost exclusively grown are a pretty salmon-pink, the top petals being a deeper shade than the middle ones, and the old flowers fading to a very pale color. This variation in color is only noticeable when you look closely at the plant; from any distance the effect is a lovely misty pink. The leaves are dark green palmate, that is, lobed or divided in a palmlike fashion. The flowers are well above the foliage and always numerous. A most rewarding annual, it flowers and flourishes with no special demands or requirements. In fact the one possible drawback is that it seeds itself so freely as to become almost a pest. There is some diversity of opinion about the colors of these self-sown seedlings, most authorities claiming they all revert to the unattractive muddy pink of the wild species. My experience has been that you cannot count on them. Most of my self-sown plants have been a good pink color but occasionally I get one with the undesirable look. To be sure of your color scheme it is best to start every year with fresh seed.

Classification and recommended varieties. Only three varieties are in existence, and the pink is the only one that is grown to any extent. An occasional catalogue lists the yellow form. I tried seed this year and it never even came up—or at least, I don't think it did. I was erroneously looking for the same type plant as the pink form, while actually it is not at all similar as I found out when I saw a plant at a seed farm. The yellow form has a 6-foot tall, weedy looking plant, and small, golden yellow flowers which do not compare in interest to the pink ones; it does not seem worth growing to me. The white form is a sport of the pink one and is pure white with even larger, fuller heads than PINK QUEEN. Elizabeth Lawrence in *A Southern Garden* says that it is pure white, and one of the most beautiful of the heat-tolerant annuals, with a bold leaf pattern and domes of delicate, long-stamened flowers, that it grows 3–4 feet in height and spreads as much, that it self-sows, and that even the white self-sown seedlings come into bloom the end of June, continuing until hard frost.

PINK QUEEN is the standard pink variety. All-American

winner. Huge heads of delightful pink flowers. Grows to 4 feet tall.

Rose Queen is a Harris development. It is listed as an improvement of Pink Queen with a deeper and brighter color than the older varieties, and which fades less in summer heat. 3½ feet. Burpee also.

Helen Campbell. This is the white Cleome with large heads of white flowers. It is a good companion for the pink varieties.

Culture. If all flowers were as simple to raise as Cleomes, the gardener's life would be almost effortless. I should say that after the seed is once sown even a volcanic eruption wouldn't stop Cleome from growing into a lusty plant and flowering. The fact that you find self-sown seedlings producing flowers in poverty stricken, waterless soil proves this; I have seen it in bloom in soil that won't even grow weeds! So there are no culture suggestions needed. Just plant the seed and your work is done.

When to plant. Since Cleome is a very hardy annual it can be sown a week or two before the last frost date, and can also be sown any time during the spring. The following are the earliest safe dates for sowing seed in the garden: (see page 282 for Spring Frost Zone Map)

Zone A	Feb. 15 –Feb. 22
Zone B	March 1 –March 8
Zone C	March 15–March 22
Zone D	April 1 –April 8
Zone E	April 15 –April 22
Zone F	May 1 –May 8
Zone G	May 15 –May 22

How to plant. Cover the seed with about ¼ inch of soil, and when the plants have their first or second set of true leaves, thin or transplant to stand 2–3 feet apart. The young seedlings grow very rapidly. Do not delay transplanting too long, although they can stand being moved even when a foot or so tall.

Care and cultivation. Cleome blooms well without any attention at all, but the flowers will open more fully and look better if the plants are watered once a week during hot dry spells.

Uses and planting combinations. Because Cleome is a tall plant it is used as a background or bedding plant, and for either of these uses it is almost unexcelled. It is also good as a hedge, or for a mass planting in front of shrubbery. In spite of the fact that the color is not a brilliant one, the flower heads are so large and numerous that a planting is effective from a long distance. I had beds of it at the end of a large lawn one summer, and they were a lovely soft pink all summer, very cool and airy looking.

Some suggested planting combinations are:

Background—Cleome PINK QUEEN,—middle ground—white, pink, and lavender Asters; edging—Alyssum CARPET OF SNOW and ROSIE O'GRADY.

Background—Cleome HELEN CAMPBELL; middle ground— GLEAM Nasturtiums mixed; edging—yellow and apricot Violas.

Background—Cleome PINK QUEEN; middle ground—mixed Larkspurs; edging—Alyssum CARPET OF SNOW and VIOLET QUEEN.

Background—Cleome PINK QUEEN; middle ground—white, yellow, and rose GIANT TETRA Snapdragons; edging—*Lobelia* CAMBRIDGE BLUE.

Background—Cleome PINK QUEEN; middle ground—Petunias WHITE, PINK, and PURPLE JOY; edging—yellow, salmon, and white Portulaca.

Cosmos [koz-mos]. *Compositae* family. There are 20 species, native to tropical America.

History. The name Cosmos comes from the Greek, meaning ornament or beautiful thing, and it is the only name the plant has, since no common names have become attached to it. The plants were introduced into Europe from Mexico, which is the native home of the species we grow in our gardens. Until 1895 there were only three colors, white, pink, and crimson and the flowers were small 1-inch ones. In 1896 a new yellow species was introduced but not listed in our catalogues, and it was not until 1935 that the original three colors were extended to include an orange Cosmos (hybrid), and a yellow followed in 1942. The hybridists have also been working on the form of the flowers, and there are now double and crested ones.

Description

HEIGHT: 3–6 feet

PLANTING DISTANCE: The 3–4 foot varieties should be 1½ feet apart, and the tall ones require 3 feet of space

COLOR: White, pink, crimson, yellow and orange

TYPE: Tender

GERMINATION TIME: 5–9 days

SEED TO BLOOM: 10 weeks for the earliest varieties, 12 weeks at least for the later ones

BLOOMING PERIOD: Until frost

IS INDOOR OR COLDFRAME START REQUIRED? The late varieties take such a long time to bloom that an early start of 3–4 weeks is advisable

CAN BE TRANSPLANTED: Yes

SELF-SOW: Yes, but not to any great extent

FALL-SOW: No

Cosmos is a lovely plant with large attractive flowers. The light, airy feathery green foliage makes an ideal background for garden beds. Some varieties provide about the tallest annuals we have but because of the delicacy of the foliage the effect is never heavy. However, the very tall varieties tend to look straggly and take so long to bloom that they have barely begun to flower when frost kills the plant. One of the most important developments in the field of annuals has been the new EXTRA-EARLY and SENSA-TION types which bloom in about 10 weeks instead of 3–4 months. They are not as tall, about 3–4 feet high, but have large 3- 4-inch flowers and the plants are massed with them. The flowers have good clear, pronounced colors. The white is a really definite white, and the crimson beautiful; all the pink varieties are mauve-pink, and pleasing. The orange and yellow varieties have darker green foliage than the others; it is not as finely cut, but the general effect is still not heavy. Recent introductions include flower forms in which the usual yellow center has been replaced by raised disks the same color as the petals; in the few trials I have seen the percentage of flowers with the so-called crested center was comparatively small. However, the single Cosmos is a beautiful flower and I may be reactionary but I can see no need for changing the form. Cosmos are good plants for the South and temperate climates, since as natives of Mexico, they bloom continuously during hot weather.

Classification and recommended varieties. Cosmos are usually classified according to the blooming dates, though the yellow and orange varieties are classified separately. The Cosmos growing picture was drastically changed in 1936 when the new quick-blooming SENSATION type was introduced; before then Cosmos took 4–5 months to flower which meant either early indoor or coldframe start or almost too late a blooming period to bother about. For that reason the old standard type Cosmos LATE MAMMOTH or LADY LENOX is not often grown and in fact is not even listed by many seedsmen. The best types for general use are SENSATION and KLONDIKE.

Sensation type. This is the most popular type. The flowers are the largest, 4 inches or more across, on very long stems. The 4-foot plants are well-branched and have lacier foliage than KLONDIKE. The single flowers resemble daisies and the colors are white, pink, and crimson. The crimson is more on the purple than the orange side. The plants start blooming 10 weeks after the seed is sown and continue flowering until frost. There are several variations.

PURITY. Large pure white

PINKIE. Bright clear rose-pink. Largest and earliest.

DAZZLER. All-American Selection. Amaranth-crimson (almost magenta red).

RADIANCE. All-American Selection. The first bicolor and an interesting one. Deep rose with a dark crimson center zone.

EXTRA-EARLY DOUBLE CRESTED (anemone flowered). White, pink, and crimson mixed. Park's.

Note: Double Cosmos have several layers of petals. All the flowers will not actually be double.

MYSTIC MIX. Semi-double SENSATION type. Each flower center has a crown of small, upright, waved petals surrounded by a single row of broad outer petals. Pink, red, and white. Harris.

CANDYSTRIPE. White and rose-red flowers, 3 inches across. Blooms about 2 weeks earlier and a little smaller than the other SENSATIONS. Park's.

Klondike type. Earlier and smaller than the SENSATION type. Bushy 3-foot plants with denser, broader-leaved foliage. The plants are base-branching and produce many wiry stems. The 2-inch semi-double flowers are yellow, orange and vermilion red.

DIABLO. All-American Selection. New bright red variety, deeper than SUNSET with dark green foliage. Easy to grow, blooms in 2 months, especially good in hot areas.

BRIGHT LIGHTS. A mixture of 4 radiant colors—yellow, gold,

orange and red. A blend of GOLDCREST, SUNSET, and a bright new yellow not yet available separately.

SUNSET. All-American Selection. Orange-scarlet.

GOLDCREST. Early flowering. Many rich golden yellow multi-petaled flowers all summer into late fall. Good companion for SUNSET.

Culture. Cosmos are readily grown tender annuals. The seed should be sown out of doors about the last frost date, preferably in soil that is not too rich so that the plant will concentrate on flowers rather than a vigorous luxuriant foliage. When the plant is about half grown, or 2 feet tall for the varieties recommended here, pinch back to make fresh side branches and to make bushier and more symmetrical. However, do not delay the pinching back too long or you will slow up the flowering. Also there will be more flowers since all the additional branches and shoots will bear them.

When to plant. Although Cosmos should not be planted until danger of frost is past, the planting should not be postponed much after the given dates. It takes long enough to flower as it is, and delayed planting means later flowers and smaller plants. In the South where the fall is very late, planting in June or July will produce short stocky, fall-blooming plants. But as a rule, plant as soon as the weather is warm in the spring.

Earliest safe dates for planting seeds in the garden are: (see page 282 for Spring Frost Zone Map)

Zone A	March 1 –March 15
Zone B	March 15–April 1
Zone C	April 1 –April 15
Zone D	April 15 –May 1
Zone E	May 1 –May 15

Zone F   May 15 –June 1
Zone G   June 1 –June 15

How to plant. Plant the seed directly in the garden and cover with ¼ inch of soil. Thin or transplant when the plants have their first or second set of true leaves; they transplant easily. When only the late, tall varieties were available it speeded up the flowering if the seed had an early start, and this is still the best procedure if you want Lenox (Late Mammoth) Cosmos. Since the seed germinates quickly and the young plants make a rapid growth, the seed should not be started more than 3–4 weeks before the outdoor planting date; otherwise they will tend to be leggy and not as husky as they should be. But the newer strains flower so much sooner than the older ones that early starting is not necessary.

Care and cultivation. The tall older varieties of Cosmos grew so tall that they toppled over unless staked. The newer strains are shorter and so much bushier that staking is unnecessary. The only attention needed is pinching out, as explained previously, if you wish to make the plants bushier and more floriferous.

Uses and planting combinations. Cosmos is generally used for background planting because of its height and decorative foliage. Because of the color range, a Cosmos can be found to use with almost any color scheme. It can also be planted in the cutting garden since the flowers are so decorative, or it may be planted in a shrubbery border (the white Cosmos is best for this).

Good bedding combinations are:
Background—Cosmos Sensation Purity; middle ground—
    yellow and orange Calendula and *Centaurea cyanus* Blue
    Boy.

Background—Cosmos GOLDCREST; middle ground—Dahlia UNWIN'S HYBRIDS mixed.

Background—Cosmos SENSATION PURITY, PINKIE and RADIANCE; middle ground—Verbena ANNAPOLIS BLUE; edging—Alyssum CARPET OF SNOW.

Background—Cosmos CANDYSTRIPE; middle ground—Petunias WHITE MAGIC, HAPPINESS and MALIBU; edging—Snapdragon dwarf white.

Background—Cosmos SENSATION PURITY; middle ground—white, lavender and purple Asters; edging—Alyssum CARPET OF SNOW and VIOLET QUEEN.

Background—Cosmos SENSATION PURITY; middle ground—Snapdragons LITTLE DARLING; edging—Nasturtiums GLOBE PRIMROSE.

Dahlia [dal'-ya]. *Compositae* family. There are 20 species with their origin in Central America.

History. In 1570, Philip II of Spain sent Francisco Hernandez, a renowned naturalist, to Mexico to study plants, animals and minerals. He found a plant which was described as having single, dull red flowers with a yellow center, and this was the first recorded Dahlia. Before it was finally introduced into Europe, about two hundred years later, Aztec gardeners had already hybridized the plants and the colors had been increased to crimson, white, yellow and lilac. In Europe they were named Dahlia to honor a Swedish botanist, Dr. Dahl, who was a pupil of Linnaeus. In 1820 The Royal Horticultural Society reported 6 varieties, in 1914 there were 3,000, and by 1934 there were 14,000 named varieties, most of them double.

Description

HEIGHT: 18–24 inches
PLANTING DISTANCE: 12 inches
COLOR: Wide range of bright gay colors, although usually only available in mixtures: yellow, salmon, pink, white, crimson, dark red, buff, peach, copper, lavender
TYPE: Tender
GERMINATION TIME: 5–10 days
SEED TO BLOOM: 8–10 weeks
BLOOMING PERIOD: Until frost
IS INDOOR OR COLDFRAME START REQUIRED? No
SELF-SOW: No
FALL-SOW: No

Annual Dahlias are like miniature editions of the usual tall ones, and many people do not realize just how attractive and easy to grow they are. The plants grow about 18 inches high or possibly 2 feet in very congenial soil and climate. They are erect, bushy and compact and produce a quantity of flowers similar to the large dahlias but only about 3 inches across. The foliage is dark green, the flowers an amazing variety of colors, all bright gay clear ones. Single and double flower-forms are available, both of them good, but as a rule the colors are only obtainable in mixtures although you can store tubers of especially desirable colors to replant another year. These flowers are charming and not too well known, and I can honestly recommend them without any qualifications. They have continuous, colorful bloom which makes them ideal for bedding.

Classifications and recommended varieties. The main difference is whether the flowers are single or double, and there is a slight difference in height. All of the varieties have semi-double or double flowers except COLTNESS. The varieties are available only in mixture, but, as I will discuss later, tubers can be saved if you want to keep separate colors. The color range is lovely and includes white, buff, yellow, orange, soft pink, deep rose, salmon, coral, scarlet, crimson, and lavender.

UNWIN's DWARF HYBRIDS. This is one of the two popular standard varieties. The plants are semi-dwarf, about 18 inches tall with green leaves and 3–4-inch flowers.

COLTNESS is the other standard variety, very similar to UNWIN's but the flowers are single. The 18–20-inch plants are neat and bushy.

EARLY BIRD MIXED. This is an earlier and dwarfer strain of UNWIN's, with 12–15-inch plants.

REDSKIN. All-American Selection in 1975 as well as recipient of other honors. The distinguishing feature is the glossy, dark, bronzy red foliage in contrast to UNWIN's green. It is very early with 15-inch plants and 3-inch flowers.

RIGOLETTO. Very early blooming, two weeks earlier than EARLY BIRD, dwarfer and more compact.

Culture. Dahlias are simple enough to grow. They are grown from seed which should be sown directly in the garden when all danger of frost is past, although they can be started in the coldframe for earlier bloom. They start blooming in 8–10 weeks and continue until frost. They have no diseases or pests. The plant produces a small tuber which can be stored indoors during the winter and replanted the following spring. The plants from these tubers will be taller than seed-produced plants, and the color of the flowers will be the same as that of the original plant. I never bother keeping tubers because it is so easy to grow new plants from seed, and I like the dwarf habit of growth, but tubers can be kept of an especially desirable color.

When to plant. Dahlia seed is tender and should be sown within a week or two of the last frost date. The seed will not germinate well if the weather is cool; on the other hand do not delay planting after the specified date or you will also delay flowering. The earliest safe dates for planting seed in the garden are: (see page 282 for Spring Frost Zone Map)

Zone A	March 1 –March 8
Zone B	March 15–March 22
Zone C	April 1 –April 8
Zone D	April 15 –April 22
Zone E	May 1 –May 8
Zone F	May 15 –May 22
Zone G	June 1 –June 8

In parts of the country where the summers are very short, the seed can be started in the coldframe a month before the outdoor planting dates.

How to plant. Seed sown in the garden is most easily planted by putting 3–4 seeds in spaces 12 inches apart. When the seeds germinate, thin to leave just one plant in each position. If you are growing a quantity of plants for a large bed, you can sow the seed in a row with the seeds planted 2 inches apart and then transplant into permanent positions when there are two sets of true leaves.

Care and cultivation. The plants themselves require no special care except for routine cultivation and watering if the soil is very dry. To store the tubers, when frost kills the top of the plant, carefully dig them up, being sure you do not bruise them. Shake off the dirt, dry indoors for a few days, then pack in a box of vermiculite (see page 21). Sand or earth can also be used, but vermiculite is inexpensive and so much more satisfactory that I strongly recommend its use. Storing tubers is often more easily said than done; they either get too dry and shrivel up, or they are too wet and turn mouldy. Vermiculite is said to be almost human in the way it regulates humidity and removes the guesswork. The storage place should be cool but the temperature should not go below freezing.

Uses and planting combinations. The best use for Dahlias is in beds by themselves, either with an edging or a background planting. There is so much variety of color in the flowers that the effect of a group planting is lovely and gay. They are ideal plants for front walk beds. They can also be planted in a mixed bed if the color of the other flowers is chosen judiciously.

Good bedding combinations are:
Dahlia DWARF UNWIN edged with Marigold LEMONDROP.
Dahlia COLTNESS hybrids edged with Phlox dwarf SALMON, YELLQW and WHITE BEAUTY.
Dahlia DWARF UNWIN edged with *Lobelia* CAMBRIDGE BLUE.
Dahlia DWARF UNWIN or COLTNESS hybrids with background of Cosmos SENSATION PURITY.
Dahlia DWARF UNWIN or COLTNESS hybrids with background of Cosmos GOLDCREST.

Bed of Dahlia Dwarf Unwin, Calendula Lemon Beauty, Cynoglossum Firmament; edging of Alyssum Carpet of Snow.

Dianthus [di-an'-thus]. This plant is a member of the *caryophyllacae* family with 250 species in Europe, Asia, and Africa.

History. *Dianthus* was so named in 300 B.C. by the Greeks and the name means "divine flower" probably because of the clovelike fragrance of the perennial species. It has been cultivated for thousands of years. Apparently 2000 or more years ago the Arabs in North Africa used the spicy petals to improve the flavor of a tonic they made of bitter herbs to relieve fever. They were mentioned in Chaucer's time and were known to Elizabethans as Gillyflowers and Sops in Wine because the petals were added to wine. Shakespeare said:

> "The fairest flowers of the season
> Are our Carnations and streaked Gillyflowers."

The common name of Pinks was given them by the Irish, and refers not to the color but to the fringed or "pinked" edges of the petals. It has been a garden favorite in this country for years, and still **is.**

Description

HEIGHT: 10–15 inches

PLANTING DISTANCE: 8 inches apart

COLOR: White, rose, pink, scarlet, crimson, violet and bicolors

TYPE: Half-hardy

GERMINATION TIME: 6–10 days

SEED TO BLOOM: About 3 months

BLOOMING PERIOD: Until frost, if the dead flowers are removed

IS INDOOR OR COLDFRAME START REQUIRED? No, although they may be planted in the coldframe to hasten blooming

CAN BE TRANSPLANTED: Yes

SELF-SOW: In some climates, and the plants sometimes live over the winter

FALL-SOW: They may be

The Dianthus family is a large one, but there are far fewer annual than perennial members, and the annual species have been collectively grouped together and are known to botanists as *Dianthus chinensis.* The plants are 10–15 inches high with tufted green foliage which is branched, and in large plants has a tendency to sprawl. The 1½–2-inch flowers are carried on slender stems and are either solitary or two or three grow together. The flowers are charming, and grow in a variety of sizes and shapes. There are both single and double forms, both of them good, and the flowers have fringed edges or laciniated ones which are deeply cut. The colors are clear and definite and in a lovely range, and many are interesting bi-colors with different color eyes or edges or curious petal markings. Perennial *Dianthus* has a delightful characteristic fragrance, but the annual has almost no fragrance at all.

The flowers are excellent for cutting and garden and bloom profusely and steadily all summer long. In many sections of the country they will live over and produce even larger and better plants the second year.

Classification and recommended varieties. There are two types of Dianthus. One is *Dianthus chinensis* (Chinese) and the other the Japanese *Dianthus Heddewigii*. The Japanese has large open flowers, while *D. chinensis* grows more rapidly and has longer stems. This information is purely for the record; it means little to the average gardener, who needs only decide whether he wants double or single flowers, and what color they are to be. My own favorites are the single ones but that is obviously an individual matter. There are no undesirable Dianthus varieties. You could choose one blindfolded and be sure of good flowers, and because the colors are all so beautiful the mixtures are satisfactory if you are using the plants in the cutting garden or a bed by themselves.

Mixtures. They all have flowers in shades of pink, salmon red, crimson, and scarlet, sometimes speckled and sometimes edged with white, as well as pure white.

BABY DOLL. Single. Plain-edged large flowers are the regular Dianthus colors as well as many bicolors. Dwarf 8-inch plants loaded with flowers. For rock gardens or borders.

MAGIC CHARMS. Single. All-American Selection 1974. Early flowering with many fringed 1½-inch flowers.

CHINA DOLL. Double. All-American 1970 winner. Usual colors with fringed picotee edge, as well as interesting color combinations. 12-inch plants.

GAIETY. Double. Large fringed flowers in a galaxy of rich gay colors. 1-foot plants.

Separate colors. There is not much choice here.

QUEEN OF HEARTS. All-American winner. Masses of single
bright scarlet red 1½-inch flowers cover 12-inch plants.

White. Called SNOWFLAKE or SNOWDRIFT, the large single
flowers are pure white and fringed.

Culture. The culture of Dianthus is a simple matter. It is
a half-hardy annual that can either be sown right in the
garden about the date of the last spring frost, or it can be
planted in the coldframe 2–3 weeks before for earlier
bloom. I usually plant a 1-foot row in the coldframe about
the first of April for early July flowers. They do best in
poor soil with plenty of sun. If the plants have a light
cover some of them will probably live over the winter,
in fact a few of mine usually do even without protection.
The second year plants bloom very early, in late May or
early June and should be dug up when through flowering.

When to plant. The earliest safe dates for planting seeds
in the garden are: (see page 282 for Spring Frost Zone
Map)

Zone A	Feb. 15 –March 1
Zone B	March 1 –March 15
Zone C	March 15–April 1
Zone D	April 1 –April 15
Zone E	April 15 –May 1
Zone F	May 1 –May 15
Zone G	May 15 –June 1

Seeds that are to be planted in the coldframe can go in
two weeks before the earlier of the two dates given above.
Since it takes Dianthus a relatively long time to bloom,
the seed really should be planted promptly. However,
late sowings will provide good plants for the following
spring.

How to plant. The seed should be covered with ¼ inch of soil and the seedlings either thinned or transplanted when they have their first or second set of true leaves. The young plants are very sturdy and can be transplanted readily.

Care and cultivation. Dianthus is one of those happy annuals that can go right on growing and flowering without any special care or attention. Light stakes will keep them from sprawling and dragging the flowers in the dust. If you want the plants to winter over, plant in a well drained spot. They can stand severe frosts but will die if exposed to low temperatures in wet places.

Uses and planting combinations. Dianthus is best used in a mixed bed or border, in a rock garden, to border walks, or in the cutting garden. If the seeds are started early, the plants can be used in solid beds and one of the mixtures is good for this.

Good ways to use Dianthus are:
Bed of Dianthus MAGIC CHARMS; edging of Alyssum CARPET OF SNOW.
Bed of Dianthus QUEEN OF HEARTS and SNOWFLAKE; background of Morning-glories HEAVENLY BLUE.
Bed of Dianthus CHINA DOLL and BABY DOLL; edging of *Lobelia* CAMBRIDGE BLUE.
Background of Cosmos SENSATION PINKIE and PURITY; middle ground of Dianthus GAIETY.

Eschscholzia [esh-sholt'-zi-a]. California Poppy. This plant is a member of the poppy family, and a native of California.

History. In 1815 a Russian naturalist and physician, Dr. Johann Eschscholtz, came to this country with an exploring expedition led by Otto von Kotzebue. They found these pretty flowers growing in what is now called California, and the plant's name commemorates him. The type flower is orange or yellow, but the color range has been considerably extended and there are now double as well as single flower forms. It is not a true Poppy but a close

relative. It is the state flower of California and there it is
seen growing wild everywhere.

Description

HEIGHT: 12–18 inches

PLANTING DISTANCE: 12 inches apart

COLORS: Orange, yellow, white, coral-pink, carmine, apricot,
mahogany-red, and a few bicolors

TYPE: Very hardy

GERMINATION TIME: The seed is slow to germinate, especially
if the seed is planted early in the spring when it may take
2–3 weeks

SEED TO BLOOM: About 2 months

BLOOMING PERIOD: Unpredictable, although it is never longer
than 3 months and often is shorter

IS INDOOR OR COLDFRAME START REQUIRED? No, in fact it is impossible since the plants should not be transplanted

SELF-SOW: Yes

FALL-SOW: Yes

The California Poppy is a most beautiful and accommodating plant. The flowers are large open 4-petaled,
poppy-shaped with lovely colors and a satiny sheen. When
the plants are growing wild the flowers are only 1–1½
inches across, but in good cultivation and with selected
seed they are at least 2 inches wide. They close at night
and on dull cloudy days, but stay wide open in sunlight.
The foliage is a light silver green and finely cut, with
slender upright stems. The plants are spreading, branch
freely and are full of flowers. In their native state Eschscholzia self-sow everywhere. I am told that it is a marvelous
sight to see them blooming early in spring in fields with
blue Lupines. Even here in New England the plants readily
self-sow and these seedlings often make the largest and
strongest plants. The flowers of the self-sown plants are
always yellow or orange; I do not know whether they

revert to type or whether the other colors do not self-sow, but since both these colors are good it does not matter. Unlike many flowers which self-sow, these seedlings are a welcome sight when they spring up.

Classification and recommended varieties. There are single and double California Poppies, and some plants are more erect than others. However, the most important classification seems to me to be that of color.

Not many separate colors are listed, or for that matter not many varieties either. So the following is a complete list of all the varieties I found in five catalogues, and the sources are given for the separate colors.

Separate colors.
AURANTIACA. The original California Poppy, pure bright yellow. Single. 1 foot. Burnett, Burpee, and Park's.
CARMINE KING. Carmine rose. Burnett.
DAZZLER. Bright scarlet. Burnett.
GLOAMING. Soft coral pink. Burnett.
GOLDEN WEST. Golden yellow, deep center. Burnett.
WHITE. Burnett.
BALLERINA YELLOW. Burpee. See below, BALLERINA MIXED.

Mixtures.
MISSION BELLS. Lovely, outstanding double and semi-double flowers, shades of pink, scarlet, copper, orange and yellow, many with crinkled petals and picotee edges. As well as the solid colors there are some color combinations such as rose and white, scarlet and yellow, orange and gold, and pink and amber. 1 foot.
BALLERINA MIXED. Double and semi-double, curiously fluted 3–3½-inch flowers on 10-inch plants. Color range includes yellow, orange, pink, rose carmine, scarlet and crimson. Burpee.
SUNSET MIXED. Cream to red. 1 foot. Burpee.

Culture. Eschscholzia is a hardy annual which should be fall-sown or planted early in the spring. Although plants come up during summer from seed dropped by early blooming plants, whenever I try sowing seed late in the spring it either germinates poorly or not at all. Early sown seed grows very slowly at first; it takes a long time to germinate and it seems as if the little plants are never going to start growing. Then before you know it the plants are flowering.

Although it is often stated that the period of bloom is short, I have had plants bloom from the middle of June to early September. The flowers get increasingly smaller and the plants do not look well, but it is certainly not a fleeting bloom. A Massachusetts Agricultural Experiment Bulletin says that the plants will flower in 38–52 days, but my own experience is that they usually flower in 50–60 days from the time that early spring seed is sown. It is only in cool climates like Massachusetts that seed can be sown as late as June, and it was from late sown-seed that these figures were based. California Poppies do best in poor dry soil, and will sometimes live over the winter if protected by a light loose mulch. As a rule Poppies are not satisfactory cut flowers, but if cut in the bud early in the morning, they will open and last for several days.

When to plant. The California Poppy is a hardy cool weather plant, and like Calendula, Sweet Pea and Larkspur, should be planted as early as possible in the spring or be fall-sown. The seed is indestructible so you need have no fear about frost, and these early-sown plants will bloom quickly and for a long time. Only in the coolest parts of the country will late sown-seed amount to anything; the plants really need cool weather during the first part of their growth. In the South if seed is planted in

September the foliage is attractive in the winter and the plants will start flowering; and this is the only time it is worth-while planting seed there.

The earliest spring dates for sowing seed in the garden are: (see page 282 for Spring Frost Zone Map)

Zone A	Feb. 1
Zone B	Feb. 15
Zone C	March 1
Zone D	March 15
Zone E	April 1
Zone F	April 15
Zone G	May 1

How to plant. The seed must be sown where it is to bloom since it should not be transplanted. I usually plant them before the ground is ready for much working over, and just stir the top of the soil a little with a rake or cultivator to make a rough surface which will hold the seeds—otherwise there may be unequal distribution owing to rain washing them all into one spot. Then I broadcast the seed and forget about it until suddenly one early June day flowers are in bloom. Sometimes, however, because the seed germinates slowly, I have an unhappy feeling about two weeks after the seed was planted that it was old seed and that I shall be without these favorite flowers. Luckily I am always wrong.

Care and cultivation. The plants should be thinned to give each one about a square foot of space since they spread a lot. That is all the care they require, and they will flower well without even that. I have not tried this, but I have read that if you cut the tops of the plants off even with the ground after they have set seed that they will grow quickly and bloom as freely as ever.

Uses and planting combinations. Although California Poppies often bloom during the summer months, their best use is for early spring bloom. If the seed is planted in fall or early spring, these plants will be about the first to flower, blooming about the same time as self-sown *Centaurea cyanus* and self-sown or fall-sown Larkspur. So at least two weeks before the last frost date broadcast seed of Eschscholzia and Cornflowers in a bed, and it might well be one in which you are growing bulbs. Although it is often said that the young plants will conceal the dying bulb foliage, this is not strictly true—the young plants at first are too small. However, once they start blooming they certainly perform this needed task. Let the California Poppies bloom for 6 weeks or so and then replace with Zinnia plants.

Good combinations for summer bedding are:

Background—Cleome PINK QUEEN and *Salvia farinacea*; middle ground Eschscholzia GLOAMING, BALLERINA YELLOW and WHITE; Scabiosa blue, white, and pink shades; edging—*Lobelia* CRYSTAL PALACE and Alyssum CARPET OF SNOW.

Background—Zinnias PURITY and CANARY BIRD; middle ground—GLEAM Nasturtiums, Eschscholzia DAZZLER, AURANTIACA, and GOLDEN WEST; edging—Phlox dwarf YELLOW and WHITE BEAUTY.

Background—Helianthus SUN GOLD; middle ground—Eschscholzia MISSION BELLS and *Alyssum maritimum*.

Larkspur. *Ranunculaceae* Family. There are probably 300 or more species in the north temperate zones around the world.

History. Larkspur is the annual form of *Delphinium*. The name, *Delphinium,* comes from the Greek, meaning dolphin, because as Gerarde says: "The floures, and especially before they be perfected, have a certaine shew and likenesse of those Dolphins, which old pictures and armes of certain antient families have expressed with a crooked and bending figure or shape; by which sign the heavenly Dolphine is set forth." *Delphinium* was known to the Greeks and Romans and described by Pliny. The wild species have been growing for centuries on the shores of the Mediterranean, and when the annual form reached England the spur on each flower resulted in the name "larkspur." The name of one species, *Delphinium ajacis,* traces its name to the myth of Ajax who stabbed himself in a moment of frenzy at the seige of Troy, and this flower sprang up where his blood fell (presumably it was blue blood).

Description

HEIGHT: 3–5 feet

PLANTING DISTANCE: 2 feet apart

COLOR: White, various shades of pink, rose, and crimson, lilac and purple (called blue)

TYPE: Very hardy

GERMINATION TIME: This varies considerably depending upon the weather. It is always slow, 2–3 weeks, and if the weather is hot it will not germinate at all

SEED TO BLOOM: 2–3 months

BLOOMING PERIOD: This is so irregular that definite dates cannot be given; see **Culture**

IS INDOOR OR COLDFRAME START REQUIRED? No, in fact Larkspur does not transplant well so is inadvisable

CAN BE TRANSPLANTED: Not easily

SELF-SOW: Yes

FALL-SOW: Yes, in fact this is the best procedure

A. Clutton-Brock says: "No garden flower in existence is more beautiful than the Belladonna Larkspur with its flowers of a silvery pale blue and no less perfect in form than in colour." It must be because Larkspurs are so beautiful that they are one of the six most popular flowers in the country. Their culture is more demanding than that of many annuals, their blooming period is not a continuous one from early summer to frost, but they surely are one of the loveliest of the tall annuals. The plants are upright and branching, with dark green, rather feathery foliage not at all similar to *Delphinium* leaves. The flowers are produced on long spikes filled with small individual single or double florets packed tightly together. Both flowers and foliage have a light graceful look not common in tall plants. The flowers are good for cutting and for garden display. Plants produced from fall- or self-sown seedlings are the tallest and sturdiest; I measured some of mine and the tallest was 67 inches with 18 branches and 2–3 stalks on some of the branches. As you can imagine, the effect is spectacular. Spring-sown seed, at least in my garden, never is as tall or as branching, but it blooms longer. The early tall ones are about the first flowering annual we have, blooming at the same time as self-sown *Centaurea cyanus* and California Poppies, which is early June here, and they flower for about a month. Early spring-sown seed has plants which are 3–4 feet tall, with fewer branches. These begin flowering in mid-July and continue, if planted early, until fall and often until frost.

Incidentally, like other so-called "blue" annuals (Asters and Petunias for example), the blue is not a true blue but a lavender shade, and the "dark blue" Larkspurs are really purple.

Classification and recommended varieties. The old-fashioned Larkspurs were called stock-flowered and the plant consisted of a main stem with branches along the stem and the flowers topping the branches. The present plants are base-branching; they are more compact, the flowering spikes are longer and more floriferous, and the flowers are larger and more double.

There are two strains of Larkspurs, the GIANT IMPERIAL and the newer REGAL strain. Although the REGAL one is supposed to be superior and is the only one listed by Harris and Burnett, Burpee on the other hand lists only the IMPERIAL strain, while Park's has both.

GIANT IMPERIAL. The upright plants are 4–5 feet tall with long
  Delphinium-like spikes of double florets.
WHITE KING. Pure white. Burpee.
BLUE SPIRE. Intense deep bluish purple. Burpee.
SUPREME. Violet purple. Park's.
BLUE BELL. Azure blue. Park's.
PINK PERFECTION. Shell pink. Burpee.
LOS ANGELES. Soft salmon pink. Park's.
DAZZLER. Deep carmine, almost red. Park's.

The REGAL strain also has base-branching 3–4-foot plants with unusually long stems. The double florets are large and placed close together. They are more shatter-resistant and usually bloom most of the summer. White, pink, salmon rose (Burnett), rose, light blue (Burnett), lilac, dark blue.

Culture. The one essential phase of Larkspur culture which must always be kept in mind is that it is a cool weather plant which demands cold weather for germination and while the seedlings are young. It is useless even to attempt to grow Larkspur unless you plant the seeds in fall or very early spring, at least two weeks before the last spring frost dates. Plant it, if possible, where it can be allowed to self-sow (which it will do readily if given half a chance). Although self-sown plants are often claimed to be inferior to newly planted ones, that has not been my experience. Mine are taller, stronger, and the colors are good.

Planting the seed in fall or early spring is the only trick needed for successful Larkspurs. The fall or self-sown ones do not bloom too long, maybe a month or six weeks. The ones planted early in the spring take a long time to germinate, and the early growth is very slow. Then suddenly they grow very quickly. These plants bloom all summer long if the summer is not too hot and dry. I usually have good bloom in the middle of September from plants that have been blooming for at least two months.

When to plant. The point about Larkspur being a cold weather plant has already been stated. Even in the northern zones the seed should be sown in March if possible, never later than early April. It can be fall-sown in any locality except where there is hard frost all winter but not much snow; then early spring planting is better. In the South, you can only have success with fall-planted seed. The fall seed should be planted in October or November so that in frost areas it will not germinate before the cold weather sets in.

Unlike many hardy annuals which can be planted late in spring, if Larkspur is not planted early, forget about it. Late-planted seed often will not germinate at all, and if it does the plants do not amount to anything; the growth will be stunted and the flowers negligible.

The earliest safe dates for sowing seed in the garden are: (see page 282 for Spring Frost Zone Map)

Zone A	Fall plant
Zone B	Fall plant
Zone C	Fall plant

Zone D   March 1 –March 15
Zone E   March 15–April 1
Zone F   March 15–April 15
Zone G   March 15–April 15

How to plant. Fall-sown seed can be broadcast on the surface of the ground, which of course is the way self-sown
seeds get planted. Spring-planted seed can be covered
with $\frac{1}{4}$ inch of soil, but if the ground is still hard this is
unnecessary. Germination is slow and often poor, so I
always plant very thickly. Then when the plants are 2–3
inches high they can be thinned to stand 18–24 inches
apart. Theoretically it is possible to transplant them, but
the plants get such a set-back that they never amount to
much.

Care and cultivation. No special factors are involved in
caring for Larkspur. The plants will benefit from one or
two applications of commercial fertilizer. If you wish the
plants to self-sow, let some of the stalks produce seeds and
stay in place until the seed pods ripen and loose their seeds.
In the fall, you can even take a plant or two and rub the
seed pods to loosen the seed and shake them over the
ground.

Uses and planting combinations. Fall-sown plants will
bloom in the spring, and will make lovely beds with some
of the other early annuals. Spring-sown seed will begin
blooming in July, and bloom for the rest of the summer,
and the colors harmonize with many other annuals. Since
the plants are tall they should be placed either in the background of the beds, or the summer blooming ones can be
used in the middle ground. They are also excellent cut
flowers.

Some suggested planting combinations are:

FALL-SOWN: Larkspur BLUE SPIRE and WHITE KING; mixed single Shirley Poppies.

FALL-SOWN: Larkspur BLUE SPIRE, BLUE BELL and WHITE KING; Calendula LEMON BEAUTY.

FALL-SOWN: Larkspur DAZZLER, LOS ANGELES, BLUE SPIRE and WHITE KING: edging—Pansy MOON MOTH.

SPRING-SOWN: Background—Larkspur DAZZLER, BLUE SPIRE and WHITE KING; middle ground—mixed CREGO and CALIFORNIA GIANT ASTERS; edging—Ageratum DWARF BLUE BLAZER and Alyssum CARPET OF SNOW.

SPRING-SOWN: Background—Cleome PINK QUEEN; middle ground—Larkspur BLUE SPIRE, LOS ANGELES and WHITE KING; edging—Alyssum CARPET OF SNOW and VIOLET QUEEN.

SPRING-SOWN: Background—Larkspur BLUE SPIRE and WHITE KING; middle ground—Petunia CORAL CASCADE; edging—AUREA and ALBA Portulaca.

MARIGOLDS

Marigold. *Tagetes* is the genus, the family *Compositae* with its origin in Mexico; there are 20 or so species ranging from New Mexico and Arizona southward into Argentina.

History. French Marigolds are not French, and the African ones do not come from Africa. Both originally came from Mexico. Vernon Quinn says that according to tradition the deep reddish brown color which marks so many of the flowers is due to the blood of slain Indians as the Conquistadores fought their way upward from the coast to Montezuma's rich capital. Padres who accompanied Cortez sent Marigold seed from Mexico to Spain, and from there it was sent to monastery gardens in France (1573) and Africa (1596). By the time Marigolds reached northern European gardens no one knew their real origin. The species that were sent to Morocco were probably introduced into England after the battle of Tunis and called Marigold (Mary's Gold) because of the orange and yellow colors. To differentiate them from the native European Marigolds (today called Calendula or Pot Marigold) they were called African Marigolds, while the French ones were called French Marigolds. Now they have a strong religious significance in some countries; devout Spaniards put them on altars, and they are the funeral flower in India.

Description

HEIGHT: French Marigolds 9 inches to 2 feet
        African Marigolds 1–3 feet
PLANTING DISTANCE: French Marigolds 12–15 inches
              African Marigolds 18–24 inches
COLOR: The tall African Marigolds are orange and yellow. The dwarf French ones are orange and yellow and combinations of these colors with mahogany-red, copper and scarlet
TYPE: Tender
GERMINATION TIME: 4–5 days
SEED TO BLOOM: 7–10 weeks, depending upon the variety
BLOOMING PERIOD: All summer until frost
REQUIRE INDOOR OR COLDFRAME PLANTING? No
CAN BE TRANSPLANTED: Yes, even in bloom
SELF-SOW: No
FALL-SOW: No

Marigolds are one of the three top annuals in popularity all over the country. They are of the easiest culture, blooming quickly from seed and blooming well and continuously even during the most severe heat until frost. In fact, they are so heat-resistant that they are one of the few annuals recommended for prolific summer flowering in the deep South. It is not only their capacity for bloom under adverse conditions, however, that makes them so popular. The hybridizers have worked wonders with this flower, and now such a beautiful assortment of sizes and colors exist that there is a Marigold for every use. There are no half-way measures with this flower. Either you love the bright dramatic colors and the pungent odor—or you don't. I, myself, cannot imagine having a garden without them.

There are two species of Marigold which vary considerably in habit of growth. The African Marigolds *(erecta)* are 1–3 feet tall, and the flowers are double with great diversity of form, and either orange or yellow. The dwarf French Marigolds *(patula)* range in height from 6–7 inches to 2 feet. The flowers are single and double, and the color range is wider with red and mahogany-red and copper flowers as well as yellow and orange ones, both in solid colors and in combinations of colors. There is also a third type which is a hybrid between the African and French and has varied colored flowers.

The foliage is deep green and finely cut. The flowers are high above the foliage, and the plants are erect with a compact, bushy neat growth. They start branching near the ground so the plant has an abundance of flowers. The dwarf varieties are especially remarkable in this respect— a single plant will have literally dozens of flowers in bloom at one time.

The characteristic smell is called various things from pungent to foul! For exponents of the latter, the smell has been bred out of some of the varieties and you can now have "odorless" Marigolds.

Classification and recommended varieties. There are quite a few types of Marigolds, and like most flowers which the hybridizers have been working on extensively for the past 25 or so years, there is some duplication and overlapping. New varieties appear every year, some sensationally good and others very similar to ones already on the market.

Instead of trying to be all-inclusive in the following list-ing I will give you the main types with the varieties for each. Burpee's have done much of the hybridizing, and their catalogue lists about 50 Marigolds which is rather a bewildering number; it is interesting to note that an 1881 catalogue has only 3 varieties.

African (tall) Marigolds, sometimes now called **American.** These are 1 to 3 feet tall, with large flowers which are at least 2–4 inches across, and sometimes even bigger. The flowers are yellow or orange; the so-called primrose is yellow too, but a soft shade. These plants bloom later than the dwarf French. They can be divided into 2 groups, based on flower form: Carnation and Chrysanthemum flow-ered.

Carnation Flowered. For my money this is the loveliest flower form of the African Marigolds. The petal arrange-ment is loose and fluffy, rather than stiff and formal. The following varieties vary in height from 20 inches to 3½ feet and are all good for display and cutting.

ALASKA. Light cream yellow, nearest to white. Flowers are 3½ to 4 inches across, plants 20 inches high.

CREAM PUFF. Creamy pale primrose. One of the best near-to-white. 3½-inch flowers on 2-foot plants.

ORANGE HAWAII. Deep orange, 4-inch flowers are slightly fra-grant, foliage odorless. 2½ feet.

GOLDEN HAWAII. Golden orange, 4-inch flowers on 2½-foot plants.

SMILES. Golden yellow, 3–4-inch flowers on semi-dwarf 2-foot plants.

SENATOR DIRKSEN. Golden yellow 4-inch flowers named in honor of the late Senator Everett McKinley Dirksen. For more than 10 years the late Senator worked to make the American Marigold the national floral emblem of the United States. Burpee. 2 feet tall.

SUNSPOT. The first F_1 hybrid with odorless foliage. Deep orange 3- to 4-inch flowers on $3\frac{1}{2}$-foot plants.

GOLD COIN SERIES. F_1 hybrids. Tops in the giant African Marigolds. The sturdy 3-foot plants have huge well doubled flowers up to 5 inches across with long cutting stems. The petals are deeply ruffled, and the plants are earlier than the older strains.

DOUBLE EAGLE. Light orange

DOUBLOON. Pure yellow

SOVEREIGN. Rich golden yellow

Two CLIMAX Marigolds are added to this list to complete the color range.

TOREADOR. All-American Selection. Deep orange.

PRIMROSE CLIMAX. Light lemon primrose, lightest color.

JUBILEE SERIES. Semi-tall. Hedge type F_1 hybrids. This new group of large flowering Marigolds won two All-American awards. The 26–30-inch plants are so upright and the growth so uniform that a row looks like a clipped hedge. The large 4-inch flowers are fully double. They are considerably earlier and bloom much more freely than the standard tall Marigolds.

DIAMOND JUBILEE. Clear bright yellow

GOLDEN JUBILEE. Deep golden yellow

ORANGE JUBILEE. Bright orange

LADY SERIES. Semi-tall. Earliest and most compact of the hybrid African Marigolds. The plants are 18 to 20 inches high and at maturity spread to about 20 inches across, making almost round, compact plants that stay neat all summer. Since sometimes there are 50 or more blooms on a plant they almost hide the foliage. The well doubled flowers are up to $3\frac{1}{2}$ inches.

FIRST LADY. All-American Selection. Clear light yellow.

ORANGE LADY. Bright deep orange

GOLD LADY. Golden yellow

Chrysanthemum Flowered. The flower form is something like that of the greenhouse florist's Chrysanthemums. It has a tighter, more formal look than the Carnation Flowered ones. It is a type often seen and grown.

FANTASTIC ORANGE. Bright orange tubular petals with flared twisted and curled ends. 3½-inch flowers, 2½-foot plants.

FANTASTIC MIXED. Yellow, gold and orange. 3½-inch flowers on 2½-foot plants.

FLUFFY MIXED. 3- to 3½-inch flowers with gracefully interlaced petals, tight center. Yellow, gold and orange. 2½ feet.

GLITTERS. Large light yellow, similar to MAMMOTH MUM but earlier. 2½ feet. Burnett.

MAMMOTH MUM. Hugh rich lemon yellow flowers 4 to 5 inches across like double chrysanthemums. 3 feet. Burnett. DWARF.

SPUN GOLD. All-American Selection. Early flowering, start to bloom in 7 weeks, bushy uniform 12-inch plants. Profuse all-season bloom. Burnett, Park's.

SPUN YELLOW. Another All-American winner, Sunshine yellow 2½- to 3-inch flowers on compact 12-inch plants.

GOLD GALORE. All-American Selection in 1972. Golden yellow fully double 4-inch flowers on 18- to 20-inch plants. Start blooming while the plants are still small.

CUPID SERIES. Stocky 10-inch plants with 2½-inch flowers. Gold, yellow, and orange.

MOON SERIES. Large ruffled 3-inch flowers and quantities of them on low-growing 14-inch plants. MOONSHOT (clear yellow) and APOLLO (bright orange).

French Marigolds. The French and African Marigolds differ in size, color and flower form. The French Marigolds are not as tall; there are dwarf ones that never grow more than 6 inches high, and the tallest varieties are about 18 inches; all the plants are as wide as they are tall. The color range is magnificent with many shades of copper-red as well as the usual orange and yellow flowers, and fascinating combinations of color. And there is both a single and double flower form. The French Marigolds fall into three types.

1. **Dwarf Double French.** Various catalogues list a number of this type, and they do not all have the same ones. Here is a partial listing. The thing to look for is the color you want. Some of the reds tend to be what I consider a dull rusty color.

BOLERO. All-American 1970. 2½-inch gold and mahogany bicolor on 8- to 12-inch plants.

TANGERINE. 2-inch tangerine orange flowers, 14-inch plants.

KING TUT. 2-inch mahogany red flowers with large bright yellow crest. 10- to 14-inch plants.

BUTTERBALL. One of the older varieties. The fully double 1¼-inch flowers are bright yellow and the center petals are tipped with maroon. This tipping is very slight and the flowers are most attractive. 6 to 10 inches.

LEMONDROP. Canary yellow, compact plants.

GOLDIE. Deep golden yellow 2-inch flowers with mahogany red markings at base of petals. 10-inch plants.

SPANISH BROCADE. Golden yellow and light orange 2-inch flowers flecked with mahogany red, 14-inch plants.

RED BROCADE. Rich mahogany 2-inch flowers with thread of gold at edges of petals. Good with SPANISH BROCADE.

PETITE SERIES. Extra dwarf, very early and free flowering. All double flowers on neat compact 6–7-inch plants.

PETITE GOLD. All-American winner. Golden yellow.

PETITE YELLOW. Clear strong yellow.

PETITE ORANGE. All-American Selection. Bright orange.

PETITE HARMONY. All-American winner. Mahogany red, golden crest center.

PETITE SPRY. Mahogany red, yellow crest.

2. **Dwarf Single French.**

NAUGHTY MARIETTA. Golden yellow petals with a mahogany blotch at the base of each one. and the same colors tip the center yellow disk petals. 2½-inch flowers on 1-foot plants. Very effective.

DAINTY MARIETTA. Newer. 2½-inch soft yellow flowers with contrasting maroon marking on each petal. 6-inch plants.

SUNNY. 2-inch pure golden yellow flowers. A favorite of mine which is hard to find. Burnett has it.

3. In the last few years a new type of Marigold has been developed which is a hybrid. The African Marigolds which have only yellow and orange flowers were crossed with the French ones in their red shades, and the results are larger than the French ones and the color is brighter.

BURPEE'S RED AND GOLD HYBRIDS are double and beautiful flowers. The plants are about 1½ feet tall, the flowers larger than any of the double French ones, and the colors a lovely mixture of varying shades and combinations of velvety copper-red and golden-yellow, with some solid so-called red ones. It blooms quickly from seed.

RED SEVEN STAR. Very rich, reddish scarlet overlaid on gold. Fully double 2½-inch flowers on 14-inch plants. Early and free-flowering.

SHOWBOAT. All-American Selection, Early with rich yellow 2½-inch flowers on 13-inch plants.

Culture. Marigolds are sun-loving plants which grow well in hot climates. One of the reasons for their enormous popularity is undoubtedly their ability to bloom abundantly during the heat of summer. They are a half-hardy annual which should not be planted out of doors until the weather is reasonably warm. I have had late spring frosts catch all my seeds and young plants, so I now wait until the weather is fairly certain to be frost-free. Since they like heat, trying to hasten the blooming season by early planting in the open ground does not avail you much. You can, however, start them either indoors or in the coldframe 2–3 weeks before the earliest outdoor planting date and have flowers blooming in the garden within two

months. I planted seeds of 10 varieties indoors one year
in one large seed flat on March 29th and transplanted
them into the garden the middle of May, when some of
the little French ones were in bud. All but the tallest
African Marigolds were blooming on June 25th. And I
had almost 250 plants from the one seed flat. Flowering
plants are usually obtainable at local nurseries as soon as
it is time for outdoor planting, and, since they transplant
so readily, are good buys to fill in bare spots in the garden
and provide early bloom when most annuals have not
yet started to flower.

When to plant. Marigolds are not fussy about planting
dates, as long as there is no danger of frost getting them.
The young seedlings will stand cold weather but not actual
frost, even a light one. They can be planted in open
ground about the date of the last spring frost, or any time
within the next 6–8 weeks. They are one of the least fussy
annuals about weather conditions for germination, for
they seem to come up with no attention at all even late
in the season when the soil is sometimes quite dry.

The earliest safe dates for planting seed in the garden
are: (see page 282 for Spring Frost Zone Map)

Zone A	Feb. 15 –March 1
Zone B	March 1 –March 15
Zone C	March 15–April 1
Zone D	April 1 –April 15
Zone E	April 15 –May 1
Zone F	May 1 –May 15
Zone G	May 15 –June 1

Seed that is to be started indoors should be planted
about 2 weeks before the earlier of the above two dates.
The seeds germinate so quickly (usually within 4–5 days
indoors) and the plants grow so well that unless you have

room to transplant the seedlings they will grow leggy indoors if started too early.

How to plant. Marigold seeds are fairly large and should
be covered with about 1/4 inch of soil. When the first or
second set of true leaves has appeared, the plants can be
thinned or transplanted the proper distance apart. Since
the plants are very bushy, they need plenty of room to
branch well. Although ideally they should be transplanted
when the plants are very small, they are tough enough to
stand transplanting even when in flower as long as they
are kept watered for a few days. I should say that given
water, it is almost impossible to kill a Marigold.

The seeds that are started indoors are best sown in
vermiculite, see page 21. I sow the seeds in rows in a very
large flat, with a row for each separate variety. All they
need is watering until it is time to put the plants in the
garden. If you want to grow enough Marigolds for a large
bed, the easiest way to handle them is to sow your seeds
in short straight rows, one row for each variety, and transplant them into the bed when they have a set or two of
true leaves.

Care and cultivation. Fading flowers turn an unattractive
dark brown, so your plants will look better if you keep
these dead-heads cut off, although they will bloom well
regardless of this attention. Marigolds are also a favorite
of Japanese beetles. The beetles can be kept in check by
hand picking and dunking them in kerosene (a rather
sadistic but satisfying form of entertainment) or by one of
the new DDT sprays. Just give the plants enough room
and not too rich a soil.

Uses and planting combinations. Marigolds have numerous uses. They are ideal bedding plants, either alone or with other annuals (providing the colors are carefully chosen). The dwarf French Marigolds are good edging plants, especially Yellow Pygmy. The tall African Marigolds are good for background planting. The little ones— SPUN GOLD, SPUN YELLOW, or BUTTERBALL—provide all-summer plants for narrow beds along walks or driveways, or for flower pots or window boxes. They are also excellent for cutting.

Good planting combinations

Marigold bed: background—ALASKA and ORANGE HAWAII; middle ground—BURPEE's RED and GOLD HYBRIDS, GOLDIE, TANGERINE; edging—PETITE GOLD and ORANGE.

Narrow bed of Marigold SPUN YELLOW; edging—Alyssum CARPET OF SNOW and *Lobelia* CRYSTAL PALACE or CAMBRIDGE BLUE.

Narrow bed of Marigold SUNNY; edging—Ageratum MIDGET BLUE or ROYAL BLAZER.

Background—Zinnia ELDORADO; middle ground—Petunia SNOWSTORM; edging—Marigold CUPID yellow.

Background—Marigold FLUFFY MIXED; middle ground—Petunia MOON GLOW; edging—Dianthus SNOWFLAKE.

MORNING-GLORIES

Morning-glories. *Ipomoea* [ip-po-mee'-a] is the genus, and there are over 400 species of which more than 200 are found in tropical America, mostly in Mexico.

History. *Ipomoeas* are found growing wild over a large part of the United States and tropical America. They are very similar to *Convolvulus* which is a rampant weed (although attractive). The common Morning-glory came originally from the American tropics and the flowers were either bright purple-magenta or white. In 1895 a species from Japan was introduced here, which at one time was so admired and sought after by the Japanese that in 1830 single seeds of rare varieties sold for $15.00. These flowers apparently were beautiful, having many colors and forms. Today there are not many colors, but those we do have are lovely, especially the blue which is a great improvement over the wild ones with their purple centers and stripes. The name is derived from a Greek word meaning "like bindweed," and refers to the twining stems.

Description

HEIGHT: 10 feet or more

PLANTING DISTANCE: 1 foot apart

COLOR: Blue, red, and white

TYPE: Tender

GERMINATION TIME: 5–10 days

SEED TO BLOOM: About 3 months

IS INDOOR OR COLDFRAME START REQUIRED? Not required, but preferable for early flowering

CAN BE TRANSPLANTED: No

BLOOMING PERIOD: From mid-summer to frost

SELF-SOW: The wild varieties do self-sow, you see them in every field and fence in Bermuda for instance, but the cultivated ones do not seem to seed themselves, at least not in my part of the country

FALL-SOW: No

Morning-glories are the most popular and widely grown annual vine. They have heart-shaped, medium-green leaves, and flowers in great profusion. The vine itself is twining, so it needs something to wind around unlike the tendril-bearing vines which will cling to a surface. They thrive in poor soil and will grow anywhere as long as they have sufficient sun. In dull weather the flowers stay open most of the day, but on sunny days they close up about noon, and really hot weather wilts them very early in the day. If the plants are placed so that they do not get direct sun in the early morning, they will stay open longer. The plants start flowering when very small, just a few inches high, and, as they continue to grow, new flower buds form along the vine so that there are always flowers in bloom. The flowers, as everyone knows, are incredibly beautiful, especially the new variety **HEAVENLY BLUE** which must be the most exquisite shade of blue in the world.

The plants are healthy and strong growing. A few vines can cover a wide area. They can be grown to climb a fence, arbor, wall, or bank, and are seen to a very good advantage if grown, as shown in the illustration, to climb around a stone vase or jar. In my garden there is a low brick wall with a stone vase in the center, and the Morning-glories climb around an old Ampelopsis vine, drape themselves over the vase, and are a mass of bloom every morning. Moonflowers were planted with them which bloom from late afternoon until mid-morning and the result is a beautiful continuous flowering.

Moonflowers are *Ipomoea Mexicana alba* and are native Mexican and tropical American plants. The vines are a little longer than Morning-glories, the leaves larger and darker green, and the huge white flowers are fragrant, have a long white tube, and the stamens are quite prominent. They do not open until late afternoon and close in the morning.

Classification and recommended varieties. The only Morning-glory classification is by color, and very few varieties are available.

HEAVENLY BLUE. Sky-blue flowers with yellow throats shading to white, the best Morning-glory variety. The only reason this is not an All-American winner is that it was introduced before these awards were given.

SCARLET O'HARA. Gold Medal All-American winner. New climbing strain which climbs vigorously, unlike the older strain. Crimson-carmine.

EARLY CALL ROSE. 1970 All-American winner. Extremely early
   flowering habit, far earlier than the standard varieties.
   Free flowering 4-inch flowers stay open well into the day.
   Clear rose with white throats.
EARLY CALL BLUE. Counterpart of EARLY CALL ROSE. Deep
   violet-blue flowers with creamy throats.
PEARLY GATES. Silver Medal All-American Selection in 1942.
   The flowers are a creamy white and a good size. I prefer
   planting Moonflowers for white flowers because they
   bloom at night, but PEARLY GATES are lovely.
MEXICANA ALBA (Moonflower). Huge white 4–4½-inch flowers.
   They are perfect flowers to grow near a porch or terrace
   because the white flowers, when they open in the evening,
   really seem to glow.

These are the five standard Morning-glories; a few
others are listed in different catalogues. One unusual type
is the JAPANESE IMPERIAL GIANT MIXED (Burpee, Parks).
The colors are described as brilliant red, rose, pink, white,
purple and light blue, with huge showy flowers. They are
indeed that, and I grow them in pots all years. But the
only colors I have had are a deep red and purple, sometimes with white edges, and a lovely very light lavender.

Culture. Morning-glories are essentially hot weather plants,
and should not be planted outdoors until the weather is
warm, or about 1–2 weeks after the last frost date. If
planted while the weather is cool and damp, they will just
rot. Since the blooming period is long, it is a good plan
to hasten it by planting some seeds indoors a month or so
before the outdoor planting date. If sown directly in the
garden, plant the seeds where they are to bloom since they
do not transplant well.

You can also grow regular Morning-glories indoors if
you have an east or south exposure, and I can assure you
that a HEAVENLY BLUE Morning-glory is a most welcome

sight on a dark February morning. Soak the seed (see below) and plant in 7-inch pots. Thin to about 4 plants per pot and support with a light stake or inverted wire coat hanger. As the plants start climbing, pinch out the tops. They will bloom in 8 weeks and continue for a long time.

When to plant. Seed which is planted directly in the garden should not be sown until 1–2 weeks after the latest spring frost date. Indoor planting should be made 3–4 weeks earlier.

The earliest safe dates for planting seed in the garden are: (see page 282 for Spring Frost Zone Map)

Zone A	March 8 –March 15
Zone B	March 22–April 1
Zone C	April 8 –April 15
Zone D	April 22 –May 1
Zone E	May 8 –May 15
Zone F	May 22 –June 1
Zone G	June 8 –June 15

How to plant. Morning-glories have seeds with hard coats, which makes the germination slow. It can be speeded considerably by soaking the seeds overnight in tepid water. Then they will germinate in a day or so instead of 5–10 days. Plant 3–4 seeds in the garden in all the spots you want the plants to grow, and keep the ground watered until the seeds germinate, since often at this time in the spring the ground is dry. When the plants have their first set of true leaves, thin to leave one plant in each place.

For indoor seed planting, you should sow the seeds in individual containers since the plants cannot be transplanted. Paper containers or small flower pots can be used. Sow 3 seeds in each one, cover with a $\frac{1}{4}$ inch of soil, and keep moist until the seeds germinate. The first leaves are enormous, especially of the Moonflowers, and the plants should be thinned as soon as the first leaves have appeared, leaving one plant to each pot. The seeds germinate irregularly, so don't despair of the slow ones. When you are ready to put the plants in the garden be careful not to disturb the roots. Morning-glories are one of the few plants that seem well worth starting indoors to me. They are easy to grow and a dozen or so plants do not take up much room. A package of seed costs maybe 40¢, and will supply more than a dozen plants. In my vicinity, grown-plants are very expensive to buy from a florist. In 1948 my seeds planted April 6th indoors had their first flowers on July 4th, and were full of bloom every day until frost. Moonflowers, planted the same time, were much slower to bloom but flowered profusely until frost.

Care and cultivation. Morning-glories are so eager to climb that if you do not give them a support they will climb over anything they can find. If there is not a natural support such as a lattice fence, you can give them some strings or thin brush. Although they require care in the way of heat and water to start the plants off, once started, there is no stopping them and they are no trouble at all. The flowers will be more abundant if the plants are not given fertilizer and the soil is not too rich.

Uses and planting combinations. Morning-glories make an excellent background for any flower bed that has a sunny wall or fence behind it. I would suggest always planting at least one or two Moonflowers with the Morning-glories; mine are so sensational that I cannot imagine a garden without them. If you have Morning-glories along a wall there are a number of low annuals you can plant at the base for an attractive effect.

Some suggested planting combinations are:

WALLS OR FENCES

Ipomoea HEAVENLY BLUE and Moonflower, with border of Marigold yellow LEMONDROP.

Ipomoea HEAVENLY BLUE, SCARLET O'HARA and Moonflower, border of Ageratum dwarf ROYAL BLAZER.

Ipomoea HEAVENLY BLUE and Moonflower, with border of Dahlias UNWIN's HYBRIDS.

FLOWER GARDENS WITH WALL OR FENCE

Background—Ipomoea HEAVENLY BLUE and Moonflower; middle ground—orange and yellow Calendula and *Centaurea cyanus* BLUE BOY; edging—Alyssum CARPET OF SNOW.

Background—Ipomoea HEAVENLY BLUE and Moonflower; middle ground—Zinnias Zenith FIRECRACKER and CARVED IVORY; edging—Viola WHITE PERFECTION.

Background—Ipomoea EARLY CALL BLUE, EARLY CALL ROSE, and JAPANESE IMPERIAL MIXED; middle ground—Snapdragons ROCKET FROSTY ROSE, LEMON, PINK, WHITE and ORCHID; edging—Alyssum CARPET OF SNOW, ROYAL CARPET, and ROSIE O'GRADY.

There are other Ipomoeas, besides the Morning-glories, which are occasionally grown. Some are Convolvulus, sometimes classified as Ipomoeas and sometimes not; even the standard reference books are not consistent about this. At any rate, they are first cousins, and can stay here for the sake of simplification, since the culture is the same for all.

Cardinal Climber. *Ipomoea quanoclit* [kwan'-o-klit]. This rapid-growing, very attractive vine has finely cut, bright green foliage and small 1-inch, trumpet-shaped flowers which are a lovely shade of cardinal-red. The foliage, because it is fine, does not give much shade but the vine is good because of the flowers. It will grow about 10 feet in a season.

Cypress Vine. This vine also has fernlike foliage, and grows about 15 feet long. The flowers are 1- 1½-inch, star-shaped, and offered in two separate varieties, scarlet and white.

Alamo or Mile-a-Minute Vine. *Ipomoea Alamo.* This vine is not often listed by seedsmen and I have never seen it growing. Elizabeth Lawrence says in *A Southern Garden* that she planted it the end of April and first buds came on September 16th. The white of the corolla is set off by the dark wine color of the throat. The leaves are a beautiful dark green and intricately cut. It grows thickly and makes a neat flat screen. It is drought resistant, but does not grow as fast as mile-a-minute would indicate.

Crimson Rambler. *Convolvulus.* This is a fast-growing, Morning-glorylike vine with deep red flowers which have white throats. It will grow about 10 feet in a season.

Dwarf Blue Ensign. *Convolvulus.* Very seldom listed but a lovely plant. It grows about 1 foot tall and does not climb, but has foliage and flowers like Morning-glories. It is a neat growing plant which could be used for edging. The flowers are purple and white, with yellow throats, and stay open all day. I tried the new Dwarf Pink under admittedly poor cultural conditions; one poor little flower finally made an appearance. It would probably do better with more attention.

NASTURTIUMS

Nasturtium. The genus of Nasturtiums is *Tropaeolum* [tro-peé-o-lum]. There are 45–50 species of wild Nasturtiums ranging throughout tropical America from Southern Mexico to Chile.

History. Nasturtium means literally "nose twister," and refers to the pungent smell. The generic name was given in 1737 by Linnaeus. Before then in England the plant had been called Indian Cress; the leaves and flowers were often served as a salad and the green seeds were pickled as an alleged delicacy. Since the name Nasturtium applies to all the cresses, Linnaeus called the plant *Tropaeolum* (trophy) to distinguish it, and apparently considered that the shield-shaped leaves and helmetlike flowers were suggestive of the trophies of war. The original plant was yellow, and took a long time to bloom; hybridists have worked to extend the color range to red and orange colors, to hasten the growth, and to produce a compact non-spreading plant.

Description

HEIGHT: The three types are 12 inches tall, about 24 inches, and the climbing variety will grow at least 6 feet

PLANTING DISTANCE: 12 inches apart

COLOR: A good range in yellow, orange and red colors

TYPE: Tender

GERMINATION TIME: 8–13 days

SEED TO BLOOM: 7–8 weeks

BLOOMING PERIOD: Until frost

IS INDOOR OR COLDFRAME START REQUIRED? No

SELF-SOW: In temperate climates, not otherwise

FALL-SOW: No

Nasturtiums are popular because they are extremely easy to grow, the flowers come in a marvelous range of gay bright colors, and the plants will bloom profusely through hot dry weather and in poor soil. There are few lovelier sights than a large mass of Nasturtiums, and on the West Coast the plant perpetuates itself and the size makes our Eastern ones look faintly dwarfed. The Government Bulletin on Annuals says: "For three or four months of the season (Nasturtiums) make a better display than almost any other plant. No annual will produce such a profusion of flowers for so long a time with the same outlay of time and labor. It never flags through the hottest weather. It is said that a good bed, 6 x 20 feet, will yield about 1,000 flowers each day." The large leaves are light green and have a smooth texture. If grown in soil which is not too rich, the flowers rise well above the foliage and bloom in great profusion, a dozen flowers on one small plant being a frequent occurrence. In spite of the name "nose twister" the sharp fragrance is pleasing. There are single and double flowers, and usually only the climbing Nasturtiums.

are offered in the single form, although a few seedsmen list a dwarf single mixture. However, many of the "doubles" produce single flowers. All of the Nasturtium colors are lovely, clear and vivid. The two dwarf types are usually sold in separate colors in the Nasturtium range which is bright orange, light yellow, deep golden-yellow, scarlet, a good dark velvety mahogany-red, a bright salmon-cerise, and Burpee's CHERRY-ROSE. The best way to buy Nasturtiums, I think, is to get one package each of every available variety in whichever type you want. If you buy mixtures you will get a preponderance of orange flowers. A few seedsmen list a type which has blackish green foliage, and frankly I do not know whether it is attractive or not; usually these rather freakish dark foliages are not especially appealing.

Classification and recommended varieties. There are three distinct types of Nasturtiums.

1. **Dwarf Nasturtiums,** called GEM OR GLOBE, are about 12 inches tall, have a compact or globular form and are without runners. since they are bred for a uniform runnerless form. Available varieties are: WHIRLYBIRD (brilliant red), GOLDEN, MAHOGANY, ORANGE, SCARLET, PRIMROSE (light yellow), CHERRY-ROSE (a lovely watermelon pink which flowers early and profusely; a must for a Nasturtium bed) and MIXED.

2. **Gleam Hybrids** are about 20 inches tall, with double and semi-double flowers, and the plants have short runners. These are good for bedding and also for cutting since the stems are long.

GOLDEN GLEAM. Gold Medal All-American Selection in 1933. The first double sweet-scented Nasturtium and still very popular. Also: SCARLET, SALMON, ORANGE, MAHOGANY and MIXED.

3. Climbing Nasturtiums. This type has vines up to 8 feet tall which are fine for a quick screen effect. The plants develop rapidly from seed sown in May and bloom profusely. The flowers are single and the Harris color range includes shades of crimson, scarlet, yellow, orange and bicolors. The fragrance is the typical spicy one. Its runners can be trained on strings or a trellis and are useful for climbing poles and for camouflaging old fences, stumps and so on. They are also very good when the plants are allowed to hang. In the Jack Gardner Museum in Boston these Nasturtiums hang from a balcony on the fourth floor of the enclosed patio and almost come down to the ground floor level, making a spectacular sight. However, these plants are greenhouse grown and carefully fed and probably none of us could duplicate such splendor.

Another member of the *Tropaeolum* family is an attractive vine, CANARY BIRD VINE, *(Tropaeolum peregrinum)*. The 1- 1½-inch flowers are light yellow, and oddly shaped, although so small you do not notice them particularly and just get the effect of the canary-yellow color. The foliage is finely cut and light green. The plant grows about 10 feet long and, unless planted in a climate with a long cool growing season, the seeds should be started indoors in individual pots about a month before the outdoor planting date for Nasturtiums.

Culture. Nasturtiums are of the simplest possible culture. Sow the seeds outdoors when the weather has warmed up, about a week after the latest spring frost date. Poor soil is preferable to rich. If the soil is rich the plants produce lavish leaves which not only hide the flowers, but to some extent prevent their production. Once the seeds are in, the plants require no further attention, but they need plenty of sun.

Before I knew enough about gardening to find out that

Nasturtiums should not be transplanted, I started some seeds indoors and transplanted them successfully into the garden. However, they do not transplant easily and it is better practice to sow them where they are to bloom. For extra early bloom (this is really only important if you are planting the climbing ones and want a good display— the others bloom quickly) you can plant seeds in individual paper pots, see page 21, about one month before the outdoor planting date, and then the plants can be put into the garden without disturbing the roots.

When to plant. It is wise to time Nasturtium planting rather carefully. Seed should not be planted if there is any danger of frost. On the other hand, if not planted when the weather is still reasonably cool, the germination is poor and the plants definitely smaller than they would otherwise be. One year I planted one lot of seed on May 10th, another lot in the same bed about two weeks later, and the latter were very inferior to the first. Seed planted here (Zone E) on May 10th will start to flower by July 4th.

The earliest safe dates for sowing seed in the garden are: (see page 282 for Spring Frost Zone Map)

Zone A	March 1 –March 15
Zone B	March 15–April 1
Zone C	April 1 –April 15
Zone D	April 15 –May 1
Zone E	May 1 –May 15
Zone F	May 15 –June 1
Zone G	June 1 –June 15

How to plant. Nasturtium seeds are large and should be planted about an inch deep, otherwise the plants may get uprooted. The easiest way to plant a bed of any size is to poke holes with a pencil in the soil, about 6 inches apart, and drop the seeds in them. Cover and tamp down the earth. When the plants come up, thin to a foot apart. Sometimes Nasturtium seeds are full and plump, and sometimes they look dried up. This difference is due to varieties and not to the soundness of the seeds, so you can plant the dried up ones without worry.

Care and cultivation. The only insects that attack Nasturtiums are aphids; these small black lice crowd the stem and eventually suck the leaves, causing them to wither. In this locality we are sometimes bothered with them, but mostly do not have any trouble. A Black Leaf 40 or a Pyrethrum spray once or twice should control them. One garden magazine reader said she pounds moth balls into small pieces and puts a handful around each sprouting plant and that this entirely prevents aphids. Scientists apparently snort at this home-made cure, but it is not the first time I have seen it recommended.

Uses and planting combinations. Nasturtiums have many uses. The dwarf GEM type can be used for edging reasonably tall plants, or for low bedding, especially along narrow walks or drives. The GLEAM type is excellent for bedding and for window boxes. The climbing Nasturtiums, although not robust for some vine uses such as screening a porch, are fine for low walls, sunny banks, or hanging baskets.

Some suggested planting combinations are:
Background—Cleome PINK QUEEN and *Salvia farinacea* or Cynoglossum FIRMAMENT; middle ground—Petunias PALEFACE; edging—Nasturtium GEM CHERRY-ROSE.
Background—Cosmos BRIGHT LIGHTS; middle ground—GLEAM Nasturtiums MAHOGANY, ORANGE, GOLDEN, SCARLET, SALMON; edging—Alyssum CARPET OF SNOW.

Background—Cosmos Sensation Purity; middle ground—
Gleam Nasturtiums Golden, Scarlet, Mahogany,
Salmon; edging—Marigold Sunny.

Background—Cleome Pink Queen; middle ground—Nasturtiums Cherry-Rose; edging—Alyssum Carpet of Snow.

Pansies and Violas [vye′-ol-uh] The exact family origin of pansies and violas is not certain. They are descended from the *Viola tricolor;* however it is possible that other species have contributed to the modern flower.

History. The word Pansy comes from the French *pensée,* meaning thought. Pansies have been garden favorites for centuries as proved by the long list of common names, some of which are: heartsease (because it was used medicinally to cure the pangs of love), call-me-to-you, love-true, three-faces-under-a-hood, Johnny-jump-up-and-kiss-me, stepmother, kiss-me-at-the-garden-gate, ladies-delight, bird's-eye-none-so-pretty, tickle-my-fancy, and finally what is claimed to be the longest English plant name meet-her-in-the-entry-kiss-her-in-the-buttery.

Violas and Pansies are cousins, well removed. Their common ancestors was the *Viola tricolor,* better known to most of us as Johnny-jump-ups. Even the huge modern hybrids are descendants of this tiny flower. The actual steps in the transformation are hard to trace because plant breeders have been working on them for such a very long time, and during the past 100 years English, Scotch, French, German, Swiss and American hybridists have produced extraordinary changes.

Description

HEIGHT: 6–8 inches

PLANTING DISTANCE: 6 inches apart

COLOR: Pansies now come in every color except a bright red. Violas are white, yellow, lavender, purple, apricot, and a ruby-red

TYPE: Very hardy

GERMINATION TIME: 8–14 days

SEED TO BLOOM: About 3 months

BLOOMING PERIOD: Violas bloom all summer. Fall-sown Pansies bloom from early spring until early summer, spring-sown ones start blooming about 3 months after the seed is sown and continue for several months

IS INDOOR OR COLDFRAME START REQUIRED? The culture of Pansies and Violas differs from that of the rest of the annuals in this book, and is discussed in detail in the Culture section

CAN BE TRANSPLANTED: Yes

SELF-SOW: Some varieties do, but they seldom amount to much (except for Johnny-jump-ups)

FALL-SOW: They can, and often are, planted in August

Pansies and Violas are so similar in culture that they are treated together here. Technically Violas are perennials and Pansies are usually grown as biennials, but since they both will flower in three months from early spring-sown seed, it seems excusable to class them as annuals.

Pansies are certainly far too well known to require any description of mine. Even a young child knows what they look like. Although Violas are similar in growing habit and flower form there are certain differences between the two. Violas have smaller flowers than Pansies, some of the tiny ones being only ½ inch across. Viola colors are generally pure clear solid ones with possibly a yellow eye but not many bi-color markings, and have few if any dark lines radiating from the center. Violas are very floriferous (often giving hundreds of flowers from one plant during its life) and usually bloom steadily all summer, while Pansies tend to get very leggy and small-flowered. Both plants have nice dark green foliage, and a spreading habit of growth, although Violas are more compact.

Violas have a longer period of bloom here in the New York area than Pansies do, usually lasting until frost although the plants get rather straggling and the flowers smaller as the season advances. They also often live over the winter and the plants are good the second year, while Pansies that live over seldom amount to much.

Classification and recommended varieties. In this section Pansies and Violas will be treated separately.

Pansies. A great many Pansy varieties are offered in various catalogues; some are American seed and some Swiss. Because the diversity seems confusing, I have done some eliminating, and this discussion is confined to the hybrids, Swiss seeds, Steele's, and one excellent unusual type, CLEAR CRYSTALS.

In choosing Pansy seeds the decision is basically much simpler than it is with a lot of the other annuals. The plants are all about the same height, and the flower forms are similar—some with blotches and faces and some without. Some flowers are larger than others and the large ones can be spectacular. Your choice really depends on the color of the flowers and the length of the blooming season. Although Pansy mixtures are satisfactory enough, especially Steele's BUTTERFLY HYBRIDS, if you choose separate colors carefully you will have much more effective beds and cut flowers.

As far as the season goes, Pansies used to collapse as soon as hot weather arrived, but they have now been bred to withstand heat and the new hybrids can bloom until frost.

MAJESTIC GIANTS. F_1 Hybrids. Mixed.

Few Pansies have been All-American Selections but this mixture won in 1966. The flowers are immense, up to 4 inches across, and in spite of their size bloom freely and profusely on neat 7-inch plants. They are 2 weeks earlier than the standard Swiss Pansies. and their hybrid vigor enables them to withstand summer heat, so they bloom continuously when other types are past their prime. The mixture has a wide range of colors, all with handsome blotches. Park's has 6 separate colors, listed later in the section arranged by color.

Separate colors of F_1 hybrids have all the advantages of the MAJESTIC hybrids, earlier and abundant bloom, and resistance to hot weather. The IMPERIAL series with blue, orange, and yellow flowers as well as a few other separate colors are all included in the listing by color.

SWISS SEEDS. There are 3 types.

1. SWISS GIANTS. The Swiss have been famous for their Pansy seeds for many years, and they are still outstanding. The flowers are large, firm-textured, and velvety with long stems. The plants are compact and about 6 inches tall. There is a large selection of separate colors offered by all seedsmen and listed later.

2. ROGGLI ELITE MIXED. Mr. Roggli is the Swiss originator of this world-renowned strain. The large 3- to 4-inch flowers are freely produced on long erect stems. Available only in mixtures which tend towards the deeper tones of red and blue.

3. SUPER SWISS GIANTS MIXED. Huge flowers with a velvety texture of the Swiss type, with a wider color range and

smaller blotches which make them appear more colorful.
CLEAR CRYSTALS.

Flower size midway between Violas and Pansies, 2 to 2½ inches, with beautiful solid colors without blotches or faces. Compact 8-inch plants smothered with flowers. Very early. Stokes had 8 separate colors included in the following color listing.

STEELE'S PANSIES.

These are Pacific Coast Pansies. Park's has 2 separate colors, listed later, and their beautiful BUTTERFLY HYBRIDS. Mr. Steele worked for 15 years to produce a pink Pansy, and now the pastel colors include pink, rose. apricot buff, orchid, pale gold, coral and flesh.

COLOR LISTING.

WHITE. The SWISS GIANT whites are offered under different names. Just plain WHITE, MONT BLANC, and JUNGFRAU. STEELE'S MOON MOTH has enormous pure white flowers, Park's. The F_1 hybrid MAJESTIC WHITE WITH BLOTCH (blue), All-American 1966, has enormous flowers up to 4 inches, is free-flowering and heat tolerant. MAMMOTH WHITE is another F_1 hybrid with its creamy white flowers with a small yellow eye, Harris. CLEAR CRYSTAL WHITE has very early, faceless, medium-size flowers on compact free-flowering plants, Stokes.

YELLOW. STEELE'S JUMBO PAY DIRT is the largest clear golden yellow without markings ever produced, Park's. CLEAR CRYSTAL YELLOW is also golden yellow without markings, smaller than PAY DIRT but early and very floriferous, Stokes. MAJESTIC F_1 hybrid yellow with blotch, Park's. RHEINGOLD is a Swiss yellow and SUNNY BOY is a hybrid version of it, early, deep butter yellow with blotch, Harris, Burpee. CORONATION GOLD, All-American in 1938, pure golden yellow with lightly ruffled edges. IMPERIAL YELLOW, same qualities as IMPERIAL BLUE, Harris.

RED AND PINK. ALPENGLOW is the Swiss variety with velvety garnet red large flowers with dark blotches. Park's has MAJESTIC GIANTS RED, ROSE, and SCARLET BRONZE.

Fire Beacon is a Swiss bronze, Park's and Stokes. Raspberry Rose is a Swiss Pansy with soft carmine pink flowers with a velvety center—large and lovely.

orange. Clear Crystal Orange has solid, bright orange, faceless, medium-size flowers and plenty of them, Stokes. Harris has Imperial Orange, similar to Imperial Blue; the Swiss Giant Orange is a deep bright orange.

blue. Imperial Blue hybrid, All-American 1975, has extra-large light azure blue flowers (with a dark blotch) in abundance over an extremely long blooming period. Majestic Giants Blue Shades, Park's. Clear Crystal Light Blue, faceless and early, Stokes. Paramount Azure Blue is a solid sky blue hybrid, not as large as the Majestics, but very early with a multitude of bloom, Harris and Burpee. Paramount True Blue, the same but mid-blue. The Swiss blues are Lake of Thun (Ullswater), medium blue with dark blotch; Lake of Thun, clear light blue, Burnett; Delft Blue, very light blue, blue blotches, Stokes.

black. Jet Black, 80% black during the spring, in bright weather deep purple undertones are noticeable. Typical Swiss size, Park's and Stokes.

Violas. Violas are available in several separate clear solid colors, and there are also a few varieties with more than one color. The best bred violas have no lines radiating from the center, although the lines do not detract from the appearance of the flowers. The solid colors are:

white: White Perfection. A clear pure beautiful white, a better white than that of white pansies.

Avalanche, pure white.

apricot: Another beautiful shade; to me all viola colors are lovely. Sometimes this is just listed as Apricot; the variety Chantreyland is also apricot.

red: Arkwright Ruby is a deep solid velvety ruby-red.

yellow: Yellow Perfection is a deep clear butter-yellow.

LUTEA SPLENDENS is also yellow, and so is SCOTTISH YEL-
LOW, which is large-flowered and pure yellow, Burnett.
BLUE: Most so-called blue Violas are really lavender. BLUE GEM
(Jersey Gem) has small violet-blue flowers, long bloom-
ing, Burnett. BLUE PERFECTION is larger, a deep blue.
ADMIRATION is also dark blue, Stokes. CAMPANULA BLUE
is bright blue with a yellow eye, early and very floriferous,
Park's.
LAVENDER AND PURPLE: PURPLE BEDDER is a rosy purple, Burpee.
PAPILIO is a lavender blue with a white face and, according to its admirers, one of the loveliest Violas, Stokes.
MIXTURES: Since all of the Viola colors are harmonious and
blend well together, mixtures can be a good choice.
MONARCH MIXED has large well-rounded flowers, very
freely produced. Wide range of colors, bicolors, and
picotees. TOYLAND is a new F_2 hybrid mixture, pure colors
of red, yellow, blue, purple, violet, white and apricot as
well as many color combinations, 2-inch flowers. Hybrid
vigor assures strong free flowering qualities. Burnett and
Stokes.
PLANTS: Wayside Gardens in Mentor, Ohio has unusual Viola
plants, not the ones ordinarily listed in seed catalogues.

Besides the solid color Violas there are some nice small
bicolors. JOHNNY-JUMP-UPS are an old-fashioned favorite
and when you have had some plants in your garden they
will self-sow and perpetuate themselves for years. The tiny
purple, lavender and yellow flowers are lavish bloomers
and the plant has a special charm all its own. A standard
variety is HELEN MOUNT. KING HENRY is another bicolor
of rich violet and light blue with a gold eye. These are
both from Harris.

Culture. Pansies are one of the first signs of spring. While
the weather is still cold and raw and there are no leaves
on the trees, most of us see boxes of Pansies at the florists
and can hardly wait to have them in our own gardens. So

we buy a few boxes and have flowers until about the first of June; by that time they are leggy, the flowers small, and we rip them out. The plants probably cost several dollars, and all we had was a very few weeks of flowering. Actually both pansies and violas are very easy to grow from seed, and by growing your own, you not only save considerable money but usually get infinitely better flowers. The average, small commercial plant-grower apparently does not bother at all about buying choice seed, and the result is small flowers in a heterogenous mixture of colors. The best way to illustrate my two points—money saved and superior plants—is to tell an experience of mine. Last August one of my friends got ⅟₁₆ ounce of GRAND DUKE MICHAEL pansy seed from Steele (they have a better white variety now, MOON MOTH). It cost $2.50; she sowed part of the seed and gave me the rest. I was about to leave for a vacation, and hastily broadcast the seed in a spot where I had dug up some old iris. The seed had no attention, not even watering, but by the end of September I had about 40 plants to put in the coldframe, and my friend had about 60. By the end of March some of the pansies were in bud and I picked them every day from the first of April until I dug them up the middle of July; they were still flowering then but a bit leggy and I wanted the space for something else. In other words, I had more than three dozen plants for about 35¢, all a lovely clear color, with large flowers and plenty of them. At the cheapest local grower, plants were 10¢ each with small nondescript flowers.

The real selling point is not the money saved, although that is an important factor. The essential thing is that you can grow so much lovelier Pansies yourself. The seed of both Pansies and Violas can be sown either in early spring for summer bloom, or in August for spring blooming. And you will have infinitely stronger plants than the average bought ones.

Violas are often propagated by cuttings, which is the best way to retain a desirable strain of hard-to-get varieties, since Viola plants from cuttings always come true to color. I have read some elaborate descriptions of the technique of root cutting, but learned from Mrs. Harper in Oregon that the whole thing is very simple. Pull up a plant and take it gently apart into pieces with some roots and a few stems. Cut off the tops leaving 2–3 inches of stem, and put these shoots into the coldframe, or straight into the ground if the soil is moist where the cuttings can be shaded for at least part of the day. The cuttings should be made at least 6 weeks before the first Fall Frost Date (see page 283 so that they have a chance to get rooted before frost.

When to plant. Seeds of Pansies and Violas can be sown in early spring for summer bloom, or in August for spring blooming. When you plant them really depends on the part of the country you live in. The seed will not germinate properly and the young seedlings do very poorly if the weather is hot and dry. Also the plants tend to produce very small flowers if the weather is hot; in other words, they are cool weather plants. So if you live in the South or Middle West, it is best to plant the seeds in August for early spring blooming. The seed should also be fall-sown in ideal climates like the Pacific Northwest and parts of California, because plants will bloom there from early spring throughout the summer. In the cool climates of the East and Middle West, in Zones E, F and G, these plants can be spring-sown in a coldframe, planting the seed the middle of March or the first of April. Seed planted in my coldframe March 30th started to bloom June 25th, and I had flowers until hard frost November 10th.

How to plant. AUGUST PLANTING. The earlier in the month the seed is planted the better, although even late August is all right if you do not get your first frost until the middle of October. It is a good idea to weed and water the ground a week or so ahead and then at planting time pull out any weed seedlings that have sprouted. Pulverize the soil with a rake, and sow the seed broadcast or in rows. Water well. Many growers cover the seeds with burlap until they have germinated although I never do. If the weather is dry, keep the seed bed moist but not too wet. Seeds germinate in about a week, and in a month or so have a set of true leaves and can be transplanted.

They can be put in a coldframe or right in the garden. They are very hardy and should winter well out-doors in any climate with a little protection. I prefer putting them right into the garden because then the roots get a good start in the fall and the plants are not set back by transplanting in the spring. Mr. Steele does all his transplanting in the fall and winters his plants in the open with a manure and peat moss mulch between the plants, not over them. The one danger is that the plants may heave with alternate frost and thaws, and if uprooted may die. Hard frosts or severe winters do not bother them. These plants will bloom early in the spring, and be strong and floriferous. Plants that have been wintered in a coldframe can be transplanted in early spring, and will flower a little later than the ones which were put directly into the garden.

SPRING PLANTING. Pansies should be sown as early as possible in the spring, either indoors or in the coldframe. If seed planting is delayed until the weather is warm, the plants will do very badly. The seed is hardy and can be put in the coldframe any time during March. Cover with $\frac{1}{8}$ inch of soil. Usually the seedlings can be put into the open garden without any intermediate transplanting. The plants start flowering while they are very small, about 8–10 weeks after the seed is planted.

Violas are not quite as fussy about climatic conditions

and can be planted any time during the spring, right in the garden if you wish. Early coldframe planting will prolong the blooming period.

Care and cultivation. It is important to keep the dying flowers cut, because seed production slows up flowering. However, it is also advisable not to pick every flower as soon as it opens, because the flowers will have short stems, and the plant wears itself out trying to produce new flowers.

For very large flowers and strong plants, Mr. Steele advises feeding the plants every 2 weeks. Dissolve 2 tablespoons of Vigoro in a gallon of water, and pour a cupful around each plant. Plants that have been put into the garden in the fall need a light covering. Hay or straw should be put over them when the ground has frozen hard; do not use a heavy covering such as leaves since they might smother the foliage.

If plants get leggy during the summer, cut them back to within an inch or so of the base, and new flowering shoots will form.

Uses and planting combinations. Pansies and Violas can be used for bedding, window boxes, or to grow in flower pots.

Fall-sown seed does not usually bloom long enough to do for summer bedding, but spring-sown seed will flower all summer.

Some suggested planting combinations are:
Middle ground—Pansies MAJESTIC GIANTS MAMMOTH WHITE, WHITE WITH BLOTCH and YELLOW, SWISS RASPBERRY ROSE, CLEAR CRYSTAL LIGHT BLUE and ORANGE, LAKE OF ZURICH, JET BLACK; dwarf Snapdragons SWEETHEART mixed; edging—Violas WHITE PERFECTION and YELLOW PERFECTION.

Solid bed of Pansies BUTTERFLY HYBRIDS; edging—Alyssum
  CARPET OF SNOW.

Background—*Salvia farinacea*; middle ground—Petunia APPLE-
  BLOSSOM; edging—Pansy MOON MOTH.

Middle ground—Petunia SKY CASCADE; edging—Viola CHAN-
  TREYLAND.

Petunia [pe-too'-ni-a]. *Solanaceae* family. About a dozen species are known with a South American origin.

History. Petunias in their native land are small-flowered plants which grow as rank as weeds. They are related botanically to tobacco, potatoes and tomatoes. The name comes from the word "petun" which it is believed means tobacco. In 1823 a white Petunia was discovered in the Argentine and seeds were sent to France and England. In 1830 a rose-violet (magenta is probably a better description) was found in Uruguay. Today there are many species but probably all are derived from these two flowers, and it is interesting to notice in our own gardens how often self-sown seedlings, regardless of the parents, turn out to be either white or magenta. Although hybridizers have been working on Petunias for over 100 years, the really fancy hybrids are not more than 35 years old, and work constantly is being carried on, with new varieties listed every year.

Description

HEIGHT: 6–18 inches

PLANTING DISTANCE: 6–10 inches apart

COLORS: White, yellow, many shades of pink, rose, crimson, and dark mahogany reds that look almost black, blue-lavender, mauve, purple, and many bi-colors

TYPE: Some Petunias are half-hardy and some are tender; discussed in detail in culture section

GERMINATION TIME: 6–10 days for the dwarf and bedding varieties, 10–12 days for the large-flowered fringed and double ones

SEED TO BLOOM: 2–3 months

BLOOMING PERIOD: All summer until frost

IS INDOOR OR COLDFRAME PLANTING REQUIRED? Not for the dwarf and bedding Petunias, but advisable for the large-flowered and double ones

CAN BE TRANSPLANTED: Yes, even when the plants are flowering.

SELF-SOW: Yes, but they usually revert to white, magenta or a rather dull pink

FALL-SOW: No

I suppose Petunias are the most popular annual in the United States (one commercial seed house sells 5 tons of Petunia seed yearly). Their very easy culture, wide variety of color, and constant bloom from early summer to frost under any conditions of heat and drought makes them almost indispensable for any garden. I hold no brief against the prevalent universal use of Petunias, but I do make a plea for readers to select varieties with judicious care. There are literally dozens of varieties of Petunias and they are far from being uniformly good. Some Petunias are as beautiful as any flower that grows, but many seen in summer gardens are dull and uninteresting—horrid, hot pinks, small nondescript whites, and the ever recurring magenta.

It is just as easy to grow good Petunias as dull ones for it is simply a case of buying good varieties. This is true of many annuals, of course, but applies more to Petunias because of the enormous difference in color, habit of growth, and flower form. The height varies from the dwarf, 6-inch plants to trailing, spreading ones which grow at least 1½ feet long. There are small single flowers, large single ones, flowers with ruffled edges, flowers with fringed edges, some with five-pointed petals like a star, and double flowers that look almost like roses. The color range is tremendous and includes not only many colors, but an enormous range within these colors. Many of the varieties are bi-colored, or colors combined with white. The choice is bewildering, and I cannot help repeating that good varieties are so very lovely and poor ones so dull that it is of essential importance that you buy and raise the best.

Another factor to consider when choosing Petunias is where they are to be used. Dwarf varieties make good edging plants. Taller, erect plants can be used for bedding, while the balcony Petunias grow tall and sprawling and are suitable for hanging baskets, window boxes, or covering sunny banks. The beautiful large single-fringed and ruffled Petunias are a bit trickier to grow and produce less flowers than the small-flowered small ones, but they are easily grown if you go at it the right way, and you can have beds full of them for very little money although if you buy nursery plants they are quite expensive.

Petunias are not only of easy culture but some of the varieties are as floriferous as any flower that grows; some plants will produce 400–500 flowers in one season. The foliage varies from deep to light green, and shows very little in some of the bedding varieties, while the large leaves of the fringed and ruffled types are quite conspicuous. One Petunia characteristic is the stickiness of the foliage; another is the pleasant light fragrance.

Classifications and recommended varieties. The great number of Petunia varieties makes trying to choose the best from seed catalogues difficult. But Petunias can be classified quite simply, and I shall discuss each classification briefly and recommend a limited number of varieties.

The big change in Petunias is the development of so many F_1 hybrid varieties. The superior qualities of the hybrids are, to quote from the Park's catalogue: *greater vigor* (faster, stronger, growth, quicker bloom, larger flowers, brighter colors; heat resistance to last the summer in good condition), *greater production* (more plant—more flowers), *greater uniformity* (flower color and plant habit show almost no variation) and *new colors* (many offered here were not possible except as hybrids).

The only disadvantage with the hybrids is that the seeds should be planted indoors 6 to 10 weeks before the last expected frost. But this is not difficult and is discussed on page

Petunias can be classified into 6 groups:
1. F_1 Hybrid Grandiflora (large flowers). Single.
This is probably the most popular of the hybrids—Stokes lists about 70 varieties. The beautiful huge flowers are much larger than the old Grandifloras and should be used where their size and colors can be seen and appreciated. The plants are approximately 1 foot tall.

WHITE

GLACIER. The large 4½-inch flowers are heavy satin textured with chartreuse in the throats.

WHITE MAGIC. An old standard with pure white ruffled 3-inch flowers which are rather small for a Grandiflora but the plants are early and vigorous bloomers.

SNOW MAGIC has slightly larger 3½-inch flowers.

YELLOW

SUNBURST. The first yellow F_1 Grandiflora with ruffled beautiful light lemon yellow flowers.

ORANGE

TANGERINE. Tangerine orange 3½-inch flowers with prominent white throats. Stokes and Comstock, Ferre.

SALMON

APPLEBLOSSOM. All-American 1965. 3- to 3½-inch flowers slightly variegated from light pink to light salmon pink, lightly veined.

BALLERINA. An All-American Selection in 1952. Large fringed salmon orange flowers with darker veins.

MAYTIME. Slightly fringed 3½-inch clear light salmon pink with darker veins in a white throat.

PINK AND ROSE

PINK MAGIC. For many years a favorite bright rose pink.

HAPPINESS. Stokes calls this variety their most popular bright rose-pink, and Park's says it is their finest rose-pink Grandiflora. 4-inch flowers.

RED

CANDY APPLE. Large smooth-edged vivid scarlet red.

EL TORO. Deep cherry-red 3-inch flowers.

TANGO. Fringed scarlet red.

SCARLET MAGIC. 3½-inch bright scarlet, golden throats.

BLACK OPAL. 4-inch velvety wine red. Harris original.

BLUE AND PURPLE

BLUE LACE. Wide-throated 3-inch flowers of light orchid blue ruffled and veined with deep violet blue.

MALIBU. Earliest medium blue with 3-inch deep flag blue flowers opening more violet.

BLUE MAGIC. Slightly fringed 3½-inch deep violet blue.

BLUE LUSTRE. 3-inch deep purple flowers. Burnett, Stokes.

BICOLORS

CALYPSO is the bicolor listed by most of the seedsmen, and is the most popular one. Fringed 3½-inch flowers are scarlet with white 5-pointed star.

SABRE DANCE. Slightly ruffled dark crimson and white.

FIESTA. Large 4-inch bright rose pink and white.

FANDANGO. 3½- to 4-inch ruffled violet and white flowers similar to CALYPSO.

BLUE PICOTEE is a new bicolor with deep violet blue flowers with a white border. Burpee and Park's.

CASCADE SERIES, F_1 Hybrid Grandiflora. Single. This series has extra large 4- to 4½-inch flowers on 14- to 15-inch plants, suitable for window boxes as well as for bedding. Early.

WHITE CASCADE. Pure white ruffled 4-inch flowers.

CORAL CASCADE. Coral salmon with white throats.

PINK CASCADE. Slightly ruffled clear bright pink, light yellow throat.

RED CASCADE. Scarlet red

SKY CASCADE. Light blue. Stokes.

ROYAL CASCADE. Deep velvety purple, new. Stokes.

BICOLOR CASCADE. Pink and white. Burnett.

2. F_1 Hybrid Multiflora (many flowers). Single.

This group has all the high qualities of the Grandifloras with medium-size plain edged rounded flowers and plenty of them. The plants are more erect than the Grandifloras which makes them very showy for window boxes and pots. Approximately 1 foot tall.

WHITE

PALEFACE. All-American 1955 winner, pure white 2½-inch flowers with creamy throats.

WHITE SATIN. Early pure white on free-flowering plants.

WHITE JOY. Pure white, early, uniform 10-inch plants.

YELLOW
MOON GLOW. Masses of creamy yellow with deeper centers.

ORANGE
ORANGE BELLS. Opens orange-scarlet with bright cream throat, matures orange-pink.

SALMON
PINK JOY. A new rich medium salmon pink which is very early on uniform 10-inch plants.
PEACH SALMON. A soft salmon pink. Burnett, Comstock, Ferre.

PINK AND ROSE
SUGAR PLUM. Deep orchid pink heavily veined with rich orchid purple.
PINK SATIN. Rose-pink with light throats.
DAWN SATIN. Lovely light pink. Burnett.
ROSE JOY. Early clear rose-pink with white throats.

RED
CORAL SATIN. All-American 1961. Opens cherry-red, changes to coral rose.
RED SATIN. 3-inch scarlet red with light yellow throats.
COMANCHE. All-American 1953, rich scarlet red.
RED JOY. 2¼-inch intense scarlet, early.

BLUE AND PURPLE
MERCURY. Finest pure light blue, compact plants stay neat and unfading all summer.
PURPLE PLUM. Rich plum rose heavily veined with fuchsia red.
BLUE JOY. Medium violet-blue.
PURPLE JOY. Pure deep violet. Burnett, Comstock, Ferre.

BICOLORS
GLITTERS. All-American 1955, rosy red-barred white.
STARFIRE. Striped evenly with sharply defined rich scarlet and white. Most intense color, and best plant habit of any bicolor.
STAR JOY. Deep carmine rose with white star.

POLARIS. Beautiful violet-blue with white star.

3. F_1 Hybrid Grandiflora (large flowers). Double.

These are the largest of the double Petunias, and the edges are usually frilled or fringed. Generally 1 foot.

WHITE

SONATA. Pure white with large fringed 4-inch flowers.

BRIDAL BOUQUET. Another pure white with 3½-inch flowers, yellow throats.

SALMON

LYRIC. 3½-inch light salmon pink flowers.

SALMON BOUQUET. Also a large-flowered light salmon pink.

ALLEGRO. A deeper salmon.

ROSE AND PINK

CAPRICE. Deeply-fringed bright rose-pink.

RED

GRENADIER. 3½-inch well fringed intense scarlet-red.

VALENTINE. Ruffled lighter red 3-inch flowers.

BLUE AND PURPLE

BLUE DANUBE. Light lavender blue with dark violet.

ORCHID BOUQUET. 3½-inch pale lavender flowers with deeper orchid veins.

BLUE MONARCH. Velvety large violet-blue flowers. Park's.

NOCTURNE. Midnight purple. Burnett.

BICOLORS

CIRCUS was an All-American in 1972, the first double since 1947 to win an award. The large 3½-inch flowers are bright salmon red edged well with white.

PRESTO is carmine rose and white variegated.

FANTASY has 3-inch dark blue and white fringed flowers.

4. F_1 Hybrid Multiflora (many flowers). Double.

This type of double Petunia is fine for all summer bloom since they are more rain-resistant and free flowering than the larger Grandifloras. The medium size 2- to 3-inch flowers smother compact 1-foot plants.

WHITE
SNOWBERRY TART (SNOW BIRD), pure white, prolific.
WHITE DELIGHT. Also pure white, compact.

SALMON
HONEY BUNCH (PEACH TART), soft clear salmon.

PINK AND ROSE
PINK DELIGHT. Pale pink with crimson veining.
RASPBERRY PINK (PINK RICHES). Lovely soft pink.
PLUM DOUBLE. Bright orchid pink, pencilled deep purple.

RED
CARDINAL RED RICHES (APPLE TART). First bright scarlet.

BLUE AND PURPLE
LAVENDER DELIGHT. Rosy lavender. Comstock, Ferre.
BLUE EMPRESS. Violet-blue. Burpee.

BICOLORS
CHERRY TART. Cherry-rose, edged well with white.
STRAWBERRY TART. Strawberry red and white. Burnett.
PEPPERMINT. Rose-pink stripes. light pink background.
POLKA DOT. White with small bright blue center tuft. Park's.

5. Giants of California.

The distinguishing feature of this group is the enormous size of the flowers, 4 to 6 inches across and ruffled and frilled with heavy veining. The plants are 8 to 12 inches high. Available only in mixtures.

6. Giant Single and Bedding Petunias. Inbred Varieties.

The F_1 hybrids are so popular that some of the leading seedsmen do not list any other Petunias. But this group still has a place in the garden since some of them have large flowers, and others have dwarf, more compact plants. And, above all, they can be planted directly in the garden. Burnett offers the largest number of varieties, and Olds and Stokes have a few.

Culture. The culture of the edging, bedding and balcony Petunias is an easy matter. The large-fringed, ruffled, and double ones are the result of painstaking hybridizing and require more care and coddling for they are the incubator babies of the Petunia family.

The seed of dwarf, bedding and balcony Petunias is hardy and can be planted out of doors about the date of the last spring frost. They flourish and flower in any soil, can be transplanted at any stage of their growth (even when flowering), and will thrive under the most adverse conditions. Seed of the fancy varieties should be started early indoors where the temperature is warm and they will have personal attention. The method is discussed in **How to plant.**

When to plant. Although seeds of the dwarf, bedding and balcony Petunias are hardy and can be sown early, they seem to like warm weather and seed planted May 1st–15th, in Zone E, blooms as quickly as seed planted two weeks earlier. These seeds bloom quickly, usually in two months or less. Self-sown seedlings sometimes start flowering as soon as July 1st (I dumped some compost in a neglected part of my garden one spring and found a blooming Petunia there before the first of July), and seed planted May 1st blooms soon after that. I suggest planting the seeds in the garden about the time of the last spring frost date, or a week or so later. The earliest suggested dates for planting seed in the garden are: (see page 282 for **Spring Frost Zone Map**)

Zone A	Feb. 15	–March 1
Zone B	March 1	–March 15
Zone C	March 15	–April 1
Zone D	April 1	–April 15
Zone E	April 15	–May 1
Zone F	May 1	–May 15
Zone G	May 15	–June 1

The seed can also be planted a month or so after these dates for late plants. Seed of the fancy varieties should be planted indoors about a month before these dates.

How to plant. The only point to bring up in connection with outdoor seed planting concerns covering the seeds. One reason why some people have trouble with Petunias is that they insist on burying the seed. I have had people tell me they planted the seeds an inch deep and then wondered why the poor plants never came up. It is very fine seed and should be scattered on the surface of the ground and pressed in.

The fringed, ruffled and double Petunias really should have an indoor start. They do best if it is warm; the seed is very fine, germinates slowly and the young seedlings get off to a slow start. Also they take about 3 months to flower. However, since they are slow and small, it is possible to grow a great many plants in a limited space. I have grown 60 double Petunia plants in one 6-inch bulb pan, and they were flowering the end of June and continued until frost.

I suggest sowing the seeds in vermiculite following the general directions on page 17. Plant them about a month before the last spring frost date. Do not cover the seeds, but press them into the surface. Cover with a piece of paper and glass, and keep the vermiculite dampened but not too wet. The seed will germinate slowly, over a period of days, from 10 days to 3 weeks. Remove the cover as soon as the first seeds have germinated, but keep even the tiniest late seedlings because often these laggards produce the best plants.

The seedlings do not require any attention except watering. I never even thin or transplant them. They may be crowded but are small and it will not matter. Of course, if you start them too early they will have to be transplanted, but it will speed up the flowering date. Seed planted here April 1 (last spring frost date April 15–May 1st) produces plants to put in the garden the middle of May and are flowering a month or so later. Choice Petunia plants are very expensive, but by growing your own you can save money and have your choice of varieties.

It is incredible how quickly even tiny seedlings with two or four true leaves will grow when they are put in the garden. Once they are started even the fancy ones grow very quickly and will often start flowering when only 4–5 inches high.

Care and cultivation. Once Petunias, even the fanciest and largest, get started, they ask no attention except routine care and watering during hot spells. Some of the older varieties used to get very straggly looking and full of old seed pods unless they were kept cut. But the newer ones are obviously bred for compact plant growth and this care is not required of many of them. You can always cut some long-stemmed flowers for the house if the plants start to get out of hand. DDT sprays will help keep over-attentive Japanese beetles in control if you are unlucky enough to have them—they were particularly fond of my double flowers. Otherwise I know of no bothersome pests or diseases.

Uses and planting combinations. The uses of Petunias have already been mentioned. Actually there is a Petunia for every garden use except background planting.

Good combinations of Petunias for solid beds
Petunia RASPBERRY PINK. Edging of Alyssum CARPET OF SNOW and/or *Lobelia* CAMBRIDGE BLUE.
Petunia SNOW MAGIC, TANGO, and CALYPSO.
Petunia WHITE JOY, MOON GLOW, and PURPLE JOY.
Petunia PINK CASCADE, SKY CASCADE, and WHITE CASCADE.
Petunias California Giants mixed.

Good bedding combinations

Edging—Petunia SONATA; middle ground—Snapdragons BRIGHT BUTTERFLIES.

Background—*Celosia plumosa* CRUSADER and GOLDEN TORCH; middle ground—Petunia MOON GLOW.

Background—Cleome PINK QUEEN; middle ground—Petunias WHITE MAGIC, PINK MAGIC, and FIESTA; edging—Portulaca AUREA, ROSEA, and ALBA.

Phlox drummondi. Annual Phlox is a native of **Texas,** often called Texas Pride, and there is only 1 species.

History. Perennial Phlox has been growing in English gardens for about 300 years. Linneaus named the plant *Phlox,* which means flame. Vernon Quinn says that witches liked Phlox, so there was a theory that it should be planted in front of the house and behind it, "for any witch landing beside the patch would be so delighted she would busily gather it and haste away, leaving the house unmolested." In 1835 an English botanist, Thomas Drummond, found annual Phlox on the plains of Texas and sent seeds to England, where it was called *Phlox drummondi.* It was described in an English publication of that time as either "light, or deep carmine on the inner surface of the corolla, and a pale blush on the outside, which sets off wonderfully the general effect. A bed of this plant has hardly yet been seen for it is far too precious and uncommon to be possessed by anyone, except in small quantities."

Description

HEIGHT: The dwarf varieties are 6–8 inches tall. The tall varieties are about 15 inches high

PLANTING DISTANCE: Dwarf varieties 4 inches apart. Tall varieties 8 inches apart

COLOR: White, yellow, chamois, red, rose, salmon, purple, lavender, many with white eye

TYPE: Hardy

GERMINATION TIME: 8–17 days

SEED TO BLOOM: 60–70 days

BLOOMING PERIOD: Will bloom all summer until frost if kept moist and given a little fertilizer

IS INDOOR OR COLDFRAME START REQUIRED? No

CAN BE TRANSPLANTED: Yes

FALL-SOW: Can be fall-sown, but early spring planting best in all but temperate climates

SELF-SOW: Yes

The flowers have 10–15 individual 1-inch round florets on one flower head, and several heads on a plant. The heads are carried well above the foliage and make a very showy effect. The leaves are medium green and lance-shaped, and the plants are branching. Although inclined to sprawl, the dwarf varieties have a neat appearance; the tall ones get a bit shabby looking. The plants will continue to bloom for a long time if given a little attention, and if summers are not too hot. There are few annuals which are more easily grown from seed, and which bloom as quickly and well. This phlox is one of the best annuals to use for edgings and dwarf bedding because of the striking color effect when planted in masses.

The color range is large and Phlox colors are definite

and uniform. The white is a clear pure white; the salmon-pink and the buff the best in any annual I know. The reddish purple is not unattractive, in fact it is as good a magenta as there is, but it does not blend well with some of the other colors. This list gives some idea of the color variety in a mixture which is available: salmon self-color, carmine with white eye, watermelon-pink, flesh-pink with salmon eye, purple, white with peach eye, all crimson, carmine with darker eye, lavender with white eye, fuchsia with red eye, salmon with white eye, white, red with white eye, very pale pink, and violet with purple eye.

Classification and recommended varieties. There are three main types of Phlox, and two more specialized ones. The three main ones are:

1. **Dwarf Compact Large-Flowered.** *Phlox drummondi nana compacta.* The plants are 6–8 inches high, branching and compact. This is the best type for edging and low bedding.

BEAUTY SERIES. The individual florets are very large, in fact, they are almost twice the size of the other dwarf strains.
PINK BEAUTY. Soft pink
SCARLET BEAUTY. Scarlet red
WHITE BEAUTY. Snow white
YELLOW BEAUTY. Canary yellow
SALMON BEAUTY.
BLUE BEAUTY. A rare color in Phlox.
GLOBE MIX. Many branches from the base result in a compact mound or globe 6 to 8 inches tall and 8 to 10 inches across. The colors are white, pink, red, and violet.

2. **Tall Large-Flowered.** *Phlox drummondi grandiflora.*
Tall isn't exactly the word for these since they are only 12–15 inches high. The flowers are not as large as the Giant ones, but those are only available in mixtures and Burnett has the Grandifloras in separate colors: chamois, rose, crimson, yellow,

purple and white. The mixtures have both solid colors as well as flowers with different eyes, either white, starred or dark.

3. **Tall Giant-Flowered.** *Phlox drummondi gigantea.*

This strain is a beautiful one. The flowers are enormous and the colors are lovely. Available only in mixtures. The Burnett color illustration shows red flowers with fringed white eyes, rose flowers with starred white and red eyes, salmon with white eyes, rose with dark eyes, solid white and buff, and violet with purple eyes.

There are two other Phlox types, GIANT TETRA and STARRED PHLOX.

GIANT TETRA (short for Tetraploid) is the result of treating seeds with colchicine which apparently doubles the chromosomes with surprising results. The flowers are larger with stronger stems and a lusher appearance. GLAMOUR is the only variety. It was an All-American Selection and has large mid-salmon flowers with creamy white eyes. The plants are 14 inches tall and, being a TETRA, they are extra-vigorous and free-flowering.

STARRED PHLOX. TWINKLES. All-American winner. First dwarf star Phlox. The Harris catalogue says: "Without question the best starred Phlox to grow. Compact plants blanketed with clusters of tiny, bright flowers, distinctly star-shaped with pointed petals. Solid colors and bicolors in shades of red, pink, salmon, rose, lavender, blue and white. 6 to 8 inches tall." Park's has two separate varieties, RED SHADES and SALMON SHADES.

Culture. Phlox is a hardy annual that can be planted early in the spring, or any time until about June 1st. It blooms quickly, often in about 6 weeks if the weather is warm; and in most climates, if kept watered during hot dry weather, will bloom until frost. It can also be fall-planted, and that is the usual procedure in the South. Fall-planted seed bloom early in the spring, and I have read that if the plants are sheared back when the first bloom fades that you will get a second bloom which will last until frost. In the New York region, seed planted about the last frost date blooms until frost without any special care. It reseeds itself.

When to plant. In the South and other mild climates Phlox can be fall-sown, and is often grown as a winter annual since it is hardy enough to stand a cold snap and continue blooming. In the rest of the country a first planting can be made as soon as the frost is out of the ground, which is usually about two weeks before the first spring frost date, or any time during the spring. In fact, Phlox is so adaptable that you can sow it almost whenever you wish.

The earliest dates you can sow Phlox in the spring are: (see page 282 for Spring Frost Zone Map)

Zone A	Feb. 1
Zone B	Feb. 15
Zone C	March 1
Zone D	March 15
Zone E	April 1
Zone F	April 15
Zone G	May 1

If you wish to be assured of continuous flowering until frost, make a second planting about a month later than the above dates.

How to plant. There are no special factors to consider in planting Phlox seed. It should not be covered with more than 1/8 inch of soil, and the plants should be thinned when quite small (when they have their first or second set of true leaves) if they are to branch properly. Crowded plants do not branch and are spindly and bear very few flowers. Although it is sometimes stated that Phlox should not be transplanted I have done it often enough with no visible harm to the plant.

Care and cultivation. Phlox is one of the easiest and most adaptable annuals. To maintain a more compact growth and longer blooming period flowers should be cut so that seed pods do not have a chance to form. The tall Phlox get the same scraggy look that some Petunias get when seed pods are permitted to form along the stems. They also benefit from a feeding of a commercial fertilizer once in the middle of the summer, and a thorough soaking if the soil is very dry.

Uses and planting combinations. Phlox are excellent for edging (the dwarf ones), bedding, window boxes, and narrow beds along walks and driveways. It can also be planted around shrubs, and I have read that fall-planted seed will really bloom early enough to solve the problem of covering up dying bulb foliage, and that since Phlox self-sows one planting will last for several years. It is certainly worth a try.

Some suggested planting combinations are:
Middle ground—Phlox GLAMOUR; edging—*Lobelia* CAMBRIDGE BLUE and Ageratum SUMMER SNOW.
Background—Cosmos SENSATION PURITY; middle ground—Phlox tall YELLOW, PURPLE, and WHITE; edging—Zinnia PINK BUTTONS.
Middle ground—Nasturtiums CHERRY-ROSE, PRIMROSE, GOLDEN GLEAM, SCARLET GLEAM, ORANGE GLEAM, SALMON GLEAM; Edging—Phlox dwarf TWINKLES.
Middle ground—Dahlias COLTNESS; edging—Phlox dwarf WHITE and PINK BEAUTY.

PORTULACA

Portulaca [por-tew-lak'-a]. Purslane. The family is *Portulacaceae*, with about 40 species in the tropical and temperate regions, mostly American.

History. This plant is often called Rose Moss. It was first described in 1829 by Hooker in the *Botanical Magazine.* He said the flowers were "orange-colored, or of a very bright reddish purple." It was "discovered by Dr. Gillies, growing in light sandy soil, in various situations between the Rio del Saladillo, or western boundary of the Pampas, and the foot of the mountains near Mendoza. On the western side of Rio Desaguardero plants were in great profusion, giving to the ground over which they were spread a rich purple hue, here and there marked with spots of orange color, from the orange-colored variety which grew intermixed with the others."

Description
HEIGHT: 3–6 inches
PLANTING DISTANCE: 6 inches apart
COLOR: White, yellow, apricot, pink, rose, scarlet, salmon, some
   striped

TYPE: Half hardy
GERMINATION TIME: 5–10 days
SEED TO BLOOM: 40–50 days
BLOOMING PERIOD: Usually until frost
IS INDOOR OR COLDFRAME PLANTING REQUIRED? No
CAN BE TRANSPLANTED: Yes
FALL-SOW: No
SELF-SOW: Yes, particularly in the southern part of the country

Portulaca is a gay and accommodating garden flower. It flowers profusely in the poorest and driest ground as long as it gets full sun. It seeds itself, and although the double varieties revert to the single form (no catastrophe to me), the colors of the self-sown seedlings are good. The small plants are very spreading and soon form a thick carpet, with flowers topping the branches. The foliage is succulent, with thick stems and short, narrow fleshy leaves. The colors are clear good ones, and the Government Bulletin on annuals calls it "unrivaled for brilliancy among plants of low growth." The flowers open only when in full sun, closing at night and on cloudy days. But there is something about them that makes you feel light-hearted and cheerful.

Classification and recommended varieties. The only Portulaca classification is flower form. Both single and double varieties are available, although many of the so-called doubles are in reality single. Portulaca is usually offered only in mixtures, and while there will be an assortment of colors in a mixture the predominant color is a rather hard deep pink. In one planting of *Portulaca grandiflora* double mixed, these are the colors I noted: clear salmon, yellow, orange, white, cerise (the typical Portulaca pink), apricot, deep pink, glowing red and white with pink blotches. The striped ones have their stripes so close together that at any distance the flowers appear to be a solid color. I cannot find the single form in many colors, but the double is offered in several colors. All are available from Park's.

ALBA. White. The flowers have yellow stamens and are most attractive when planted by themselves.
COCCINEA. Scarlet
ROSEA. Rose
AUREA. Yellow
RED FOUNDLING. Extra large-flowered, carmine-red.
DAY DREAM. Very brilliant red strain with sparkling color range.

There is a new Portulaca variety called Jewel. The single flowers are supposed to be 4 times as large as usual; they actually are very large and the plants do not sprawl so much. Park's has two separate varieties, JEWEL, which is crimson, and WHITE JEWEL.

Culture. Portulaca is very simple to grow. They will grow in any soil, even the gravelly kind around garages or in cracks between stones on terraces. It should be planted in full sun so that the flowers will stay open. The plants do not require any attention aside from thinnings.

When to plant. Although classed as a hardy or half hardy annual, the seeds do not germinate until the weather gets warm, so there is no point in planting until about the date of the last spring frost. Even self-sown seeds do not germinate until well after frost. It can also be planted any time in the spring; the seeds germinate readily in hot weather and bloom in about 6 weeks, so plantings can be made as late as July 1st.

The earliest dates for sowing seeds in the garden are: (see page 282 for Spring Frost Zone Map)

Zone A	Feb. 15 –March 1
Zone B	March 1 –March 15
Zone C	March 15–April 1
Zone D	April 1 –April 15
Zone E	April 15 –May 1
Zone F	May 1 –May 15
Zone G	May 15 –June 1

In the South and in mild climates Portulaca self-sows so freely that it is self-perpetuating. However, since the color of these self-sown plants is so often pink, fresh seed should be sown if you wish to have other colors.

How to plant. The seed is usually just broadcast on the surface of the soil. Since the plants are so spreading it is best to thin them to allow 6 square inches for each plant if you want them to branch. If you do not thin, the plants will flower, but there will only be a few stems. The plants can be transplanted, although usually all you do is scatter the seeds and forget about them.

Uses and planting combinations. Portulaca is generally used in places where the soil is poor and a spot of bright color is needed: to line a walk or driveway, around garages, on sunny banks, and between stepping stones on a walk or terrace. Seed can be broadcast over rock gardens to fill them with color when the perennial rock garden plants have finished flowering. Portulaca can also be used as an edging for flower beds.

Some suggested planting combinations are:
Background—Rocket Snapdragons Lemon; middle ground—
    Cut-and-Come-Again Zinnias Canary Yellow, White,
    Salmon; edging—Portulaca Aurea, Red Foundling and
    Alba.

Middle ground—Pansies BUTTERFLY HYBRIDS; edging—Portulaca WHITE.

Narrow border—with background Ageratum BLUE CHIP; middle ground—Snapdragon FLORAL CARPET WHITE; edging—Portulaca RED FOUNDLING.

Narrow border—Verbena MARILYN, Portulaca ALBA on both sides.

Middle ground—Gleam Nasturtiums; edging—Portulaca WHITE, SALMON, and YELLOW.

Scabiosa [skay-bee-o'-sa]. This plant is a member of the *Dipsacacaea* family, of which there are about 70 species in Europe, Asia and Africa.

History. The name Scabiosa comes from the Latin word *scabo,* meaning itch and was given to the plant because it was supposed to cure skin eruptions. An article in the *National Geographic* says that the old name Scabious is a linguistic legacy of that lusty period in our history when bathing was both a luxury and a social affectation. Old European gardens were not complete without a plot of Scabious, cure for the "scabies" or itch. Scabiosa is also called Pincushion Flower because the light-colored stamens look like pins stuck into the darker rounded flower head;

this effect is especially noticeable with the dark varieties. Other popular names are Sweet scabious, Mourning Bride (one variety has very dark flowers), and Glass Flower. The plant is a weed in Europe, with a small 1-inch lavender flower. In California it self-sows and seems to be naturalized. The hybridists have enlarged the flowers and increased the color range. There is a dwarf as well as a tall form.

Description

HEIGHT: Dwarf varieties 18 inches high. Tall varieties 3 feet high

PLANTING DISTANCE: 8 inches apart

COLOR: Lavender, pink, old rose, maroon

TYPE: Half hardy

GERMINATION TIME: 15–20 days

SEED TO BLOOM: About 3 months

BLOOMING PERIOD: Until frost

IS INDOOR OR COLDFRAME START REQUIRED? No

CAN BE TRANSPLANTED: Yes

FALL-SOW: No

SELF-SOW: In some climates; freely in California

Scabiosa is not a particularly attractive plant, but the flowers are pretty and good in a mixed border or for cutting. The plant flowers well during hot dry weather, which makes it useful in climates where summers are hot. The old standard form is a tall 3-foot plant with few leaves of a nondescript green, and very long stems. Since the flowers are only about 1½–2 inches across, the proportion of stem to flower seems unbalanced and the plants look leggy. The newer, less tall, forms are much better in this respect. The colors are pastel shades, lavender, white and light to deep pink; the lavender Scabiosa is the prettiest lavender of any annual that I have seen. There is also a very dark maroon which to me is not appealing either as a garden flower or for cutting.

Classification and recommended varieties. There are two classifications of Scabiosa: since the plants are similar, the choice depends upon which height you wish.

1. **Tall Double.** GIANT IMPERIALS. This type is 2½ to 3 feet tall. The large 2½- to 3-inch flowers are about 2 inches deep and they look ball-shaped. The protruding white-tipped pistils give the flowers a frosted effect. The stems are long and wiry and therefore excellent for cutting. The seed is usually available only in mixtures in which the colors include white, shades of pink, coral and salmon, scarlet, crimson and maroon as well as lavender and blue.

Burnett has the following 7 separate colors. 3 feet tall.

BLACK KNIGHT. Velvety black-purple
BLUE MOON. Rich, deep lavender blue
CORAL MOON. Lovely salmon shades
FIRE KING. Fiery scarlet
LOVELINESS. Delicate salmon rose
OXFORD BLUE. Large, deep blue
SILVER MOON. Pure white of enormous size

2. **Semi-dwarf.** Compact 18-inch plants for beds and cutting. The flowers are not quite as large as the GIANT IMPERIALS but they more than make up for this in numbers so some gardeners prefer the shorter plants, especially since the flower stems are still long enough for lovely multi-colored bouquets. The flowers are well-rounded with dense flower heads. Available only in mixtures and the colors include white, pink, rose, scarlet, blue, lavender and maroon.

When to plant. Scabiosas are half hardy annuals and should be planted directly in the garden about the date of the last frost, although they may also be planted up to a month later and will produce large, good flowering plants.

The earliest safe dates for sowing seeds in the garden are: (see page 282 for Spring Frost Zone Map)

Zone A	Feb. 15 –March 1
Zone B	March 1 –March 15

Zone C   March 15–April 1
Zone D   April 1 –April 15
Zone E   April 15 –May 1
Zone F   May 1   –May 15
Zone G   May 15 –June 1

How to plant. Plant the seeds right out in the open and cover with ⅛-inch of soil. They germinate quickly, and as soon as the first or second set of true leaves have formed, the plants can be thinned or transplanted to stand about 8–10 inches apart. This is not much space for such a tall plant, but since the plants are rather spindly they do not need much room, and they look better if placed close together.

Culture. Scabiosas have no bugs or diseases, germinate and flourish without any special attention, start flowering 2½–3 months after the seed is sown, and continue until frost. The ease of culture and abundance of flowers are two reasons why Scabiosa are popular.

About the only attention Scabiosa needs, aside from routine weeding and watering, is keeping the old flowers cut to prevent seeding and to prolong the flowering. When you see self-sown plants flowering in poor soil and unlikely places in California, you realize that this is not a demanding plant.

Uses and planting combinations. Scabiosa should be grown either in a mixed border, or in the cutting garden.

Background—Morning-glories HEAVENLY BLUE, Scabiosa blue, white and pink shades, Snapdragons tall ROCKET PINK AND GOLDEN; edging—Phlox dwarf WHITE BEAUTY.
Background—Cosmos SENSATION PURITY and PINKIE; middle ground—tall blue, rose, and white Scabiosa, Asters EARLY CHARM or CREGO; Petunia WHITE, ROSE and

PURPLE JOY; edging—Violas white, yellow and purple.

Middle ground—Zinnias Elegans SALMON ROSE; Scabiosa BLUE and SILVER MOON; edging—Ageratum MIDGET BLUE.

Background—Larkspur DAZZLER and WHITE KING; middle ground—Verbena ANNAPOLIS BLUE, Scabiosa SILVER MOON and BLACK KNIGHT; edging—Portulaca white and yellow.

SHIRLEY POPPIES

Shirley Poppy. *Papaver rhoeas*. This is a form of the **Corn** Poppy, usually known now as the Flanders Field Poppy.

History. Scarlet Poppies have been growing wild in the fields of Europe for years. In 1880 the Reverend W. Wilkes, Secretary of the Royal Horticultural Society in England who lived in Shirley, England found a poppy growing in his garden which had a thin white edge on the petals and yellow stamens; the usual pollen and stamens were very dark and disfigured the flower when it ripened. He saved the seed, planted it and the next year out of the

200 or so plants there were 4 or 5 with the same white line. He worked patiently for years, as one inevitably does with hybridizing, and finally produced all the lovely colors we have today in Shirley Poppies, all with light centers.

Description

HEIGHT: 12–18 inches

PLANTING DISTANCE: 8 inches apart

COLOR: White, and shades of pink, rose, red, scarlet

TYPE: Very hardy

GERMINATION TIME: 6–12 days

SEED TO BLOOM: 51–70 days

BLOOMING PERIOD: About 4–6 weeks

IS INDOOR OR COLDFRAME START REQUIRED? This plant cannot be transplanted, so early start is not possible

CAN BE TRANSPLANTED: No

SELF-SOW: Yes

FALL-SOW: Yes

Poppies are truly beautiful flowers, with their delicate silken petals and the bluish green foliage. The colors of the Shirley Poppies are particularly lovely, with all shades of pink from very pale ones to a deep watermelon color, pure white, the typical scarlet color, and both single and double forms. The flowers are not long lasting, many bloom only a day, but the plants keep on opening new flowers daily during the relatively short time they flower. The flowers are on long wiry stems, and the buds hang their heads until just before they open, apparently because nature carefully protects them—they will rot if rain-drenched before they open. After they bloom there is a large upright oval capsule which contains an enormous number of seeds, some of which self-sow.

Classification and recommended varieties. The usual classification of Shirley Poppies is by flower form—single and double. Both are lovely, although I like the single ones better. The seed is often offered only in mixtures, and the plants will have a large and varied color range. There will be self-colors and plants with white-edged petals and others with beautiful color combinations. In one day, I had the following colors in bloom: plain red, red with white edge, watermelon-pink, light pink and white zones, scarlet, rose-pink, shrimp-pink shading into lighter pink edges, all with white centers and yellow stamens. The scarlet and pinks clash a bit but not unpleasantly; probably because the flowers are so lovely that you just cannot find fault with them.

The seed is usually offered only in mixtures, either single or double. I could only find two separate colors in any of the catalogues I have.

SINGLE MIXED. Papery silk-like petals in tones of pink, salmon, apricot, terra cotta, yellow, red and so on.
DOUBLE MIXED. Same color range, which also includes white, rose, and scarlet.
SWEET BRIAR. All double, fluted deep rose-pink.
FLANDERS FIELD. Single, orange scarlet, black cross.
AMERICAN LEGION. Single, orange scarlet, white cross at base.

Culture. The Shirley Poppy is a hardy annual which can be fall- or early spring-sown, and can also be planted any time in the spring. The seed must be sown where it is to bloom since no Poppy likes transplanting. The plants bloom quickly; seed planted in my garden about the first of April, flower by the end of June; while seed planted when the weather is warm bloom in less than 2 months. Easily grown in any sunny location, the only drawback is that the bloom does not last very long. You can have a long period of bloom only by making three plantings about 6 weeks apart. Where the summers are really hot these

Poppies should only be grown for spring-flowering since they do best in reasonably cool moist weather.

When to plant. The first spring planting can be made as soon as the ground can be worked. You do not even have to wait for the ground to be frost-free; just work the surface over with a rake or cultivator. The seed can also be fall-planted for very early flowering. No matter how early you plant seed in the spring the plants never bloom as soon as fall-sown seed—this is true of many other hardy annuals too.

The earliest safe dates for planting seed in the garden are: (see page 282 for Spring Frost Zone Map)

Zone A	Jan. 15 –Feb. 1
Zone B	Feb. 1 –Feb. 15
Zone C	Feb. 15 –March 1
Zone D	March 1 –March 15
Zone E	March 15–April 1
Zone F	April 1 –April 15
Zone G	April 15 –May 1

Except where the summers are very hot, these **Poppies** can also be sown any time during the spring.

How to plant. Poppies should be broadcast on the surface of the ground and not covered. When the plants are 2 inches or so high, thin so that they will stand about 8 inches apart.

Care and cultivation. Once thinned, Shirley Poppies will grow and branch well, and require no further care. They are not bothered by insects or diseases. At the end of their blooming period, the plants become tall and leggy, and the foliage begins to die. It is best, therefore, to pull up the entire plant as soon as flowering is over.

Uses and planting combinations. Since the blooming period is short, Shirley Poppies do not make good bedding
plants. One excellent way to use them is to fall plant with
either white and dark blue Larkspur or with *Centaurea
cyanus*. They will bloom early in spring, and when flowering is over, the bed can be planted with Zinnia or Petunia
plants.

Spring-planted Shirley Poppies can be used in beds with
white, pink, lavender or yellow flowers, such as Alyssum,
Cosmos, Scabiosa, Snapdragons and the pastel Zinnias.
See the suggested planting combinations for those flowers,
and you can plant some Shirley Poppies in any of those
beds. Or they can be planted on a sunny bank, or in any
sunny out-of-the-way place for naturalizing.

There are two other annual Poppies besides the Shirley
Poppies.

Argemone. [ar-jem'-o-nee]. PRICKLE POPPY. Mexican
Poppy.

The name comes from the word *argema,* a cataract of
the eye. The plant was supposed to have certain medicinal
qualities. This Prickle Poppy is a stunning plant and, unlike most of the Poppies, stays in bloom for a long time.
The plant is about 3 feet tall with grayish green, white-
veined leaves which have real prickles along the edges. In
fact, the plant is so prickly that it is hard to handle. The
flowers are large, single, open 3-inch ones and are either a
reddish violet or white with yellow centers. The white is
the better color of the two. The petals are usually fringed
or a little frilled. The flowers are followed by prickly seed
pods. It is a hardy annual and can be sown early in the
spring, at least two weeks before the earliest of the two
last spring frost dates. It should be sown where it is to
bloom. Here in Zone E it starts flowering about the first of
July from an April 1st planting, and is still flowering in

the middle of September. It even blooms all summer in the South, which is unusual for a Poppy. The plants are branching and tend to sprawl, and staking is needed if you wish the plants upright. It is not often listed by seedsmen, and I cannot find the colors separated, but Rex D. Pearce has the mixture.

Hunnemannia. [hun-nee-man'-i-a]. Mexican Tulip Poppy. Santa Barbara Poppy. This is a Mexican plant named in honor of John Hunneman, an English botanist. It is an upright 1½-foot plant with long finely cut thick almost gray leaves. The flowers have a deeper cup than the other Poppies, and are canary-yellow with salmon-pink centers in the variety Sunlite which won a Silver Medal in the All America Selections in 1934. Hunnemannia should not be planted until the weather is very warm, about two weeks after the latest spring frost date, where it is to bloom. It will flower in 6–8 weeks and continue for a long time, often until frost. It often self-sows and is perennial in warm regions. It is considered by some people the best of all the Poppies, probably because it blooms for a longer time than either the Shirley or Eschscholzia. It also lasts several days as a cut flower.

SNAPDRAGONS

Snapdragons. The genus is *Antirrhinum* [an-tir-rye'-num], and there are 40 or so species which are native to the warm climate of Southern Europe.

History. The generic name means "noselike," supposedly in reference to the shape of the flowers. The name Snapdragon seems more natural because the flowers are so formed that they will snap when pinched, which presumably is customary with dragons. Other common names in the past have been lion-snap, rabbit's-mouth, dog's-mouth, toad's-mouth, and calf's-snout. This flower was grown in the ancient Latin world, and has been cultivated for centuries in European and American gardens. The early colonists grew them here in pre-revolutionary days. The original flowers were yellow, and until recently there were only three colors—white, yellow and red. Seed catalogues of sixty years ago listed only one tall and one dwarf variety. Today there are numerous colors and varieties.

Description

HEIGHT: Dwarf varieties 8 inch. Tall varieties 18–32 inches

PLANTING DISTANCE: Dwarf 4 inches apart. Tall 8–10 inches apart

COLOR: Many variations and combinations in shades of white, pink to deep red, yellow, bronze

TYPE: Half hardy

GERMINATION TIME: 8–14 days

SEED TO BLOOM: About 4 months

BLOOMING PERIOD: Usually until frost

IS INDOOR OR COLDFRAME START REQUIRED? Since the plants take a relatively long time to bloom, an early start is advisable

CAN BE TRANSPLANTED: Yes

FALL-SOW: No

SELF-SOW: Yes, but in regions with long winters, self-sown plants come up too late to be of much use

Snapdragons are a very popular garden and florist's flower. The beautiful flower spikes in their gorgeous colors are familiar to all of us, although many people do not think of them as possible garden flowers. They are not as simple to grow as many annuals, not because of any quirk in their culture, but because they take longer to bloom than most annuals. But once they start flowering, they are so constant that they repay the effort spent in starting the seed early.

The flower spikes rise on long stems from the crown, and the effect is very colorful even when we have fewer spikes than the catalogues say we should. The colors are good ones. I particularly like the solid whites, lemon-yellow and dark velvety reds but there are pinks and interesting bi-colors as well. The plant is really a perennial treated as an annual, and in the South often lives through the winter to bloom early in the spring. Plants that survive the winter in northern regions are not worth bothering about.

Rust formerly made Snapdragon culture difficult, but a majority of varieties are now rust-resistant.

Classification and recommended varieties. There is no consistency in the way Snapdragons are classified in catalogues, but this is not really important. They are a big florist's flower; they grow them for cutting so for them stems are essential. But home gardeners should choose a type that is suitable for use in the garden. The heights available vary from dwarf 8-inch plants to tall 3-foot ones, so they can be put in borders, the middle of beds, or in the background.

There is a choice of varieties in all heights, especially in the tall ones. The following list is not complete but there are well-recommended ones in each of the height groups.

1. Dwarf. FLORAL CARPET. 6 to 8 inches
2. Dwarf. SWEETHEART. 12 inches
3. Dwarf. LITTLE DARLING. 12 to 15 inches
4. Medium. BRIGHT BUTTERFLIES. 2 to 2½ feet
5. Medium. MADAME BUTTERFLY. 2 to 2½ feet
6. Tall. GIANT RUFFLED TETRAS. 2½ feet
7. Tall. ROCKET. 2½ to 3 feet

1. Dwarf. FLORAL CARPET. A new type of extra dwarf hybrid Snapdragon only 6–8 inches high. Its hybrid vigor results in bushier and more compact growth and an amazing amount of bloom—as many as 25 short spikes at one time, and since new shoots keep forming there is continuous flowering until late fall. Keep picking to extend the display. The colors in the mixture are pink, rose, red, bronze, yellow, orchid and white. Park's and Stokes have separate colors.

2. Dwarf. SWEETHEART. This is a dwarf version of a new hybrid Snapdragon flower from BRIGHT BUTTERFLIES described further on. These plants are only 12 inches high but have stems long enough to cut. Sold only in mixtures.

3. Dwarf. LITTLE DARLING. All-American winner in 1971. Only 12 to 15 inches high, this is also a dwarf hybrid version of the pentstemon-flowered BRIGHT BUTTERFLIES, with very husky base-branching plants. Plenty of bloom on stems long enough to cut. Mixtures only with a full range of Snapdragon colors.

4. Medium. BRIGHT BUTTERFLIES. The "Butterflies" have been called the first really new flower form in many years. This variety was an All-American Selection in 1966. The flowers are often compared to pentstemons with wide-open faces and flaring florets rather than the usual snap jaws. The husky hybrid plants are 2 to 2½ feet tall and prolific with about 10 or 12 flower spikes on long tall stems. If cut back after blooming they will produce second or third crops. Sold in mixtures which have many beautiful colors: crimson, red, apricot, rose, light pink, bronze, yellow, white.

5. Medium. MADAME BUTTERFLY. The same height and flower form as BRIGHT BUTTERFLIES, and also an All-American winner. The only difference is that this variety has new well-doubled flowers sometimes compared to Azaleas.

6. Tall. GIANT RUFFLED TETRA. 2½ feet tall. Spectacular in the garden and as cut flowers. The sturdy base-branching plants probably have the largest florets of any Snapdragons—

2½ inches deep and 2 inches wide—most of them ruffled and placed closely together on long massive spikes. Burnett has 6 separate colors and Burpee has 5: crimson, rose, white, yellow and bright scarlet. Park's has WHITE RUFFLES, huge, ivory-white frilled.

7. Tall. ROCKET. 30 to 36 inches. F_1 hybrid bred especially for garden use and hot weather tolerance. Like the TETRAS, there are long, strong spikes with many closely spaced florets. Full of bloom in mid-summer, and if the spikes are cut back to the top of the leaves they will bloom again in the fall. Park's has 12 separate colors: cherry red; FROSTY ROSE (white with bright rose lip); scarlet; rose (medium rose with faint yellow lip); GOLDEN (bright yellow with white throat); lemon; red (velvety crimson); bronze; pink; TORCH (scarlet); white; orchid (rosy lavender with yellow lips).

Culture. Snapdragons are not as easy to grow as most annuals. You cannot carelessly plant a package of Snapdragon seeds in the garden in May and have Snapdragons blooming two months later. They are half-hardy perennials and to grow good plants they must be planted and have their early growth while the weather is cool. In most sections of the country, that means an early start. An indoor planting is probably the best method, about 6–8 weeks before the date for outdoor planting (which is the earlier of the last spring frost dates). But it should not be indoor planting in a hot room; the plants need a cool temperature, preferably about 45°F. The plants are then put into the coldframe, and later into the garden. All this is time-consuming but worth it if you love beautiful Snapdragons.

Another easier method, and the one I use, is to start seeds in the coldframe a month before the outdoor planting time. This still gives the plants a long, cool growing-season, and although they bloom a little later than those started indoors, they will continue to bloom until frost. They grow very slowly at first. To encourage branching and stocky plants, the tops should be pinched out when the plants have four or six sets of leaves.

When to plant. The dates given below are the outdoor planting dates, for plants not seeds. The seed takes a long time to mature and during early growth the plants require cool weather, so that unless seed is started at least a month before the earliest outdoor planting time it is almost useless to sow it. Seed to be sown indoors should be started 6–8 weeks before these dates.

The earliest safe dates for putting plants into the garden are: (see page 282 for Spring Frost Zone Map)

Zone A	Feb. 15	–March 1
Zone B	March 1	–March 15
Zone C	March 15	–April 1
Zone D	April 1	–April 15
Zone E	April 15	–May 1
Zone F	May 1	–May 15
Zone G	May 15	–June 1

How to plant. Indoor planting. The point in starting seeds indoors is to hasten the outdoor blooming date, but with Snapdragons demanding cool weather, there is no point in fussing with indoor planting unless you see that the seeds and plants are kept at a low temperature. Plant the seeds in vermiculite (see page 21) to prevent damping-off which otherwise might be a problem. It is best not to cover the seeds but just sow them on the surface. When the plants have one or two sets of true leaves, transplant them so that they are 2 inches apart each way; they can either be put in flats or into a coldframe, or best of all the flats themselves can be put into the coldframe for ease of transplanting later into the garden. The plants need plenty of sunshine and cool air.

Coldframe planting. A month before the earliest outdoor planting date is the time to make coldframe plantings. Sow the seed thinly on the surface of the ground, in rows about 3 inches apart, and press into ground with your hand. Be sure that the soil does not get dry, and on fine days raise the sash so that the plants will get plenty of fresh air. These seedlings can be put directly into the garden without any intermediate transplanting.

Care and cultivation. Snapdragons are most demanding during their infancy; but once the plants get a cool weather start and are in the garden, they are very little trouble. If the tops are pinched out the plants will be bushier and probably will not need staking. This can be done either when they have four or six sets of leaves, or when they are a foot or so tall; it is best to do it earlier because then you will not delay blooming. If you cut the flowers before they fade, the plant will send up new ones.

Rust used to be a serious problem, especially in greenhouses when Snapdragons were propagated by cuttings. Although seeds are now bred for resistance to rust, Dr. Wilde's tests found many varieties which were not entirely rust-resistant. Rust forms reddish brown, powdery, pustules, sometimes arranged in circles on leaf surfaces, on petioles, stems, and seed pods. When plants are subject to it they bloom poorly and die early. If the fungicide, Fermate, combined with sulphur, is sprayed on the plants every two weeks, sound protection against both rust and mildew will be provided.

Uses and planting combinations. Because Snapdragons are of medium height, they are generally used for bedding or the middle ground of a flower border.

Some suggested planting combinations are:

Background—Morning-glory HEAVENLY BLUE; middle ground
—Snapdragons Rocket FROSTY ROSE, lemon, red, pink,
and orchid; edging—Alyssum CARPET OF SNOW and Phlox
dwarf SALMON BEAUTY.

Background—Cosmos CANDYSTRIPE; middle ground—Snapdragons BRIGHT BUTTERFLIES yellow, rose, white and light
pink; edging—Verbena RUFFLED WHITE and RUFFLED
PINK.

Background—Cosmos DIABLO; middle ground—Snapdragons
WHITE RUFFLES; edging—yellow Pansies.

Background—Morning-glories HEAVENLY BLUE and PEARLY
GATES; middle ground—Verbena ANNAPOLIS BLUE, edging
—Snapdragons FLORAL CARPET yellow, white, pink or red.

Background—Cleome PINK QUEEN; middle ground—Snapdragons MADAME or BRIGHT BUTTERFLIES; edging—*Lobelia*
CAMBRIDGE BLUE.

SWEET PEAS

Sweet Peas. *Lathyrus* [lath'-ihr-russ] *odoratus. Legumino-sae* family, with more than 200 species which are widespread in America, Europe, Asia, Africa and South America.

History. Nobody knows how many centuries the wild Sweet Pea has been growing in Sicily, but the first written record was in 1695 when it was described in a small book written by an Italian monk, Father Franciscus Cupani. The book brought requests for seeds, which Father Cupani sent to England and Holland in 1699. The original flower was small, no larger than that of garden peas now, with sky blue wings and purple standards; the plant grew 6 feet tall and the most remarkable thing about it was the exquisite fragrance (unfortunately often lacking in today's flowers). By 1718 there was a white variety, and in 1737 a pink one is mentioned. The real interest in Sweet Peas, however, was not aroused until the end of the last century. In 1876 there probably were not more than 15 varieties. But Henry Eckford, of Shropshire, England, began scientific breeding of Sweet Peas, producing new prize-winning varieties every year, and awakening interest in other breeders until in 1900 there were 264 varieties (all straight-petaled) the large majority of them Mr. Eckford's. Then, in 1904, a type called Spencer was introduced which in time completely supplanted the earlier ones. The Spencer was produced by a gardener named Silas Cole, and its petals were deeply waved or frilled. He named the flower for Countess Spencer, the wife of his employer, who lived in Althorp Park, England. The color of the first was a soft pink. Since then probably a thousand varieties have been produced, and it hardly seems possible that at one time Lord Northcliffe's *Daily Mail* gave a $5000.00 prize for a bunch of Sweet Peas in an effort to stimulate interest in developing this flower. Now, Sweet Peas are so well loved that they are one of the top six most popular annuals in commercial seed sales, in spite of the fact that they are not easy to grow, and bloom only a short time.

Description

HEIGHT: Variable, depending on the type, 8 inches to 6 feet

PLANTING DISTANCE: 4 inches apart

COLOR: White, cream, many shades of light lavender to deep
   purple, light pink to deep rose, crimson, maroon, orange

TYPE: Very hardy

GERMINATION TIME: 2–4 weeks

SEED TO BLOOM: About 2 months after germination

BLOOMING PERIOD: Variable, depending entirely upon the
   weather. All summer in cool climates, 4–6 weeks in hot
   ones

IS INDOOR OR COLDFRAME START REQUIRED? No

CAN BE TRANSPLANTED: Better not to, since it slows up blooming

FALL-SOW: In some climates (see **When to Plant**)

SELF-SOW: No

There are two types of Sweet Peas, the older one which
is tall and has tendril-bearing vines, and the newer type
which is a bush one, not as tall, and does not have any tendrils. With the tall type, when the vines are quite small
they start producing flowers, and as they continue to grow
new flowers form. In cool climates such as the Pacific
Northwest and northern New England, the vines will bear
flowers all summer long. But Sweet Peas are not a hot
weather crop, and in most parts of the country the vines
give up when hot weather comes.

The flowers themselves consist of three parts, an upright
back petal called the standard, and two lower side petals
springing from the base, called wings. The early varieties
had only two flowers on each stem, but now it is common
to have up to four, and a few may have five or six. The
stems are a good cutting length, especially in the greenhouse varieties.

The color range is extensive, and includes solid colors

as well as flowers with picotee edges (a solid ground with a different color edge). There is almost every color but yellow, though the alleged blues are really lavender and purple. There is actually a staggering list of varieties and colors, although when you see the plants growing the difference in color does not seem to matter nearly as much as with some other flowers.

The fragrance is one of the chief Sweet Peas charms, although many of the modern varieties have been bred for size and color in preference to fragrance. Even in Seattle, where the growing conditions are ideal and you see Sweet Peas climbing up garden fences everywhere (I got a huge bunch in the public market for 35¢), the flowers were only mildly fragrant. Some of the older varieties are better for this purpose than the new ones, and some particularly fragrant ones are listed in the following section.

Classification and recommended varieties. As already mentioned, there are two main types, tall vines and dwarfer bushes. There are four of the bush type listed in various catalogues, and a diversity of the tall ones. The following list is not complete, but it does include the most important ones.

1. Dwarf. Bush type. LITTLE SWEETHEART. 8 inches.
2. Dwarf. Bush type. BIJOU. 12–15 inches.
3. Medium. Bush type. KNEE-HI. 1½ to 2½ feet.
4. Medium. Bush type. JET-SET. 2½ to 3½ feet.
5. Tall. Climbing. ROYAL. 6 feet.
6. Tall. Climbing. CUTHBERTSON's FLORIBUNDA. 6 feet.
7. Tall. Climbing. GALAXY. 6 feet.
8. Tall. Climbing. Perennial. LATHYRUS LATIFOLIUS.

1. DWARF. LITTLE SWEETHEART. A new type of Sweet Pea only 8 inches high and 8 inches across growing on small, upright, compact, bushy mounds. The plants bloom early and

continue flowering over a long period. The flowers are large
ruffled Spencer-type and cover the plants. Suitable for borders,
bedding and window boxes. Available only in mixtures; the
colors are white, cream, shades of pink and rose, salmon,
carmine, violet shades and dark blue.

2. Dwarf. BIJOU. This type seems to be a favorite with seedsmen. It is called a unique bush type which blooms earlier and
longer than other earlies. The plants are 12 to 15 inches high
and according to Burpee have a "profusion of flowers which
literally covers the foliage." Although so small they produce 4
or 5 ruffled flowers on 5- to 7-inch stems—in other words, long
enough for cutting. Great for borders, bedding and window
boxes, and, like the other bush types, do not need any trellis.
Usually offered only in mixtures, Burpee's has 5 separate
colors.

PINKIE. Salmon pink on cream
SALMONETTE. Rich reddish cerise with salmon tint
SAPPHIRE. Clear mid-blue
SCARLETTE. Rich scarlet
WHITE PEARL. Pure white

3. Medium. KNEE-HI. Another bush-type Sweet Pea growing
1½ to 2½ feet tall. KNEE-HI produces as well as the best vines
but does not need any support. The flowers are large on full
length straight stems carrying 4 to 7 florets. The compact uniform plants make beds with masses of color. Available only in
mixtures which have a full range of colors.

4. Medium. JET-SET. Similar to the preceding KNEE-HI, and,
like that variety, very popular for bedding since staking is not
necessary. Mature plants reach a height of 2½ to 3½ feet in
semi-shaded areas. The large flowers are straight-stemmed with
5 to 7 blooms per stem. Only in mixtures which include white,
light salmon pink, rose, scarlet, crimson, lavender, and light
and dark blue.

5. Tall. ROYAL FAMILY. This tall 6-foot climbing variety
certainly gets raves from the seedsmen. Park's say it is "our

finest climbing Sweet Pea," and Comstock, Ferre claims that it is "the best climbing Sweet Pea to date." The reasons are that it is early-flowering, larger-flowered, longer-stemmed and more vigorous. Since it is quite heat-resistant, it also has a longer flowering period. There are 5 more blooms per stem and a full range of colors in the mixtures. Burnett's has 5 separate colors: blue, lavender, white, cream-pink, and rose-pink.

6. Tall. CUTHBERTSON'S FLORIBUNDA. In 1940 Mr. Frank Cuthbertson of the Ferry-Morse Company introduced the first Cuthbertson Sweet Peas which proceeded to win awards in the United States, Britain, and Holland. At that time the only other Sweet Peas were the Spencers. Now there are other types, but this improved Cuthbertson is still one of the best. The difference between the original and these FLORIBUNDAS is the huge yield of strong long spikes with 5 or more blooms on each one; they are more heat-resistant and therefore flower longer. There is a full range of colors in the mixtures, and separate colors are listed by Burnett, Olds and Stokes. Fragrant.

7. Tall. GALAXY. Summer-flowering Spencer type, but the bloom is better than the old Spencers, and there is more of it. Now there are 5 to 7 large waved flowers on numerous long stems, and the plants are exceptionally vigorous. Burpee's offers 9 separate colors, many of them winners of English and Scottish awards.

8. Tall. Perennial. LATHYRUS LATIFOLIUS. Similar to the annual but blooms year after year from July to September. Good for covering fences, banks, stumps and so on. The mixture has pink, white, and rosy red flowers.

Culture. Knowing how to grow Sweet Peas seems to me much more important than worrying about varieties. In the long run, there is really no such thing as an unattractive Sweet Pea, and most of us are delighted to have any. Unless you live in an ideal climate with long cool summers there is not much point in hoping to have enormous flowers and luxuriant 9-foot plants. But you can have masses of cut flowers for at least six weeks, and that is enough compensation for any trouble they might be.

Since Sweet Peas are a hardy, cool weather plant, you can plant in fall or spring, depending on where you live. The usual advice about planting Sweet Peas includes instructions for digging trenches and it sounds so elaborate that many people are scared off. Actually Sweet Peas can be grown, and will flower, if you just put the seeds in the ground, as you would Zinnia seeds, and give them some support. However, the best results are obtained by preparing the soil in the fall. Spring sowing must be very early, usually before the frost is out of the ground and before it is in any condition to be worked. Dig the ground in the fall to the depth of about a foot and if you have some good compost, mix it with the soil to increase the capacity to hold moisture. Sweet Peas require alkaline conditions. Since most of us do not worry about the exact pH at any given spot in our gardens, the easiest procedure is to sprinkle enough lime on the surface to give a light-powdered appearance. (I know this sounds indefinite, but take a trowel and scatter lime thinly on the surface).

When to plant. The dates given here are the ones suggested by Ferry-Morse, and since they specialize in Sweet Peas and sell seeds all over the country, their advice, I am sure, is sound.

In California. August to September for early spring bloom, November to early January for summer bloom.

In the Pacific Northwest. March or April.

In the Southwest, Southern Texas and Southern Florida. September or October.

In the Lower Southern States. Texas to Atlantic Seaboard—November, December, January.

In the Balance of the Country. February to about April 1, just as soon as the soil can be worked.

The "just as soon as the soil can be worked" is extremely important. As a matter of fact, you do not have to wait until all the frost is out of the ground if you have prepared it in the fall. In my region where our last frost dates are April 15–May 1, I always plan to get Sweet Peas planted by April 1st at the latest, and try to make it St. Patrick's Day, the traditional one for Sweet Pea planting. There is practically always a day or two of good weather toward the end of March when you can plant the seeds; order them in plenty of time so that you have them when the occasion comes.

How to plant. Sweet Pea germination is often poor. Since the seeds are planted early, when the ground is cold and damp, a fungus hits them as they germinate and the seedlings never appear. To prevent this, the seeds should be treated with Spergon, following the manufacturer's directions. The seeds do not require soaking before planting, in fact the Ferry-Morse people advise against it. They should be planted 1–1½ inch deep and an inch apart. Plant seeds in a double row with a 6-inch space in between; then if the germination is poor, the gaps do not show too much. Do not try transplanting the seedlings. They will take it, but it slows up the blooming and with Sweet Peas quick blooming is the aim. If you want to start some plants still earlier indoors, use individual paper pots so that transplanting will not disturb the roots, and sow the seeds about a month before the outdoor planting date.

The best location for Sweet Peas is one with some afternoon shade.

Care and cultivation. The tendril-bearing ones require some support so that they can climb properly. Brush was the old standard support, but the only way to get brush is to go out and cut it, and that takes time. Brush also can be a nuisance with the ends sticking you in the eye when you cultivate or cut flowers. Wire can be used as a support in cool climates, but in hot regions the sun makes the wire so hot it literally burns the vines. The tendrils need very little to cling to, and string works very well. There is a product called Train-etts, which is a net made of string; it lasts for several years and is very simple and effective to use. The net is attached to poles at each end of a row. The best time to put the net up so that the plants will not sprawl is just as soon as the seeds germinate, since the tendrils appear when the plants are quite small.

When the plants are about 8 inches high they will benefit from a light dressing of nitrate of soda; or water them once every two weeks with liquid manure. They should not be fertilized heavily with complete commercial fertilizers.

Because they like a cool moist soil, mulching is an excellent practice. A 2–3-inch mulch of grass clippings or straw around the roots will help considerably to keep the soil cool. The plants should also be thoroughly watered if the soil at the base of the vines begins to look dry.

The flowers should be kept cut so that the vines do not start producing seed which is a drain on them, and often seriously checks flowering. When the plants are in full bloom you will probably have to pick flowers every day or two—no great hardship!

Occasionally, if the weather has been muggy and damp, the plants may be affected by mildew, which is easily checked by a light dusting of sulphur, applied when there is no wind.

Uses and planting combinations. Since Sweet Peas have a relatively short blooming period, they are not used for any regular flower bed or border. Their best place is in the cutting garden where they can be mulched and cared for easily. I have seen it suggested that Sweet Peas be grown on a thin trellis on a sunny bank, but it seems a little impractical for ease of cutting flowers. In the few parts of the country where Sweet Peas will grow all summer, they can be used as a background planting. But by and large, growing them in a straight row in the cutting or vegetable garden is the best plan.

Verbena [ver-bee'-na]. The family is *Verbenacaea,* with about 80 species which are natives of America except for one Eurasian species.

History. *Verbena* is the Latin name for an old-established plant called Vervaine. The Verbenas we grow in our gardens today have been developed over a period of about 75 years. They are not referable to any one wild species but seem to have several parents. One was a scarlet-flowered species which grows wild in Argentina and South Brazil, and was hybridized with a purple-flowered species from Brazil and Paraguay and a whitish-flowered species which is widespread in parts of southern South America. The result of all this hybridization is a wide color range of beautiful shades. Formerly the plants were rather sprawling, but the latest development is a dwarf plant of upright growth.

Description

HEIGHT: Tall type about 18 inches. Dwarf type about 6–12
   inches.

PLANTING DISTANCE: 10 inches apart

COLOR: White, pink, rose, crimson, many shades of blue from
   light to very dark, and pure lavender, most of the colors
   being combined with white

TYPE: Half hardy

GERMINATION TIME: 10–15 days

SEED TO BLOOM: 8–10 weeks

BLOOMING PERIOD: Until frost

IS INDOOR OR COLDFRAME START REQUIRED? No

CAN BE TRANSPLANTED: Yes

FALL-SOW: No

SELF-SOW: No

Verbenas are lovely plants with very dark green leaves
and attractive flowers which grow well above the foliage
and form a mass of solid color. The plants are usually of
a very sprawling branching habit, but there is nothing
sloppy or unsightly about them; the branches do not grow
too long to get out of hand, and the leaves are large and
abundant enough to give the effect of a pleasant dark green
carpet. The flowers are borne on terminal shoots that rise
6–7 inches above the ground. The flower clusters are about
2 inches across and composed of a dozen or more tiny
florets. They are often brilliant, but usually some florets
are white or have white eyes so that there is no effect of
harshness. The plants bloom for a long time, usually from
early July until frost. Because of the long blooming period and free-flowering, Verbenas are one of the showiest
annuals we have.

Classification and recommended varieties. There are two
main types of Verbena; a tall type with plants 12- 15-inches
high, and a dwarf 6–12-inch form.

1. **Hybrida grandiflora.** This is the tall type, and the one described in the previous paragraph. It is the form generally known and grown and there have been trials of as many as 50 varieties. One thing to bear in mind about Verbena colors is that they do not seem to be very fixed, and in the large scale tests and seed-farm plantings I have seen, there is considerable variation in the color. So a color listed in a catalogue as rose, for instance, may have every shade from almost white to deep pink flowers. On the other hand, some of the varieties are listed as having varying colors.

ANNAPOLIS BLUE. Blend of light, medium and dark blue flowers with small white eyes.

MARILYN. Fiery cerise

SALMON PINK. Soft salmon pink

SNOWY WHITE. White

BEAUTY OF OXFORD HYBRIDS. Clear rose-pink to deep rose red with white eyes.

LAVENDER GLORY. Lavender blue, creamy white eye.

SUTTON'S BLUE. Deep royal blue

ROYAL BOUQUET. Different, rigid, upright growth. 15–18 inches. Many colors. Burnett.

2. Dwarf Verbenas.

GIGANTEA Type. Semi-double ruffled flowers. 10-inch plants.

RUFFLED WHITE. Very fine white Verbena. Florets tightly clustered into a pure white ball.

RUFFLED PINK. Delicate salmon pink. Perfect companion for RUFFLED WHITE.

DWARF SPARKLE Type. Neat, compact 8- to 10-inch plants completely covered with flowers.

AMETHYST. All-American Selection. Mid-lavender blue with white eye.

BLAZE. Another All-American winner. Bright scarlet flower, heads 3 inches across.

CRYSTAL. White

DELIGHT. Coral pink, suffused salmon

SPARKLE. Scarlet, white eye
SPLENDOR. Royal purple, white eye

MULTIFLORA or BUSH Type. 10 to 12 inches high and a foot or
    more across.
    FIRELIGHT. Solid red without any eye
    ROSELIGHT. Rose-pink with white eye
    SALMON QUEEN. Salmon pink
    SNOW QUEEN. Pure white
    STARLIGHT. Rich blue with cream eye
RAINBOW. Early-flowering, dwarf, upright 8- to 10-inch plants.
    Ideal for narrow borders in sunny places. Mixed colors
    only from white through shades of pink, rose, salmon,
    scarlet, and deep red as well as lavender and purple.
    Mostly eyed.

Culture. Although they are classed sometimes as half
hardy and sometimes as tender, Verbenas grow quickly
and easily when the seed is planted directly in the garden
about the time of the latest of the spring frost dates. To
allow the plant to grow to its full potential size, the seedlings should be thinned when they are quite small and
given about 10 square inches of space. Seed planted about
the first of May starts flowering before the middle of July
and continues until frost. For earlier bloom, seed can be
started in the coldframe a month before the outdoor planting date. In the South, if given a light mulch, the plants
will sometimes live over the winter.

When to plant. Unless they have the protection of a coldframe, Verbenas should not be planted until there is no
danger of frost. To be on the safe side, unless the spring
is an advanced warm one, it is better to wait until the second of the two dates listed below. Coldframe planting
can be made a month before the second date, and the
plants transplanted into the garden when the soil is warm,

about six weeks after seeding.

The earliest safe dates for planting seed in the garden are: (see page 282 for Spring Frost Zone Map)

Zone A	Feb. 15 –March 1
Zone B	March 1 –March 15
Zone C	March 15–April 1
Zone D	April 1 –April 15
Zone E	April 15 –May 1
Zone F	May 1 –May 15
Zone G	May 15 –June 1

How to plant. Both garden and coldframe seeds are covered with ⅛ inch of soil. The garden seedlings should be thinned or transplanted when small, 'to give the plants plenty of room to branch and spread. The coldframe seed should be planted thinly, so that the little seedlings will not be too crowded before being placed in the garden. As soon as the plants have enough space to spread in, they require no further attention.

Care and cultivation. The plants will flourish with absolutely no attention; I have left my garden for a month in the summer and returned to find the Verbenas in full flower. As far as I know, they are not subject to any diseases or pests.

Uses and planting combinations. The regular Verbena is used for bedding, while the dwarf form makes an ideal bright edging plant.

Some suggested planting combinations are:
Background—Cleome HELEN CAMPBELL; middle ground—Snapdragons BRIGHT BUTTERFLIES; edging—Verbena ROSE-LIGHT.
Background—Marigold DOUBLOON; middle ground—Petunia WHITE MAGIC; edging—Verbena STARLIGHT.

Middle ground—Verbena LAVENDER GLORY, Petunia MOON GLOW, Phlox GLAMOUR; edging—Ageratum dwarf ROYAL BLAZER and Alyssum CARPET OF SNOW.

Middle ground—Verbena ANNAPOLIS BLUE; edging—dwarf WHITE BEAUTY Phlox, apricot and yellow Violas.

Background—Larkspur BLUE SPIRE and WHITE KING; middle ground—Verbena SALMON PINK; edging—Alyssum CARPET OF SNOW.

ZINNIA

Zinnia [zin'-i-a]. *Compositae* or Sunflower family, with about 15 species originating chiefly in Mexico.

History. This most popular flower, with its wide variety of form and color, had a very lowly start, which probably explains some of the common names such as Poorhouse Flower, Everybody's Flower, Old Maid, Old Faithful, and

Garden Cinderella. Even in its native country, Mexico, it was called "Mal fe Ojo" or eyesore. The original flowers were a dirty orange or a washed-out magenta color, borne singly on a scrawny looking plant. The seed was introduced into Europe during the 1750's, when it was sent to Professor Johann Zinn at Göttingen University in Germany. From there the plant migrated to France, where a double form was developed and introduced in 1886. However, until 1919 Zinnias were grown chiefly because they withstood almost any soil or climatic condition, not because of any intrinsic beauty. At that time, the entirely new double Dahlia-flowered Zinnias were introduced, in a marvelous range of strong vibrant colors. Since then as much hybridizing has been done with Zinnias as with any other flower, and the result is an enormous color range and an almost bewildering number of forms.

Description

HEIGHT: Dwarf varieties 12–15 inches
          Medium-sized varieties about 24 inches
          Tall varieties 3–4 feet
PLANTING DISTANCE: Small varieties 6–8 inches each way
                    Medium-sized 10–12 inches each way
                    Tall varieties 15–18 inches each way
COLOR: About as wide a color range as any flower—white, cream, buff, yellow, golden-yellow, orange in many shades, pink, salmon, rose-scarlet, crimson, lavender, purple, in solid colors and in blended tones of different colors
TYPE: Tender
GERMINATION TIME: 5–18 days
SEED TO BLOOM: 40–60 days
BLOOMING PERIOD: Continuous from the first flowering until frost
REQUIRE COLDFRAME OR INDOOR START: No, Zinnias are a warm weather plant and an early start is actually a disadvantage
CAN BE TRANSPLANTED: Yes

SELF-SOW: No
FALL-SOW: No

Zinnias, the country over, are certainly one of the favorite and best all-purpose annuals. They are easily grown in
any soil, and in the hottest weather make a striking and
dramatic garden display; they have enough forms and
colors to fit into almost any garden bed and border, and
the prolific blooms are long lasting as cut flowers. In most
varieties the plant is upright with a large fleshy center
stem and many stiff side branches. The leaves are a pleasant light green, somewhat hairy, and arranged in pairs
along the stem with a bud in each axil. The flowers are
particularly effective because of the bold colors in an
enormously wide range with every color but shades of
blue. Until a few years ago all the colors were brilliant,
but now Zinnias are offered in soft pastel shades. Only two
things mar the perfection of Zinnias. You will find that the
plants are not entirely fixed; sometimes the flowers will
revert to single and semi-double forms, the colors are not
always true, and the flowers may have little cones or
"Mexican hats" in the center—all this because they hy-
bridize readily and because plant habits may vary greatly
in seedling plants obtained from an individual flower
head. Also, late in the season, the foliage sometimes get
unsightly from mildew, or from drought which shrivels
the leaves. But neither of these factors is really important
in the face of the many advantages: long prolific continuous bloom, ease of culture and adaptability to adverse
climatic conditions, effectiveness as bed or border plants,
and value as cut flowers.

Zinnia colors should be chosen as carefully as a trous-
seau; some of the colors are so decidedly better than others.
The pinks have a stronger tendency to veer toward their
magenta great-grandparent, and the salmon-pinks and

bright pinks are usually better than the rose-pinks which often fade out badly. The yellows are good, shading from a deep butter-yellow to the lovely pale soft lemon-yellow CARVED IVORY. The whites are fine as long as the flowers are not allowed to die and ripen seed on the plant. The orange and some of the reds are screaming colors; fine if used well, terrible otherwise. The purple is a color which an English friend identified as royal purple, the color of the king's robes. It is a much more winey purple than that of Asters, for instance. The lavenders are not good, tending toward rose-pink or magenta, and not a true lavender at all. The mixtures are almost universally full of clashing colors. There are some exceptions, but look carefully before you buy *any* mixture.

Types and recommended varieties. Classifying the numerous Zinnia varieties is quite a task, and to a new gardener the following list will probably seem appalling. In general there are three types: tall, which have large flowers, medium-height plants with medium-sized flowers, and dwarf plants with small 1-inch or so flowers. The choice depends largely on the use of the Zinnias. The tall ones are best for the back of borders, the dwarf ones for edging, and the medium-sized for the middle of a border. Either one type or all three are excellent for solid Zinnia beds. This chart lists most of the types of Zinnias available today, and is followed by a description of each and some recommendations.

1. Tall. Dahlia Flowered
2. Tall. California Flowered
3. Tall. Cactus Flowered (ZENITH)
4. Tall. TETRA GIANTS (State Fair)
5. Medium. *Elegans pumila* or Cut-and-Come-Again
6. Medium. Lilliput or Pompon

7. Dwarf. Button
8. Dwarf. Peter Pan
9. Dwarf. Gracillima (Red Riding Hood)
10. Dwarf. Linearis
11. Dwarf. Mexicana, or Haagena
12. Midget. Thumbelina

1. **Tall. Dahlia Flowered.** This type was introduced in 1919 and changed the apathetic public attitude toward Zinnias into the present-day, widespread esteem. Fifty years ago, before America started giving horticultural awards, Dahlia Flowered Zinnias were awarded a Gold Medal and an Award of Merit by the Royal Horticultural Society of England, and were considered the most outstanding improvement in flower development. The freely borne flowers are 3–5 inches across and 2–3 inches deep. They resemble Dahlias in form, and have cup-shaped, incurved petals instead of the usual flat Zinnia ones. The plants are about 3-feet tall, stocky, and begin to flower in 60 days.

2. **Tall. California Flowered.** California Flowered was first introduced in 1926, and is a companion of the Dahlia Flowered. Both are tall plants, with freely produced large flowers, and bloom in about 60 days. Sometimes, this type grows as tall as 4 feet with very long stems for cutting, whereas 3 feet is usually the maximum height for the Dahlia flowered. The flower petals are more loosely placed, each petal lying flat on the other, so that the flower is smooth topped and only an inch or so in diameter.

Recommended varieties for Dahlia and California Flowered. Some seedsmen combine the listing of the two types, calling them Giant Flowered; others list them separately. The following list is by color, since the color choice is so all-important in planning a Zinnia bed, and the type is specified.

White. POLAR BEAR. Dahlia Flowered. Pure white.

PURITY. California Flowered. Also pure white.

Yellow. CANARY BIRD. Dahlia Flowered. Good, rich, deep, buttercup yellow.

Orange. GOLDEN STATE. Dahlia Flowered. Yellow in the bud, turning orange when in full bloom. Park's.

ORIOLE. Dahlia Flowered. Orange and gold. Harris and Comstock, Ferre.

Pink, rose, and salmon. EXQUISITE. Dahlia Flowered. Most attractive with pink outer petals which deepen towards the center to a strong rose pink.

MISS WILMOT. California Flowered. Bright pink.

SALMON QUEEN. California Flowered. Salmon with scarlet tinge. Burpee.

ELDORADO. Salmon pink and lovely. Comstock, Ferre.

CHERRY QUEEN. A beautiful cherry rose, maybe the prettiest of all this group. Harris.

Red. CRIMSON MONARCH. Dahlia Flowered. Largest and best red, a deep dark color.

WILL ROGERS. Dahlia Flowered. Loud bright scarlet.

Lavender and purple. DREAM. Dahlia Flowered, rosy lavender, not a true lavender.

ROYAL PURPLE. Dahlia Flowered. Deep purple.

PURPLE PRINCE. Also Dahlia Flowered. Although the preceding variety was an All-American winner, this is a better color, a real royal, winy purple. Park's.

Green. ENVY. This is a real curiosity. California Flowered, apple green flowers with deeper green foliage. 2-foot plants.

3. **Tall. Cactus Flowered.** ZENITH F_1 hybrids. The F_1 hybrids are a newer type of giant Zinnias than the Dahlia and California Flowered ones, with a different flower form, darker green foliage, and more mildew resistance. The hybrid vigor of the plants, the larger size of the flowers, and the profusion of bloom really make them more desirable than the older types. But I would suggest taking a good look at the flowers to see whether you like the form as well.

They are described as informal or cactus flowered, with

curled or quilled petals. The huge ball-shaped flowers are
5–6 inches across and are produced on bushy 2–2½-foot plants.
The colors are all vibrant ones, with no pastel pinks, lavenders and purples, or whites. Since all the colors blend together,
this is a case where a mixture is satisfactory for a massed bedding effect or for cutting. Almost all of the separate colors
are All-American Selections.

There are less expensive Cactus Flowered Zinnias than the
ZENITHS, since hybrids cost more to produce. But the return
on a package of seeds is so rewarding in relation to the cost,
that is really false economy to try to save a few cents.

YELLOW. Clear lemon yellow
TORCH. Bright orange
LIPSTICK. Cherry crimson
ROSY FUTURE. Light salmon pink
BONANZA. Golden orange
FIRECRACKER. According to the Burnett catalogue, "the bright-
    est, most beautiful red Zinnia every produced."
WILD CHERRY. Brilliant cherry rose
CARVED IVORY. This is a most lovely light ivory yellow, a
    unique Zinnia color and much more subdued than the
    other ZENITHS.

4. Tall. GIANT TETRAS. Like the ZENITHS this tetraploid
strain has very husky plants with a high resistance to mildew.
And the flowers are also extremely large, 5–6 inches across,
with thick double blooms. In this case they are Dahlia-like,
rather than Cactus Flowered. The leaves are thicker than the
older types, and they are darker green.

There is one factor that seems like something of a problem to me. Most of the catalogues list only a mixture which
although called "gorgeous gay colors" would produce a rather
unharmonious border. These colors are pink, yellow, gold,
orange, scarlet, rose, white, salmon, lavender, and purple.
They would, of course, be all right in a cutting garden. Stokes
lists 5 separate colors: STATE FAIR SCARLET, YELLOW, LAVEN-
DER, ORANGE and PINK.

5. **Medium, Elegans, Pumila, or Cut-and-Come-Again.**
Sometimes listed as Dwarf Double Flowering, and the best
all-around medium-sized Zinnia. Plants bloom in 45 days, are
neat and compact and 2–2½ feet tall, with great quantities
of 2-inch well-shaped flowers. This is one of the oldest types,
since it was the earliest double form developed from the original single ones. It is still very popular for cutting and garden
use, since it is a good size, between the Giant and Dwarf types.
There is a nice available choice of separate colors, and a package of each makes a most pleasing middle planting and provides plenty of good cut flowers. The mixtures have lavender
and purple as well, so it is better to avoid them. The standard
varieties are: SCARLET, CANARY YELLOW, SALMON ROSE, PINK,
WHITE, and GOLDEN ORANGE (Burnett).

There are 2 newer pumila-type varieties:

PEPPERMINT STICK. About 70% of the 3-inch flowers are striped
and mottled in many gay contrasting colors. The colors
are white, yellow, orange, red and purple. The darker
ones are marked with cream and white; the lighter ones
with darker colors.

SCARLET RUFFLES. The first hybrid of this well-loved type and
a gold medal All-American winner in 1974. The fully
double, well ruffled, scarlet red flowers are borne in great
numbers on 2½-foot plants.

6. **Medium. Lilliput, Baby, or Pompon.** The plants of
this type are 18–24 inches tall and full of little 1–1½-inch
flowers; in fact, they are so floriferous that there are usually
20–30 flowers on a plant at one time. The plants are excellent for bedding and cutting. There are 7 separate colors,
available from Burpee, Burnett, and Harris-white, pink
(mid pink, salmon tint), salmon, scarlet, crimson (good deep
velvety red), orange (Harris only) and golden (Burnett
only).

Two types of dwarf Zinnias have been recently introduced
which are real breakthroughs, and have won prized All-
American awards. They are the PETER PAN and BUTTONS. The

BUTTONS are particularly spectacular with very large flowers on truly dwarf plants.

7. Dwarf. BUTTON type. Neat, sturdy, bushy, upright 12–15-inch plants with an abundance of fully double pompon shaped flowers that are 1 to 1½ inches across. BUTTONS are most useful for massed colorful plantings, borders, or pots; the stems are long enough for cutting. The three separate colors as well as the mixture are All-American selections.

PINK BUTTONS. Fine salmon pink
RED BUTTONS. Bright scarlet
CHERRY BUTTONS. Cherry red
MIXED. The mixture includes the three separate colors as well as gold, yellow, and white flowers.

8. Dwarf. PETER PAN Hybrids. These new hybrids are a sensational plant development. The plants start to bloom when they are only 6–8 inches high producing large double flowers 3 to 4 inches in diameter. The petals are broad and slightly curled, giving the flowers an extra fullness. The dwarf plants ultimately grow to 12–14 inches. Prolific bloom until frost. There are 4 separate colors and a mixture, all All-American Selections.

PINK. Coral pink with deeper salmon centers.
SCARLET. Scarlet red
ORANGE.
PLUM. Lavender rose
MIXED. The above colors as well as yellow, primrose, cream, and white.

9. Dwarf. Gracillima. (Red Riding Hood) A delightful plant which is well-branched and about a foot tall, and covered all summer with ½ inch bright red round flowers. The type was first introduced in 1870 and is still popular, in spite of all the more recent strains.

10. Dwarf. Linearis. Another excellent dwarf Zinnia, originally from Mexico, and rediscovered in Australia. The only single Zinnia, the plant is about 8–10 inches tall. The golden orange daisylike flowers are most attractive, and each petal has a light yellow stripe and a dark brown center. The plant has literally hundreds of blooms, and flowers continuously until frost, in mild climates even living over the winter. The effect, unlike most Zinnias, is one of delicacy and airiness.

11. **Dwarf. Mexicana or Haagena.** Persian Carpet is the older variety with plants that produce flowers with a great variety of color and form. The 1-inch flowers are double, semi-double and single, in a wide mixture of colors although they are all in yellow, cream, orange and wine-red tones with no bright reds. Most of them are bi-color combinations, golden-orange and maroon, wine-red and cream, golden-yellow and wine or mahogany red. Old Mexico is a newer variety with large 2- to 2½-inch flowers that are deep mahogany red highlighted with shades of yelow gold. Both are All-American winners and 18 inches tall.

12. **Midget.** Thumbelina. Harris calls this type "among the most popular annuals of all time." All-American gold medal winner. The really dwarf compact little 6-inch plants are covered with semi-double and double 1½- to 2-inch flowers, the separate colors with the larger ones. Mixed (white, yellow, pink, lavender, orange, and scarlet), Mini Pink (coral pink) and Mini Salmon (coral salmon).

Culture. One reason for the popularity of Zinnias is that they are so easy to grow. The one prime consideration is that they are warm weather, heat-loving plants, and should never be sown until both the days and nights are warm and there is absolutely no danger of frost. Trying to hasten blooming by early planting does not pay, since cold weather stunts them and they never fully recover. Planted when the weather is warm, the seeds germinate in 4–5 days and the plants grow very quickly, blooming in 40–60 days, depending upon the variety (the dwarf ones bloom first). They also do best if sown right in the garden. I tried Zinnias in the coldframe one year, sowing the seeds about April 1st. Some of the seeds never germinated, and the few plants that did come up seemed to stand still and flowered later than seed sown in the open ground May 30th. Another gardener had the same experience.

When to plant. Although two weeks after the last frost date is usually a safe time (see page 282 for map showing these dates), you have to use your own judgment. For instance, in Zone E it is usually warm enough about May 15th, but I have had to wait a week or longer before planting Zinnia seeds. Warm days *and* warm nights are needed. The following dates are recommended and choose the latter one if the season is slow: (see page 282 for Spring Frost Zone Map)

Zone A	March 15–April 1
Zone B	April 1 –April 15
Zone C	April 15 –May 1
Zone D	May 1 –May 15
Zone E	May 15 –June 1
Zone F	June 1 –June 15
Zone G	June 15 –July 1

How to plant. Sow in the open ground, and cover the seeds (they are fairly large) with about ¼ inch of soil. If the ground is very dry, you can soak the soil to hasten germination. The seeds will be up in 4–5 days, and you can thin or transplant when the plants have their first or second set of true leaves. Although they stand transplanting at almost any stage, you will have stronger, well-branched plants if you transplant or thin when the plants are small, thus giving them ample room. Although pinching out is sometimes advised, it is better not to. The first or center flower is the finest bloom, and the plants will branch freely without pinching out if they have enough room.

Care and cultivation. Once given enough room to grow in, you can forget about Zinnias for the rest of the summer if you wish, and they will go right on flowering. However the dead flowers look unattractive, so keep them picked. The foliage sometimes gets mildew which is unattractive. The first noticeable symptom is the development of a white powdery growth on the leaves. If the weather is cool and cloudy, the mildew may spread rapidly. It can, however, easily be controlled by weekly dusting with regular dusting sulphur—in fact it is a good precaution to dust Zinnias, even if there are no signs yet of mildew, if you have large plantings of them. Japanese bettles sometimes are attracted to Zinnias. They actually do not affect the plants or the flowers much, and when they disappear around the end of August the plants go cheerfully on. But according to good authorities they can be controlled by a DDT spray. I tried it last year, not too assiduously, and it seemed to curb but not entirely do away with the beetles. Possibly more regular applications would have done that.

When cultivating Zinnias it is best to do a very shallow cultivation so that you do not risk disturbing the roots. It is also better not to over-water them, since this seems to help the foliage rather than the flowers.

Uses and planting combinations. Zinnias are an all-around annual which can be used for any regular garden need.

Some suggested planting combinations are:
Middle ground—Zinnia Cut-and-Come-Again SALMON ROSE and *Salvia farinacea*; edging—Phlox dwarf WHITE BEAUTY.
Middle ground—Zinnia CARVED IVORY, yellow Calendulas, *Centaurea cyanus* BLUE BOY; edging—Alyssum CARPET OF SNOW.

Middle ground—Dahlia Flowered Zinnia CANARY BIRD, ORIOLE, CRIMSON MONARCH, California Flowered PURITY; edging—Zinnia Linearis.

Background—Zinnia Dahlia Flowered ELDORADO; middle ground—Petunia SNOWSTORM; edging—Marigold yellow SUNNY or LEMONDROP.

Background—Morning-glory HEAVENLY BLUE; middle ground —Zinnias Zenith YELLOW, ROSY FUTURE, CARVED IVORY and WILD CHERRY; edging—Zinnia MINI SALMON, Alyssum CARPET OF SNOW.

Background—Cleome PINK QUEEN; middle ground—Zinnia California Flowered CHERRY QUEEN, Cosmos SENSATION PURITY, Cynoglossum FIRMAMENT; edging—Zinnias BUTTONS mixed.

When this book was originally written some years ago, this section was called "Complete List of Annual Flowers." It included every annual I had ever heard of at that time, except for a very few rather obscure ones. Looking back, I think I was quite presumptuous to call my list "complete." In the Introduction an annual is defined as a plant that completes its life cycle from seed to natural death in one growing season. There are probably thousands of plants the world over that meet this definition. It would take L. H. Bailey's *Cyclopedia of Horticulture* (in 3 large volumes) to provide a list that is really "complete."

Now I have changed the heading and also cut down the number of annuals described. I feel that I have not left out any that the average gardener would want to plant. In an effort to make the list complete I really went all out and used every catalogue I could find. The result was that many of the annuals were found only in one unusual catalogue, and are therefore not of general interest. So now the original list has been whittled down to about eighty annuals, including some that were not in the original book. But it does include all that are listed in a good popular catalogue. It has every annual in Burpee's, for instance, and more than Harris, but less than Park's, which has a very wide selection. The material is all updated and done in more detail this time. So, with these eighty, plus the twenty-five in the preceding part of the book, the gardener has at least a hundred annuals to consider growing, which should be plenty.

The final choice was based on several considerations:

attractive looks, good color, use in the garden (vines, edging, bedding, temporary hedges and so on), tolerance for
shade, and length of blooming period. Another criterion
was availability. Every annual in the following list can be
obtained from at least one of the catalogues on page
If no source is given, you can assume the seed is generally
listed. When only one or two seedsmen have it, then the
sources are specified. There are some seed catalogues
which have more complete listings than mine. But many
of the lesser-known annuals are not commonly grown for
good reasons: perhaps they are not especially attractive, or
have a very short period of bloom, or take too long to
produce flowers from seed, or are fussy about climatic
conditions. But I think that all of the ones I have chosen
here have some or many desirable traits.

Instructions about planting distances are not given for
each flower, but a sound general rule is to space plants
apart by about half their normal height. For example,
annuals that grow about 12 inches high should be spaced
about 6 inches apart.

Acroclinium [ak-roh-klyn'-ium]. SWAN RIVER EVERLAST-
ING. Some authorities give the genus as *Helipterum*,
and it is also known as *Rhodanthe*.
This native of Australia and South Africa is one of the
most important of the everlasting flowers, mainly because
Acroclinium will last indefinitely if dried correctly. The
1½-inch double and semi-double flowers are daisylike with
strawy petals of silky appearance, borne on 12-inch plants.
The range of colors is good—white, flesh pink, chamois,
pink, salmon, apricot, and cerise, some with yellow centers
and some with dark ones. Available only in mixtures, from
Burpee, Park's, and Olds.
Sow the seeds in the open ground when the weather has
warmed up, a month or so after the last frost. The plants

will flower in 6–8 weeks and are supposed to bloom all summer. Although their use as everlastings is the one generally stressed, they can also be used for beds and cutting.

To dry the flowers for winter bouquets, see Everlastings.

African Daisy, see Arctotis.

Agrostis, see Grasses, Ornamental.

Amaranthus [am-a-ran′-thus].

This is a tall vigorous 3–5 foot plant grown primarily for its colored foliage. It is related to Cockscomb and some of the pigweed family. The loud colors are strongest in hot sunny locations; in rich soil the leaves are larger but not as brightly colored. Although half a dozen varieties are listed there are three leading ones. EARLY SPLENDOR is an improved MOLTEN FIRE, earlier, with brilliant scarlet and green leaves, often called SUMMER POINSETTIA. 3 feet tall. One catalogue claims it has "an exotic beauty not possessed by any other garden annual." ILLUMINATION is also 3 feet tall, and has crimson leaves topped with gold, with lower leaves chocolate and dark green. The plants may be kept shorter and more compact, since they produce many base branches. TRICOLOR SPLENDENS is a new improved JOSEPH'S COAT, is about 2½ feet tall, and the foliage is carmine with variegations of yellow, red, and dark green.

Seed should be sown in the garden when the soil is warm, and each plant needs 2–3 feet of space. The uses are limited, but this plant could find a place as a temporary hedge where the soil is dry and poor since it grows anywhere and is trouble free.

Anagallis [a-na-gal′-lis] TRUE PIMPERNEL.

Anagallis is sometimes called the poor man's weather glass, because the flowers stay open when the weather is fine but close as a storm warning. It is 6–10 inches tall, sometimes higher, with prostrate spreading foliage. The 5-petalled flowers are about 1 inch across, and are supposed to bloom until frost. True Pimpernel has rich deep blue flowers, one of the finest blue annuals. The only separate variety I can find is CAERULA, the typical blue. The mixture has blue, orange, scarlet and pink flowers. Only at Burnett. This plant is a hardy annual, does well in warm soil, and should be sown where it is to bloom. From my experience, it will flower under the most adverse conditions, and while not a showy flower, is an attractive and interesting one to grow as a novelty.

Anchusa [an-kew'-sa] *capensis*. CAPE OR SUMMER FORGET-ME-NOT. BUGLOSS.

The plant is 9 to 18 inches tall with wooly, grayish green foliage and long stems with sprays of blue flowers. Unlike many so-called blue annuals, which are not really blue at all but tend towards lavender and purple, *Anchusa* is a true blue. There are two leading varieties. BLUE BIRD is the older one which won a Bronze Medal in the All-American Selections in 1935, and has indigo blue flowers with a white eye; they are only ¼ inch across but grow in profusion. BLUE ANGEL is a newer dwarf variety, only 8 to 10 inches tall and about the same across. It has many sprays of intense ultramarine blue flowers with white eyes. *Anchusa* is one of the few long-blooming, blue annuals. It is a half-hardy annual which in most climates is easily grown from seed sown in the garden after danger of frost is past, and is decidedly one worth growing. In the South it should be fall sown for early spring flowering. It will bloom in 3 months and continue usually until frost.

Angel's Trumpet, see Datura.

Arctotis [ark-toh'-tiss]. AFRICAN DAISY.

This plant is one of the numerous ones with daisylike

flowers. There are two varieties, the first is worth growing. *Arctotis grandis*, called the Blue-Eyed Daisy, has an attractive 2–3-inch flower with long pointed pearly white petals which are lilac on the under side and have a dark blue center. The plant is about 2½ feet tall with long, almost leafless stems well above the foliage. The new hybrids were developed from the original orange flower with a purple disc and now the mixtures—the only way they are available—have a wide range of colors including shades of crimson, red, apricot, pink, terra cotta, yellow, orange, cream and white with striking zones of contrasting colors. The plants are about 1 foot tall, and the flowers 2 to 3 inches across. Both varieties have wooly, grayish green foliage and the flowers close up at night. The *grandis* should be sown when the soil has warmed up, and will flower in about 2 months; the hybrids are hardy and can be sown early, and will take longer to flower. They will bloom until frost if the fading flowers are removed. In the South, self-sown seedlings give good spring bloom.

Baby Blue Eyes, see Nemophila.

Baby's Breath, see Gypsophila.

Balsam [ball'-sum]. LADY'S SLIPPER. TOUCH-ME-NOT (because the seed pods readily burst open when ripe).

Balsam, a popular old-fashioned flower, originally came from India. There are two types. Tall Balsam is an erect, compact, handsome 2–2½-foot plant with a single main stem and flowers clustered in the axils of the leaves, on such short stems that often you can barely see the flowers unless you remove some of the leaves. The flowers are semi-double and double, and are justly named "camellia-flowered" since they closely resemble Camellias. The mixtures of all three types have many colors including salmon, cerise, red, scarlet, pink, white, mauve, purple and others. The colors do not exactly clash, but some are better than others, so buying separate colors is best—if you can find them. The only tall ones I can locate are SCARLET SPOTTED WHITE, brightest scarlet with splotches of white, 2 feet, Harris; and PEPPERMINT, same colors, scarlet spotted white, 20 inches, Park's. BUSH BALSAM is about a foot high and across, and is base-branching with flowers borne at the end of the branches and not hidden by the leaves. The flowers look exactly like small roses and are quite beautiful. The color range is wide, the same as the tall type. Burnett has 3 separate colors, rose (which is really a lovely shell pink), scarlet, and white. Park's has TORCH, a lovely rose-red. These plants are ideal for a rather tall edging or for bedding. Even better for edging is TOM THUMB, the first dwarf Balsam, 12-inch uniform, bushy, base-branching plants with double flowers well above the foliage. Park's has 4 separate colors: purple, scarlet, salmon, and white.

Balsams are of the easiest possible culture. They are tender annuals and therefore will not stand frost; the seed should be planted in the garden a week or two after the last frost date. The plants will bloom in 2 months or less and continue until frost. They are easily transplanted at any stage, and transplanting will dwarf the plants into a more compact shape and make the flowers more double. Gertrude Jekyll says that Balsams are one of the few annuals that will do well in the close shade of a building, and will even flower in an enclosed courtyard that receives very little sunlight.

Basil, Ornamental.

Actually this Basil serves two purposes: it is indeed ornamental and it can also be used as a herb. DARK OPAL is the variety, and it was an All-American Selection in 1962. The foliage is a striking dark purplish red, with small 2-inch

slender spikes of lavender-white flowers. The plants are a
dwarf 15 inches—regular Basil is taller. The unusual foliage makes it decorative for edging walks, borders, window
boxes, and in pots on the terrace. The plants may be cut
back and brought indoors for the winter. It is a half-hardy
annual so sow the seed about the last spring frost date. The
leaves may be picked to use as an herb, commonly asso-
ciated with tomatoes but good with many other foods.

Begonia [bi-gohn'-ya] *semperflorens*. Wax Begonia.
  There are, of course, several types of Begonias, and the
only one discussed here is the small flowered, dwarf type
that can be grown from seed to flower the first year. The
plants are 6 to 9 inches high, sometimes taller, and have
either green or bronze foliage, light or dark. The 1–2-inch
flowers are single or double, and they are all shades of
pink, rose, scarlet and red as well as white, and variations
such as white edged with pink. Sometimes it is difficult to
find separate colors when you want them because the mixtures have unharmonious colors; in this case, when the
mixtures blend well, you can find all the separate colors
you want, probably because this is a big florists' flower.
They are hybrids and usually classified by height: extra
dwarf 5 to 6 inches, dwarf 6 to 10 inches, and intermediate
9 to 12 inches.
  The dustlike seeds should be sown indoors in January or
February, put in pots when there are 4 to 6 leaves, and
planted outdoors in May or June where they will flower
continuously and profusely until frost. Before the first frost
plants can be dug up to bloom as house plants all winter.
They will bloom either in full sun, if they have enough
moisture, or in partial shade. If you do not want to start
seeds early, you can usually find plenty of blooming plants
to buy—they will just be a lot more expensive than your
own.

Bells of Ireland. Molucella [mol-lew-sell'-a].

This stunning old-fashioned annual has such an apt common name that I could not bear to put it where it belongs botanically. The plant grows about 2 feet tall with several branches which have clusters closely set together of beautiful very pale translucent green shell- or bell-like calyxes each containing in the center a curiously formed little white flower (corolla). In fact, the clusters are so full of these calyxes that there is very little room for leaves.

If you start the seed indoors, put it in the refrigerator at about 50° for 5 days before planting. It can also be sown successfully outdoors while the soil is still cold. Fresh Bells of Ireland are excellent for flower arrangements, and they are also fine dried, when they turn a light fawn color and last for months on end. To dry see Everlastings, page

Black-Eyed Susan Vine, see *Thunbergia.*

Blanket Flower, see *Gaillardia.*

Blue-Eyed Daisy, see Arctotis.

Blue Lace Flower, see *Didiscus.*

Brachycome [brak-kik'-oh-me] *iberidifolia.* SWAN RIVER DAISY.

This little Australian plant is 9–12 inches high and covered with small ½–1-inch Cineraria-like flowers. The mixture has white, rose, blue and lavender flowers, and that is the only way it is offered by several seedsmen. The plants will flower in 6 weeks from seed, and although the blooming period is not continuous until fall, they are attractive in a mild way, so interesting to try if you are looking for a novelty. The seed is hardy and can be sown anytime during the spring or early summer (although it does best if sown early) and should be planted where it is to bloom.

Briza, see Grasses, Ornamental.

Browallia [broh-wall'-i-a].

This plant was named for John Browall, a Swedish bishop and contemporary of Linnaeus. L. H. Bailey says that Linnaeus commemorated the course of their acquaintance when he named the early species: *elata,* reflecting the exalted character of their early intimacy; *demissa,* its rupture; and *alienata,* the permanent estrangement of the two men.

This flower is highly recommended for anyone who likes blue flowers and can start seeds early indoors. The small, bushy 10-inch plants have glossy green leaves and are covered with small tubular 1-inch flowers all summer until frost. They are useful plants for edging, low bedding, pots or hanging baskets. The three leading varieties are: BLUE BELLS, improved, amethyst blue flowers on 10- to 12-inch plants; SILVER BELLS, a pure white companion; and SAPPHIRE, 15-inch plants, dark blue flowers with white eyes. The only practical way to grow good plants is by sowing seeds indoors very early. They are slow to germinate and if not given attention may not germinate at all. Once given a good start, and transplanted into the garden when the weather is warm, they will bloom all summer and fall even during the hot, dry months. In the South the plants often self-sow and bloom from late June until late summer. If the bed is given some protection they may self-sow in colder climates. These plants are often grown in local nurseries, and a plant or two will provide late winter bloom for months. It should be noted that like many so-called "blue" flowers, the color has a good deal of violet or purple in it.

Bugloss, see *Anchusa.*

Butterfly Flower, see *Schizanthus.*

Calliopsis [kal-lee-op'-sis]. TICKSEED.
L. H. Bailey says this flower is almost weedlike in its ease of bloom, and that is about all that can be said in its favor from my standpoint. It is the annual form of *Coreopsis* with the same yellow, orange, brown and maroon daisy-like flowers borne on long wiry stems. There are two forms: one is 3 feet tall and the other a dwarf 1 foot. The foliage is finely cut and light green. This hardy annual can be sown outdoors about the last frost date and often self-sows. It flowers in about 40 days, but has a tendency to bloom so ferociously that the plants do not amount to much after the middle of July although the dwarf forms last longer than the tall ones.

Campanula [kam-pan'-you-la]. CANTERBURY BELLS.
This annual form of Canterbury Bells won a Gold Medal in the All-American Selections in 1933 and is a beautiful flower although not as showy as the biennial form. However, it takes 90 days for the seed to bloom, so an early start is advisable although not essential for late summer and fall flowers. The plants have 6 to 8 flower spikes, the bell-shaped flowers are about 2 inches long, and the plants are 2–2½ feet tall. As far as I know, this annual *Campanula* is available only in mixtures, and not from all seedsmen since the biennial form is the usual one. The colors are white, pink, rose, blue, and lavender blue —all lovely. Burnett, Olds and Park's.

Canary Bird Vine, see page 142 .

Candytuft, see *Iberis.*

Canterbury Bells, see *Campanula.*

Capsicum. Ornamental Pepper.

This is not a standard annual, but the plants are fun to grow and attractive, so I have listed them here. The dwarf globe-shaped 10-inch plants have an abundance of slim 2-inch fiery-hot peppers that turn from white to yellow to brilliant red. This is the variety FIERY FESTIVAL from Harris which is illustrated in their catalogue. Park's lists 7 varieties. Capsicums are grown like regular peppers, which means an early start, and will bear fruit from July to frost. Or they can be used as unusual pot plants, summer and winter.

Cardinal Climber, see page 137.

Carnation [kar-nay'-shun].

It is possible to grow lovely Carnations in the garden, but they take about 5 months to flower which means an early start in most sections of the country. The flowers are 2—3 inches across (disbud for largest flowers), clove-scented, almost all double, and carried on 15—18-inch plants. There are several strains on the market and CHAU-BAUD GIANTS and ENFANT DE NICE are good ones. Stokes has 9 separate colors of ENFANT DE NICE: salmon, crimson, mauve, pink, rose, scarlet, white, and yellow as well as striped. And Park's has 6 separate colors of CHAUBAUD GIANTS: coppery salmon, scarlet, white, yellow, deep blood red, and deep rose with white edge. The seed should be sown indoors about the first of March and the plants will bloom from early August until frost. As half-hardy perennials treated as annuals they will sometimes live over the first winter if they are protected.

Castor Bean Plant, see *Ricinus.*

Cheiranthus, see Wallflower.

Chinese Forget-Me-Not, see Cynoglossum.

Chrysanthemum [kris-san′-thee-mum] *carinatum.*
    Perennial Chrysanthemums are standbys of many gardens, but the annuals are not very well known. I first saw them in a bed at the Aquarium in Bermuda where they were in full bloom in March and made a most striking display. The flowers are sometimes called painted daisies, and are about 3 inches across with broad flat petals which have large circular zones of different colors around eyes of varied colors.
    The flowers are combinations of yellow and dark red, soft pink and purple bicolors, some with white. There are single and double forms, and the single are unusually striking. Most seedsmen offer only mixtures which are fine in this case. Burnett has separate colors including two all-white double varieties which are supposed to resemble Shasta Daisies. Burpee and Park's have separate yellow varieties.
    The plants have finely cut, fern-like leaves and long stems for cutting; they are about 2 feet tall. These annual Mums are easy to grow from seed sown outdoors as soon as the soil can be cultivated. They will bloom profusely all summer and fall, especially in locations where the summers are not too hot. They make very effective large beds.

Clarkia [clark′-i-a].
    A native of California and the Northwest, *Clarkia* was named in honor of William Clark of the Lewis and Clark expedition which was sent to the Pacific coast by Thomas Jefferson in 1806. It is an easily grown, hardy annual with

slender coppery stems and small narrow green leaves. The little double flowers are something like those of the flowering almond, and appear on sprays at every joint. The colors in the mixtures include salmon, pink, mauve, rose, carmine, purple, red and white, and the mixtures are all most seedsmen list. Seed should be sown where it is to bloom, and early so that it will bloom before hot weather. Although it is often stated that it will bloom all summer until frost, this is only true where the summer climates are cool, and it likes semi-shade. I have found that it will grow in poor soil and almost without attention.

Cobaea [ko-bee′-a] *scandens*. CUP AND SAUCER VINE. CATHEDRAL BELLS.

Cobaea is a tender, climbing and rapidly growing vine. The handsome flowers are bell-shaped, about two inches long, and are available in two varieties. The one found in most catalogues is *scandens* BLUE. The flowers open green, then they change to a rich purple blue, followed by plum-shaped fruits. The other is a WHITE *scandens* listed by Burnett.

In its native Mexico and in favorable situations in the South it is winter-hardy. In cooler climates seed can be sown out of doors during May, but for a full season of bloom it is advisable to plant them indoors in late February or early March. The seeds should be placed endwise for good germination. They will germinate in a week, and even before the first true leaves appear, the seedlings are 4 inches tall. Early in April they should be transplanted into pots with a good-sized stick to twine on. By the middle of May they are ready for the garden. They will cling to any rough surface or can be supported by a trellis or string, but they do need some support. In a sunny location the vines grow to 20—30 feet by fall.

Coix, see Grasses, Ornamental.

Coleus [ko'-lee-us]. FLAME NETTLE.

Coleus is a foliage plant, generally a house plant, and as such is almost too well known. The color of the leaves is variegated with many combinations of light jade and deeper greens, many shades of reds, pink, salmon, gold, yellow and creamy yellows, as well as some chocolate and other browns. There are also differences in the leaves: some are fringed, some oak-shaped, and so on. The flowers are insignificant and are usually pinched off. To my mind there is quite a difference between the lighter-colored pastel Coleus plants and the darker ones with brown tones which can be rather unattractive—at least to me. So I would avoid mixtures and buy separate colors, which are readily available from Burpee, and an even wider selection from Park's and Stokes.

The plants are 1–1½ feet tall. Although thought of primarily as pot plants, they make showy garden beds, and do well in semi-shade. Start the seeds indoors about April 1st and plant outside after the last frost date. Before the first fall frost either pot up your favorite plants, or make cuttings for all winter house plants. Cuttings can also be made the next spring for summer beds.

Coneflower, see Rudbeckia.

Corn, Ornamental.

Ornamental Corn is sometimes listed in catalogues with the regular corn, and sometimes with the flowers. There are two types. The one usually grown is a tall corn distinguished by the colors of the kernels, which are deep red, yellow, white, orange, blue and purple in numerous combinations. This is the corn you see in the fall in markets

and roadside stands with pumpkins, and it is purely ornamental. It has various names—Calico, Indian, Squaw, and
Rainbow—all the same corn. The other type is Strawberry
Popcorn, with mahogany red kernels on small 2-inch cobs.
When the straw-colored husks are folded back on the little
ears they are most decorative. The dwarf plants are about 3
feet tall. This type is also useful because you can pop it.
The tall corn takes about 110 days to mature, the dwarf one
a few days less. Plant after the danger of frost is past. It is
necessary to plant at least 4 rows for full pollination. The
rows should be 2½–3 feet apart, and the plants 15 inches
apart. Do not plant within 10 feet of regular corn—this
because of pollination again.

Cup and Saucer Vine, see *Cobaea scandens.*

Cuphea [kew'-fee-uh]. FIRECRACKER PLANT.
   Cuphea is a 10–12-inch erect plant, a native of Mexico,
and heat- and drought-resistant. In warm climates it will
bloom well during the summer months. The leading variety FIREFLY has small tubular fiery red flowers about ¾
inch long. The leaves are light green and about 2 inches
long. The plants are easily raised from seed and flower in
12 to 14 weeks. Good for window boxes, as pot plants, and
in hanging baskets as well as for edging. Not often listed,
but Olds and Park's have it.

Cynoglossum [sin-o-gloss'um]. CHINESE FORGET-ME-NOT.
   HOUND'S TONGUE.
   Cynoglossum is a hardy annual with lovely, true blue
Forget-Me-Not type flowers. This blue is especially good in
the garden since there are few blue annuals which will
bloom all summer until frost. The flowers are small, but
there are plenty of them growing on sprays, so the effect is colorful. The leading variety, FIRMAMENT, won a

Bronze Medal in the All-American Selections in 1939, and has indigo-blue flowers on a compact bushy 18-inch plant. The foliage is grayish green. BLANCHE BURPEE has white, deep blue and various light and mid-blues, and it is an attractive mixture. This variety was named in honor of Mrs. W. Atlee Burpee, and is offered only by Burpee's, 2 feet tall. Cynoglossum seed should be sown early in the spring for all-summer bloom. It will sometimes self-sow.

Cypress Vine, see page 138.

Datura [dah-toor'-ra]. ANGEL'S TRUMPET.

This plant has large, sweet-scented, trumpet-shaped flowers which should make a beautiful showing in the garden. Native to the Ecuadoran Andes, there the flowers are sometimes a foot long. In the South and other mild climates seed can be sown outdoors. It can also be planted outdoors elsewhere early in May for August bloom. The plants are quite spectacular, growing 3 to 5 feet tall with large leaves and a continuous display of flowers. Unless you have a huge garden, it is probably better to grow them in large pots for outdoor display. In some parts of the country a relative—the Jimson weed—is so prevalent it is almost a pest. I have seen it on a cattle ranch in California where the plants were at least 3 to 4 feet across, with a dozen or more lovely white flowers, climbing right over fences. This is a Datura of a different species from the cultivated one. The cultivated *D. meteloides* generally has white or pale lavender flowers, usually pendent. Not always listed, you can get seed of the white Datura of the single form from Olds and Stokes. Burnett has 3 separate colors—white, yellow, and lavender—but the form is double where one trumpet is formed inside another. Although I haven't seen them, they do not sound as attractive as the single, which I think are fantastic.

Delphinium [del-fin'-e-um].

Tall stately Delphiniums are one of the glories of perennial borders. Larkspurs have often been called annual delphiniums since there is some similarity. But now the plant breeders have come up with true annual Delphiniums—annual in the sense that they will bloom the first year from seed if they are started early. They are not as tall as the standard perennial ones, but they have the same beautiful flowers and plant habit. The colors of these annual are the blues—light, mid and dark lilac, lavender, purple and white. These colors are sometimes listed separately, but since they are all so lovely the mixtures are fine. There are two leading types. CONNECTICUT YANKEE is the one most commonly listed. It won a Bronze Medal in the 1965 All-American Selections. The neat 2½–3-foot plants appear as dwarf, bushy, single-flowered Pacific Giants. The mixtures have the usual colors and Park's has separate light blue and white seeds as well as plants. The plants produce masses of flowers which make superb cut flowers. After the first spikes are cut, there will be a second or even a third crop. DWARF CHINENSIS grow only 8 to 12 inches high. They are true Delphiniums but the flowers are single and smaller. The plants branch loosely and bloom heavily. Listed by Stokes and Park's; they both have separate colors as well as mixtures.

The seed should be started early in March for August bloom. The plants are hardy and can stand frost, so they will flower again the following spring, and, if cut back, will bloom again in August.

Didiscus [dye-disk'-us] *coerulea.* BLUE LACE FLOWER.

Didiscus is a popular garden and greenhouse annual, grown for its beautiful flowers which strongly resemble Queen Anne's Lace. The plant is 2½ to 3 feet tall and the flowers are 2–3 inches across and borne in a flat umbel.

There is only one variety and the color is a soft lavender blue. Seed should be sown where the plants are to bloom and they do best when the summers are not too hot and dry. Even under ideal conditions they do not bloom indefinitely, but are pretty enough to warrant some space, if you have plenty to spare.

Digitalis [dij-i-tal'-us]. FOXGLOVE.

Foxgloves are one of the most beloved biennials. Now for the first and only time there is an annual Foxglove Foxy, which won a Silver Medal in the 1967 All-American Selections. It is called an annual since it will flower from seed in 5 months the first year. It will also bloom again the second year, and like all Foxgloves usually reproduces itself for years from its own scattered seeds. Foxy starts blooming when it is about 18 inches high and eventually reaches 3 feet. The plants have compact spikes of 2–3-inch bell-shaped flowers. Available only in mixtures which have colors ranging from white through cream, yellow, pink, rose, red shades, lavender and purple-red. Some are solid colors and others have attractive contrasting spots. The florets are closely spaced on 1-foot spikes, and there is a tall center one as well as several branch spikes producing bloom over a long season.

The seed should be sown indoors 6 to 8 weeks before the last frost date. The plants do well in either full sun or semi-shade.

Dimorphotheca [dye-more-fo-thee'-ka]. CAPE MARIGOLD. AFRICAN GOLDEN DAISY.

Dimorphotheca is really a perennial but the tender varieties are grown as annuals. The plant is about 12 inches high and has quantities of single daisy-like flowers 2½ to 3 inches across. The original flowers were straw-colored or orange with dark centers, and not a bit imposing. But the newer hybrids are deep orange, salmon pink, apricot orange, bright yellow, and white. These are the AURANTICA HYBRIDS, usually available only in mixtures. However, Park's has a separate salmon pink and white, and Burnett has the same two as well as a deep orange.

Easily grown, the seed should be sown outside in May after the soil has warmed up. The plants are compact, and ideal for low beds in sunny places. They thrive in hot weather. In Bermuda, for example, with its hot, humid summers, very few annuals survive the heat, but *Dimorphotheca* bloom continuously.

Dusty Miller, see Centaurea, page 77.

Euphorbia [you-for′-bi-a].

Two species of Euphorbia are grown as garden plants. One is *Euphorbia marginata* (sometimes called *E. variegata*) which is the well known Snow-on-the-Mountain, a most attractive foliage plant. The light green leaves are edged and veined white, with the top ones almost all white. The white flowers are inconspicuous. The erect bushy 2-foot plants last until frost. This hardy annual is easily raised from seed sown in the garden, and readily self-sows in some localities to the point where it is considered a nuisance. *Euphorbia heterophylla* is called Annual Poinsettia and Mexican Fire Plant. It sounds intriguing. Apparently the leaves are dark green until early fall when the top ones turn to scarlet either all over or just at the base. The plant is 2–3 feet tall and seed should be sown where it is to grow. Snow-on-the-Mountain is readily available. The Mexican Fire Plant is listed by Burnett, Park's, and Stokes.

Evening Stock, see *Mathiola.*

Everlastings.

As the name implies, flowers classed as everlasting can be dried and will usually last for months. The flowers in this book which dry well and are thought of as everlastings are: *Acroclinium*, Bells of Ireland, Celosia, Centaurea (Bachelor's Buttons), Gomphrena, Gourds, Gypsophila, *Helichrysum* (Strawflowers), Larkspur, *Nigella*, Jewels of Opar, blue Salvia, Statice, and Xeranthemum. Everlastings which are often used and are not in this book because they are biennials are Lunaria (Silver Dollars or Honesty) and Chinese Lanterns.

People skilled at the art of drying flowers often use ones that are not commonly thought of as being everlasting. I have seen lovely arrangements using Zinnias, Roses, Delphinium, Yarrow, Chrysanthemums, Daisies, Marigolds, and Dahlias. I presume there are others.

To DRY. Pick the flowers before they are fully mature, strip off the foliage, and hang in a cool dark place upside down so that the stems will be straight. Exceptions are Gypsophila and Statice, which should be fully mature, and Gourds, which are discussed in the section about them.

There is a preparation called Silica Gel which is the best way to dry flowers since it absorbs moisture quickly, and thus, when packed around the flowers, removes the water from them without changing their color. "Instead of producing the usual washed out, half-shriveled look of dried flowers, it leaves them with all the freshness of form and brilliance of colors that would appear in the natural state." The quotation is from the Olds catalogue, and Park's also lists it and a Flower-Dri Kit with all the necessary equipment. With the kit you get a free copy of a book on preserving flowers.

Feverfew, see Matricaria.

Fire Plant, Mexican, see Euphorbia.

Firecracker Plant, see *Cuphea.*

Flax, see Linum.

Flowering Tobacco, see Nicotiana.

Forget-Me-Not, see *Myosotis.*

Forget-Me-Not, Cape or Summer, see *Anchusa.*

Forget-Me-Not, Chinese, see Cynoglossum.

Four O'Clocks, see *Mirabilis.*

Foxglove, Annual, see Digitalis.

Gaillardia [gay-lar'di-a]. BLANKET FLOWER.

Gaillardia is a native American plant from the Ozarks south to the Gulf of Mexico. In early Colonial days the seed was introduced into Europe and named for a French botanist, Gaillard. It is a very commonly grown flower, primarily because it grows easily from seed and flowers prodigiously during the hottest and driest weather until frost. There are two forms, a single and a double. The single comes in mixtures and the colors are orange-maroon, yellow and rose shades, many combined and some tipped with yellow. The plants are 18 to 24 inches tall. An attractive variety is INDIAN CHIEF which has mahogany red petals at the base which lighten to bright red, Burnett and Stokes. The double form is also available in mixtures and has 3-inch flowers with long stems. The newest type is the dwarf LOLLIPOPS with double 2½-inch ball-shaped flowers with loosely arranged fringed petals on long stems. The compact plants are 10 to 14 inches high. The mixtures have cream, yellow and mahogany solids and rosy red and gold bicolors. Park's has 3 separate colors. *Gaillardia* is a half-hardy annual which should not be planted until after the last frost date. The germination is slow, but the plants come along quickly; they will bloom in 9–10 weeks and will even survive a light frost.

Gazania [ga-zay'-ni-a].

One of the loveliest, most exciting and brilliantly colored annuals, according to one catalogue, and I consider them as attractive as any of the daisy-like group. The flowers are single and 2½ to 3 inches across. They have slender, pointed petals and the basic colors are yellow, orange, salmon, bronze, red and brown. But there are variations—many are haloed and bicolored, or have contrasting zones and different colored centers. In fact, there can be 4 or 5 distinct, sharply defined colors in a single flower. The plant is about a foot high with long narrow dark green leaves. *Gazania* is only available in mixtures. The flowers close up at night and during cloudy weather, and should be planted in a sunny position so that they will open fully. *Gazania* is a tender annual which should not be planted outdoors until two weeks after the last frost date. Elizabeth Lawrence in *A Southern Garden* says that all hot gardens should have them, that they are the sturdiest of the South African daisies, and in her experience the only ones adapted to Southern growing conditions; the crisp *Gazanias* never lose their freshness. Seed planted in the open at the end of April in North Carolina bloomed for Miss Lawrence from late July until November.

Geranium [ji-ra'-ne-um]. PELARGONIUM.

Park's calls Geraniums "the flower that has given the greatest pleasure through the ages," and although that

sweeping statement might be queried, there is no doubt
that they are the standbys of many gardens. Until recently
they were bought as plants or propagated by cuttings. But
now as a result of many years of extensive breeding Geraniums can be grown from seed to flower in 4 to 5 months,
and will bloom from some time in July until frost. The
CAREFREE SERIES of F₁ hybrids is the chief type. The
plants are about 14 inches high with large 4–5-inch flowers,
and will outbloom Geraniums grown from cuttings. Comstock, Ferre has 5 separate colors including the three 1968
All-American Selections, CAREFREE bright pink, scarlet and
deep salmon. Park's, Burnett and Stokes also have the same
5 as well as others. There are solid colors and bicolors:
PICOTEE, white petals edged with rose-red, Burnett and
Stokes; FICKLE SCARLET, white centers with scarlet edges,
Stokes and Park's; and FICKLE ROSE, rose edges, white
center, Park's. SPRINTER, another F₁ hybrid, is the popular
shade of bright red, a little earlier, dwarfer, and freer-
blooming than CAREFREE, Burpee and Stokes. Harris has
their own NEW ERA hybrids, 120 days, 20-inch plants.
Since Harris is always so reliable I am sure the series is
excellent. There are 5 separate colors: blush white, bright
red, medium salmon, scarlet and rose-pink with white eye.

For outdoor plants the seeds should be sown indoors in
February or March. After the seed has germinated, it
should be given maximum sunlight or artificial light since
the more light the plants get, the quicker they will bloom.
For house plants they can be sown any time of the year.

Globe Amaranth, see *Gomphrena.*

Gloriosa Daisy, see Rudbeckia.

Godetia [go-dee'-she-uh]. SATIN FLOWER.
Godetias are truly beautiful flowers, although not of the
simplest culture. Successful growing depends on early

sowing, a cool moist soil, and summers that are not hot and dry. The flowers are 4-petaled and cup-shaped, 3 to 5 inches across with an exquisite satiny texture. There are two types of plants, a dwarf one 10–12 inches high with single flowers, and a taller 1½–2-foot plant with double flowers. The colors in the mixtures, which is the way the seed is generally offered, are shades of pink, red, and white, and occasionally lilac. They are pleasing colors together. If you want separate colors for a special bed, Burnett has five. Sow the seed as soon as the soil can be cultivated where the plants are to bloom, since they do not transplant well. They will bloom in about 70 days and flower well in sun or light shade and in soil that is not too rich. Please note again that they prefer summers that are not too hot and dry.

Gomphrena [gom-free'-na] *globosa*. GLOBE AMARANTH.

Gomphrena originated in the East Indies. An attractive annual, it requires little attention, and has a long flowering season. The plant is about 18 inches high and branches freely, each branch having several flowers somewhat like clover. The flowers stand well above the foliage so that the effect is one of solid color. If the plant is "pinched out" it will become more bushy.

Seeds can be planted outdoors after the last frost, but for long summer bloom it is better to start them indoors in March; the plants can then be set out in the garden after the danger of frost is past.

Seed mixtures have white, rose, lavender, and purple flowers. There are two separate varieties listed occasionally. DWARF BUDDY has very neat compact 6-inch plants with uniform rich purple flowers. Good for pot plants and edgings; Burnett and Stokes. Tall purple RUBRA has 2-foot plants with purplish red flowers, Park's. *Gomphrena* thrives in full sun and warm temperatures. The attractive, strawy little ¾-inch flowers are also fine for drying for winter bouquets that keep their color and form indefinitely. To dry, see Everlastings.

Gourds.

Gourds are rapid-growing, tendril-bearing vines, grown primarily for their fruits, which come in a variety of colors, shapes and sizes. However, the large, dark green leaves and showy yellow flowers are also decorative in the garden, and one vine will cover a large area. There are both small-fruited gourds and some large-fruited ones which are really huge.

Gertrude Jekyll mentions a gourd that weighed 120 pounds! For general use, a package of mixed small-fruited gourds is best. The large fruits take about 5 months to mature (and just about as long to dry thoroughly), and have a particularly rampant growth. The mixtures have yellow, green, orange and white fruits; some striped and bicolors and many shapes including spoon, pear, apple, orange, egg and warter. If you want separate varieties, Park's and Stokes have a wide choice. Gourds are tender annuals which should not be sown until the weather is really warm, or at least two weeks after the last frost date. They should also be planted where they are to grow since they do not transplant well. Allow about 3 square feet for each plant. Gourds can be used for banks, fences, trellises, or even to cover a rubbish heap. New fruits appear daily once the vines start bearing, and are a source of great amusement for young children. Harvest them when the shell fails to respond to the pressure of the thumb (not the nail), and before they have been exposed to frost. Do not yank them off the vines but cut them with a 2- or 3-inch piece of the stem, taking care not to bruise or scratch them so they will not rot. They will also rot if they are not mature. Wash them with a strong disinfectant to remove dirt and fungi that might cause rotting. Store them in a dry, well ventilated room in a single layer without touching each other. Turn them regularly. When they are dry, which will be in 3 to 4 weeks (the seeds rattle if you shake them), wax with an ordinary floor wax and polish with a soft cloth.

Grasses, Ornamental.

These ornamental grasses seem to me to be of interest mainly as curiosities, although they can be quite effective in flower arrangements. There are two which are listed by several seedsmen.

Briza [bry'-za]. QUAKING GRASS. This has numerous grasslike stems and a few small grassy looking leaves. The spikelets look like rice crispies. They are half an inch long, and white with light green ribs turning to a straw color as they dry. Each stem has dozens of these little spikelets covering about 9 inches of the stem; they make a rustling noise.

Coix [ko'icks]. JOB'S TEARS. This grass, about 2 feet tall in the North and considerably taller in the South, has long sword-shaped leaves about 1½ inches wide. The large white or lead-colored seeds, 1½ inches across, are hard and shining and are often used as beads.

WHITE PAMPAS GRASS I know only from Bermuda, where I hear it is perennial, and the 8–10-foot plants with long silky plumes are really beautiful. Park's lists it here along with PINK PAMPAS GRASS and 11 other types.

MIXTURES. For a variety of grasses to enhance your flower arrangements these are probably your best bet. There is a wide assortment of spike shapes, form and coloring, all with long strong stems. The average height is 3½ feet.

Gypsophila [jip-sof'-fill-a]. ANNUAL BABY'S BREATH.

The perennial Baby's Breath is a well known flower. The annual form is less commonly grown although the culture is easy. This hardy annual can be sown where it is to flower any time from early spring to July. It blooms in 5–6 weeks but the period of bloom is only about 4 weeks, so a succession of sowings should be made 3 weeks apart for continuous flowering. The plant, about 18 inches tall and branching, has flowers considerably larger than perennial Gypsophila. Two separate colors are available, white and rose. The variety COVENT GARDEN IMPROVED has masses of exceptionally large white flowers—large, that is, for Gypsophila. The main use is for indoor flower arrangements since it mixes so well with other flowers.

Helianthus [he-li-an'-thus]. SUNFLOWER.

The common Sunflower is a native plant in North America and the mammoth yellow flowers with large dark centers are familiar to all of us. The plants are 10–12 feet high and the single flowers are 12–14 inches across. The standard tall variety is MAMMOTH RUSSIAN which is often grown for the prolific seeds which are very popular with birds and poultry. The main garden use is as a hedge or tall background. There are several other varieties of Sunflowers which are more adaptable for general use. Three are listed here. SUN GOLD has fully double golden yellow 4–5 inch Chrysanthemum-type flowers on 5-foot plants. The flowers are freely borne and the plants are attractive with bright green foliage. TEDDY BEAR is similar but the bush-like sturdy plants are more dwarf, only 2 to 3 feet high but with large double bright yellow 5-inch flowers. ITALIAN WHITE has single white to cream to primrose yellow 4-inch flowers with dark centers on 4-foot branching plants. Burnett, Park's and Stokes.

All Sunflowers should be planted after the last spring frost date, and, although they can be transplanted, they will grow taller and flower sooner if they are left alone. They start blooming in about 10 weeks and continue until frost.

Helichrysum [hell-i-kry'-sum]. STRAWFLOWER.

This is the most popular of the everlasting flowers. A native Australian plant, it produces quantities of flowers which are like very double daisies and have small glossy petals which rustle when you touch them. There are two types: the standard one which is 2 to 3 feet tall and has 2-inch flowers; and a dwarf 12-inch type with little 1-inch flowers. The colors in the mixtures are crimson, salmon, rose, bronze, yellow and white. The dwarf Sunflowers are only available in a mixture, and that is the way the tall ones are usually listed too. However, if you are looking for a specific color for your dried winter bouquets, Park's has 6 (red, salmon, purple, yellow, rose and white) and Stokes has 6 (bronze, yellow, white, red, pink and purple). This tender annual should be sown where it is to bloom, after the last spring frost date. Disbudding, allowing only one flower on each stem, will give extra large flowers. They are good as fresh cut flowers as well as dried. To dry, see Everlastings.

Heliotrope [he'-li-o-trope].

This well known old favorite is grown primarily for its beautiful fragrance although the purple flowers are also attractive. It is not usually grown from seed planted in the garden. It needs plenty of heat to get a good start, and is usually propagated in a greenhouse by cuttings since the seed germination is very irregular and the plants are slow to bloom. Also, since all the flowers are not fragrant, propagating by root cuttings will ensure fragrant plants. However, it can be started from seed indoors March 1st and transplanted into the garden when the soil is warm; then it will flower from July until frost. Usually only one variety is listed by seedsmen and Harris states that their PURPLE BONNET is by far the best to grow from seed, although I cannot vouch for this. Apropos of nothing in particular, bees love it.

Helipterum, see *Acroclinium.*

Hibiscus [hy-bis'-kus].

Hibiscus is a perennial which is very much a part of the landscape in a semi-tropical country like Bermuda where it blooms continuously and is perfectly lovely. A new variety SOUTHERN BELLE was an All-American Selection in 1971 and is an annual since it will bloom the first year from seed. It takes a long time, however, so it is not a proposition for the casual gardener. It should be started in January or February and then will bloom in September. But it is hardy throughout the United States so although it will die down after a hard frost it will shoot up again in the spring and will live for years—just give it a light mulch in severe climates. SOUTHERN BELLE is a mixture with deep red, rose, pink, pink with red eye, white with red eye, and pure white flowers. They are huge, 8 to 10 inches across, and the plants are about 5 feet high. Park's has 5 separate colors. If you have the proper facilities for starting seeds indoors, it should be fun to try Hibiscus since it is such a handsome plant either as a specimen or for a hedge.

Hollyhock [hol'-i-hok]. INDIAN SPRING.

Perennial Hollyhocks had been cultivated in China for probably a thousand years before 1573 when they were first introduced into England. But the annual form dates back only to 1939 when the variety INDIAN SPRING (the only annual variety to date) won a Silver Medal in the All-American Selections. The plants are about 4½ feet tall, and the flowers a lovely mixture of shades of pink and rosy carmine ranging from very pale pink to a deep rose. They are double and semi-double and many of the flowers have fringed petals; in fact, the day I was at the Burpee Seed Farm in California they were roguing the plants to eliminate the ones that were not fringed. After the main stalk stops blooming the numerous side stalks produce flowers —so the entire flowering period is longer than that of the perennial varieties. This annual form is also good in frost free climates where the perennial sorts aren't perennial because they do not get a dormant period. The seed takes 5 months to flower, so it should be sown indoors in March in parts of the country where the spring is late. It is hardy and can be planted in the garden a week or so before the last frost date.

Since the development of INDIAN SPRING in 1939 the following 3 varieties, all All-American Selections, have become available. The breeders wanted Hollyhocks that were reduced in height, improved flowers with more doubling, and earlier flowering. Only one of my catalogues now lists INDIAN SPRING, Olds.

SILVER PUFFS, All-American 1971, was the first dwarf, with 2–2½-foot plants. The very double 2-inch flowers are tissue-like silvery rose-pink. The foliage is deep green and rust resistant. 5 months from seed. SUMMER CARNIVAL, All-American 1972, is 4 to 5 feet tall with lovely flowers—each one has a double rosette center with a single outside row of broad, flat petals. The mixtures have rose, pink, crimson, yellow and white flowers. Planted April 1st, it will bloom on or about August 1st. MAJORETTE was the only new variety from the dozens of entries to be a 1976 All-American Selection. It is another dwarf 2–2½-foot plant, this time with a mixture of Hollyhock colors: crimson red, light pink, salmon, yellow and white. Easily grown from seed planted in May which will flower profusely in August.

Hunnemannia, see page 192.

Iberis [eye-beer'-is]. CANDYTUFT.

Candytuft is a native of Crete and the original flower was white and sweet-scented. Today there is a variety of colors and types. GIANT HYACINTH-FLOWERED grows 14–18 inches tall and each branch has a thick white Hyacinth-like spike. DWARF FAIRY mixed has 8-inch plants which are completely covered with a mass of flat topped fragrant gaily-colored flowers. The colors in the mixture are rose, carmine, crimson, flesh pink, white, lavender and purple. Ideal for bedding and borders. UMBELLATA mixed is about a foot tall and has the same flower form as the dwarf ones, Park's. They also have the only separate color I can find—besides the tall white—which is RED FLASH, large bright scarlet flowers centered with yellow. A foot high and just as wide. Candytuft is hardy and can be sown very early. It is also very easy to grow and not a bit fussy, so the seed can be sown any time during the spring. It flowers in 60 days and in our climate the bloom continues for about two months. It also self-sows or can be fall-sown for bloom early in the spring. Try it over bulbs.

Ice Plant, see *Mesembryanthemum.*

Impatiens [im-pa'-she-enz].

This is a plant from tropical West Africa which is a popular house plant. It is also most useful in the garden because it is very free-flowering in semi-shaded and shaded positions—it will even bloom along a north wall. So it is an important plant for growing in the shade in beds, borders, window boxes, tubs and pots. The plants are 6 to 24 inches tall with 1½–2-inch flowers and plenty of them. The main colors are various reds, pinks, and white—but there are others such as orange, orchid, fuchsia and bi-

colors. If you buy mixtures you may get colors you do not
want, and since it is easy to get separate colors I would recommend that, or buying plants.

The F_1 hybrids are far easier to grow and more satisfying in performance than the older open-pollinated seeds.
So although there is a diversity of seeds offered I would
suggest sticking to the hybrids. There are two leading
series. The dwarf ELFIN SERIES has uniform plants which
are 6 to 12 inches tall. They are base-branching and do not
require pinching. Burpee has 6 separate colors, Park's has
4, and Stokes has 7 solid colors plus a red and white bicolor. The IMP SERIES has semi-dwarf 1–2-foot plants with
large flowers. The same seedsmen have separate colors. If
you are looking for bicolors, Harris has 3 in their 8-inch
SHADEGLOW SERIES; orange and white, salmon and white,
and red and white. Park's have 2 that look lovely: A Go-
Go, 10-inch plants with deep waxy green foliage and scarlet and white flowers, available both as seeds and plants;
and BOOGALOO, a cherry-red and white bicolor, plants
only. TANGERINE is a new color, large pure golden tangerine flowers on 15-inch plants. Burnett and Park's.

Impatiens is easily grown from seed and will bloom in
about 3 months—do not cover the seed since it needs light
to germinate. It will flower continuously until frost.

Jewels of Opar. Talinum paniculatum.

I have never seen this plant, but the name is so beguiling that I could not resist including it. Here are the
descriptions in the two catalogues I have which list it.
Harris: "This exotic plant has foliage of deep glossy green
and produces numerous 1½-foot stems, bearing great
quantities of tiny, cameo pink flowers in airy clusters.
Later the stems are covered with ornamental ruby seed
pods. The plants stand summer heat well. Excellent in
arrangements as a cut flower or as dried material." Park's:

"The foliage is bright deep waxy green, growing a foot high and forming a delightful setting for the airy panicled 1½-foot stems. Great multitudes of small cameo pink flowers open early every afternoon, effecting a pink haze. Husky plants withstand summer heat, thriving and becoming more beautiful with each passing week." Even allowing for a seed catalogue's poetic license, or more accurately horticultural license, the plants still sound as though they would be interesting to try if you are feeling adventurous. To dry, see Everlastings.

Job's Tears, see Grasses, Ornamental.

Kochia [koh'-kee-uh]. SUMMER CYPRESS, BURNING BUSH.

This fascinating plant looks exactly like a small evergreen tree. The foliage is a bushy bright green and the plants are upright, oval and symmetrical and 2–3 feet tall. In the fall the foliage turns carmine red. It is the perfect plant for a temporary low hedge. It is a hardy annual which should be planted a week or two before the last frost date, and often self-sows. It lasts until late fall. There is only one variety, CHILDSII, which is readily available.

Lady's Slipper, see Balsam.

Lavatera [lav-at-teer'-uh]. ANNUAL MALLOW.

The Annual Mallow is a variety called LOVELINESS which is an attractive garden plant about 2½ feet tall, covered with light pink, single, cup-shaped flowers. Not frequently listed, Harris and Stokes have it. There is a white form, ALBA, Burnett. A newer type is the tetraploid TANAGRA which has large 2½–3-inch flowers on large upright wiry 3-foot plants which do not need staking. The color is a brilliant rose. Park's and Harris have it. In cool weather the foliage turns bronze. This hardy annual can be sown about the last spring frost date, and since it does not transplant readily should be sown where it is to bloom. It will bloom continuously until frost.

Linaria [ly-nay'-ri-a]. TOADFLAX.

The flowers are like tiny Snapdragons. The variety, FAIRY BOUQUET, has small 8-inch plants; NORTHERN LIGHTS has 12-inch ones. The leaves are slender and narrow, and the flowers are mixtures of cream, pink, rose, white, crimson and lavender with a little yellow spot on the lower lip. Seed should be sown where the plants are to bloom; scatter seed thinly in April for late June flowers.

Linum [lye'-num]. FLAX.

Perennial Flax has beautiful blue flowers. The only annual variety is GRANDIFLORUM RUBRUM which has graceful delicate foliage on bushy 18-inch plants, and single 2-inch bright crimson flowers. Not readily available but Stokes and Comstock, Ferre have this annual seed. The flowers only last one day but new ones keep appearing. It is a hardy annual which can be sown where it is to bloom a week or two before the last spring frost date, and successive plants should be made for continuous flowering since the plants only bloom for 3 to 4 weeks. Needs full sun.

Lobelia [loh-beel'-ee-uh].

Lobelia is a very popular edging plant. The plant has two forms, a dwarf erect type, and a trailing one very useful for hanging baskets and window boxes. The flowers are only about 1/2 inch wide but the plants are massed with them, and the flowering is continuous until frost.

The colors are blue, red and white and the blue is the one generally used.

In the dwarf compact type the two leading blue varieties are: CRYSTAL PALACE COMPACTA with solid rich dark blue flowers and bronze foliage; and Mrs. CLIBRAN which also has dark blue flowers but with white eyes and medium green foliage. CAMBRIDGE BLUE I think is lovely, a real light Wedgwood blue with light green foliage, not always listed but Stokes and Burnett have it. ROSAMUND was an All-American Selection and is deep carmine red with white eyes. Stokes, Park's and Burnett have pure white varieties. These are all 4 to 5 inches tall and spread a lot.

The leading trailing variety is SAPPHIRE with deep blue flowers with white eyes. Stokes and Park's have light blue varieties, and Park's also has a red one. These are all 8 inches long. This plant thrives in full sun or partial shade.

Lobelia is a tender annual which requires an early start in all but temperate sections of the country. The seed is very fine and should just be pressed into the surface of the soil but not covered. It germinates slowly and the small seedlings look very fragile and weak. However, once started, they are sturdy and grow well. Gertrude Jekyll suggests using them in a rock garden and says: "A whole large space of rock garden may be made beautiful in late summer by a June planting of dwarf bedding *Lobelia* in every empty space or chink that is available; in a large rock garden such a filling with one good plant at a time would be found restful and satisfying, and would help correct the slightly disquieting impression so often received in such a place, from too many objects of interest being presented within one range of vision."

Love-in-a-Mist, see Nigella.

Lupinus [loo-pine'-us].

Annual Lupines are not as tall or large-flowered as perennial ones, but are nice garden plants and are good for semi-shaded spots (no annual will flower properly in real shade). The plants are base-branching with 4–6 flower spikes, and the flowers are pea-like. *L. hartwegii* is the tallest strain, and is 2–3 feet high. The colors in the mixture are white, blue and rose and the available separate colors are white, blue (Oxford blue), sky blue and heliotrope. *Lupinus texensis* is more popularly called Texas Bluebonnet, is the State flower, and has intensely blue flowers which bloom in the spring. Lupines are hardy annuals which like cool weather so they should be planted as early as possible in the spring where they are to bloom. They flower in about 2 months and will bloom for several weeks if seed pods are not allowed to form.

Marvel of Peru, see *Mirabilis.*

Mathiola [may-thy′-o-la]. EVENING STOCK.
Evening Stock is so-called because the small lilac flowers resemble stocks, and when they open in the morning or in the evening they are very fragrant. The plant is 18 inches tall with long narrow leaves; a hardy annual which may be sown very early in the spring, and has a long flowering period. The standard variety is BICORNIS.

Mathiola incana, see Stocks.

Matricaria [ma-tri-kay′-ree-a]. FEVERFEW.
This plant is compact with many branches and finely cut, very pungent leaves. The flowers, like small, flat Chrysanthemums, are about 1 inch across and very numerous. There are two dwarf varieties, about 8 inches tall. GOLDEN BALL has double golden flowers, and there is a similar white one. There is also a tall white one, about 2 feet high, which Stokes calls WHITE WONDER and Burnett ULTRA DOUBLE WHITE. These closely resemble the quality which was previously only obtained from cuttings. Feverfew is a tender perennial treated as an annual, and can be sown

early in the spring, and sometimes will live over the winter.

Mesembryanthemum [me-sem-bri-an'-thee-mum].

This plant has succulent dark green foliage like that of Portulaca but the leaves are thicker and much longer. The plants have a prostrate growth and are about 8 inches high and the same width. There are two annual species. The one called Ice Plant is CHRYSTALLIUM with foliage which has little globules like tiny drops of ice. The 1-inch daisy-like flowers are white to pale pink. Burnett and Park's. CRINIFLORUM, Livingstone Daisy, makes a spreading carpet with flowers in shades of yellow, buff, cream, primrose, pink, rose and crimson. Both make excellent ground covers. Park's, Burnett and Stokes. It is hardy and can be sown about the last frost date.

Mignonette [min-yun-et']. *Reseda odorata.*

This old-fashioned favorite, grown for its fragrance, is often considered the sweetest of all. The flowers are insignificant, brownish red or white, and the small-flowered varieties are usually more fragrant than the large. This tender annual should be sown out of doors after the last spring frost date where it is to bloom since it does not transplant easily. It will bloom in about 50 days but is rather short-lived so two or three plantings are needed for continuous flowering. Just scatter the seeds throughout your flower beds every 3 or 4 weeks.

Mirabilis [mi-ra'-bil-is]. FOUR O'CLOCKS. MARVEL OF PERU.

This plant is called Four O'Clocks because that is about the time the flowers open in the afternoon and they stay open until morning. The plants have so many flowers that the effect is colorful even when they are closed. It is easily grown, long-blooming and will thrive anywhere. The plants are erect with bushy bright green foliage, about 2 feet high and useful for a quick, low hedge. The flowers, like small Morning-glories, are 1 inch wide with 1–2-inch tubes; they are fragrant and dozens bloom at a time. The seed is available only in mixtures, and the colors are clear bright yellow, red and white, with some of the flowers striped. The plant forms tuberous roots which can be stored like Dahlias, but the only point in keeping them would be if you wished to segregate a particular color. Plants are easily grown as tender annuals which should be planted in the garden a week or so after the last spring frost date; they will bloom in 60 days and continue until frost. They are perennials treated as annuals, and live over or self-sow in mild climates. There is a new variety, JINGLES, with all bicolored flowers. The colors are rose, red, yellow, orange, pink, salmon, and white. The flowers are striped, barred or flecked with a second color. Burpee and Park's.

Molucella, see Bells of Ireland.

Moonflower, see page 133.

Myosotis [my-o-so'-tis]. FORGET-ME-NOT.
   Usually grown as a biennial, *Myosotis* will flower in six weeks from seed and can be raised as an annual. The plants are 6 to 12 inches tall with white, indigo-blue or pink flowers although blue is the color most frequently grown. Since they do best in cool spring weather, I advise growing them as biennials, a sky blue carpet under spring bulbs for example, and using *Anchusa* for annual Forget-Me-Nots, and Cynoglossum or *Lobelia* for blue annuals.

Nemesia [ne-mee'-she-a].
   This plant is one of the Flower Show favorites, and it

does look charming planted there in masses. It blooms well in cool weather, but does not like hot summers. The seed must be started early indoors or in a greenhouse so that it gets a good start before warm weather, and, in hot climates, blooms before summer. Where the summers are cool, seed may be sown outdoors in April for late June blooms. The miniature orchid-like flowers are ¾ inch across and are massed in clusters 3 to 4 inches wide. There is a semi-dwarf variety CARNIVAL, about 8 inches high, and taller 1-foot varieties. Available only in mixtures, the colors are cream, orange, yellow, white, crimson, mauve, and red shades. Good for edging, the foreground of beds, and window boxes—but remember, cool summers only.

Nemophila [nem-off'-i-la]. BABY BLUE-EYES.

I first saw these lovely flowers growing wild in the Yosemite. Since then I have found they are garden favorites in a variety of climates although they are natives of California. The plants are about 6 inches tall with soft green feathery foliage and cup-shaped deep blue ½–1-inch flowers with a white center which grow in clusters at the tips of the branches. In *A Southern Garden*, Elizabeth Lawrence says: "One of the earliest annuals and one of the easiest, blooming lavishly in poor soil and in sun or part shade. Sow in September and unless the season is very late, the little plants begin to bloom in February when they are only an inch or so high, the right height for early bulbs. Later, with the tulips, they are spread into tangled masses." A Maine gardener sows seed in May and the plants bloom in July and even survive early frosts and light snow to flower until Thanksgiving. This hardy annual should be sown early, a week or two before the last spring frost date. The standard variety is INSIGNIS, sky blue flowers with white centers.

Nicotiana [ni-ko-she-ah'-na]. FLOWERING TOBACCO.

Nicotiana, a relative of commercial tobacco, has very large soft leaves and tubular 2-inch flowers with petals which form a 5-pointed star. The older varieties did not open during the day, so their main virtue was their fragrance, which became pronounced at night. But as usual plant breeders have been busy, and now there are varieties which remain open all day and the height has been reduced to make more useful bedding plants, while still retaining the evening fragrance. The leading variety is called either SENSATION or SENSATION DAYLIGHT. The plants are 1½ to 2 feet tall, and the mixtures have scarlet, crimson, rose, lavender, yellow, coral, and white flowers. There are 3 separate colors. CRIMSON BEDDER is 12 to 18 inches tall, with bright crimson flowers. WHITE BEDDER is 15 inches high with sturdy upright plants and pure white flowers, the best bedding white. A striking contrast is LIME GREEN or LIME SHERBET, aptly named for its color, 15 to 18 inches tall, Park's and Stokes. Nicotiana is easily grown from seed and will flower in 6 weeks profusely and until frost. It often self-sows.

Nierembergia [near-em-berg'-i-a]. BLUE CUPS.

Nierembergia, a tender perennial, is grown as a hardy annual. This low-growing 6-inch plant with needle-like foliage forms a dense matted mound. The variety, PURPLE ROBE, won a Bronze Medal in the All-American Selections in 1942, and has 1-inch, cup-shaped flowers which are deep violet-blue. The flowers used to fade during the summer, but now the improved PURPLE ROBE holds its color. If the plants are exposed to very hot sun, each plant produces a prodigious number of blossoms—one writer said each of his plants must have had at least 500. They take about 15 weeks to bloom so if the plants are wanted for an all-summer edging or window boxes, it is best to start them early indoors or in a coldframe. However, they flower satisfactorily if sown directly in the garden about the time of the last spring frost date, and they flower during the hottest, driest weather.

Nigella [ny-jell'-a]. LOVE-IN-A-MIST.

This attractive plant is a native of Italy and southern Europe where it grows wild in the cornfields. It is 1½ feet tall and has very fine, almost threadlike, light green foliage and the 1½-inch flowers which are surrounded with a small edging of the green, fernlike foliage. The flowers are pale blue and white and although it is not a showy garden specimen the individual plants are most interesting. After the flowers bloom they are followed by large balloon-shaped seed pods which are pale green with reddish brown markings, and may be dried—they are pretty when silvered for Christmas. Nigella is very hardy and can be either fall-sown or planted very early in the spring where it is to bloom since it does not transplant well. Seed sown in my garden about the first of April bloomed about July 1st and continued until the end of August although it will bloom longer in cooler climates, and in hot ones should be fall-sown for spring flowering. It self-sows readily. The older variety is MISS JEKYLL with Cornflower blue flowers, and Burnett has MISS JEKYLL WHITE. PERSIAN JEWELS is a newer mixture with white, pink, carmine, mauve, rose-red and purple flowers. PERSIAN ROSE is a separate color which opens light pink, turns bright pink and then a deeper rose. Park's and Burnett. To dry see Everlastings.

Ornamental Corn, see Corn, Ornamental.

Ornamental Grasses, see Grasses, Ornamental.

Ornamental Peppers, see Capsicum.

Pelargonium, see Geraniums.

Periwinkle, see Vinca.

Quaking Grass, see Grasses, Ornamental.

Reseda, see Mignonette.

Rhodanthe, see *Acroclinium.*

Ricinus [riss'-in-us]. CASTOR BEAN PLANT.
   This lush plant with fantastic foliage is a native of Africa and has a most tropical, jungle look. It grows 8–12 feet tall here although in its native, frost-free habitat it sometimes reaches a height of 40 feet. It has huge coarse leaves which in different varieties are either green, maroon, bronzy green, mulberry-colored or reddish. *Ricinus* should be treated as a tender annual and the seeds planted in the garden about a week after the last spring frost date. It has no place in a regular flower bed or border, and can only be used as a shrub or tree. In the Middle West, they are called "mole trees" because they are supposed to drive away moles. They are loved by Japanese beetles. One theory is that if you have a castor bean plant it will attract all the beetles in the garden and leave everything else free; but another school thinks that you just get all the neighbors' beetles too. It makes a quick temporary background or hedge. Available ordinarily only in mixtures, Stokes has 2 separate colors: ZANZIBARIENSIS is 15 feet tall with huge green leaves without markings; and SANGUINEUS, 8 feet, with reddish leaves. One word of warning—the seeds are poisonous and the plants are toxic.

Rudbeckia [rood-beck'-i-a]. GLORIOSA DAISY.

Rudbeckia is the hybrid version of the common wild flower Black-Eyed Susan. The plant breeders have increased the size of the flowers, added colors, and even produced a variety with green rather than brown centers. The daisy-like flowers are available in single and double forms, and the colors in the mixtures are yellow, gold and bronze, some zoned with mahogany red. The large flowers are 4 to 5 inches across, and the plants are about 3 feet tall. Separate varieties are PINWHEEL, which is a mahogany and gold bicolor, and IRISH EYES, which has golden yellow single flowers with emerald green eyes. Rudbeckia is a perennial which will bloom the first year and for years afterwards. It produces plenty of flowers all summer until frost, but I think they are more attractive growing wild on country roads than they are in a garden. However, if I were going to plant any it would be IRISH EYES since I think the green centers are more attractive than the brown ones. A hardy annual, it can be planted two weeks before the last frost date.

Salpiglossis [sal-pig-gloss'-iss]. PAINTED TONGUE.

The flowers resemble Petunias somewhat although more trumpet-shaped, and the petals are beautifully veined. The colors are many—purple, violet, pink, yellow, buff, blue, orange, rose and crimson—all intensified by gold veining and a velvety texture. These colors are either solid or bicolor combinations such as cream and yellow, silver and gold, red and gold, brown and gold, and many others. They are truly beautiful flowers and, although they are available only in mixtures, the colors are all fine together. *Salpiglossis* makes excellent long-lasting cut flowers and handsome beds. There are 3 varieties. The older one is EMPEROR with 3-foot plants. The two newer ones are hybrids, bred for bushier, more vigorous plants—the older ones have sparse foliage and slender stems—and larger flowers and more of them. SPLASH has all these superior qualities on 2½-foot plants. BOLERO is another hybrid, the same good traits, 2 feet tall. The culture is not quite as easy as it is with most annuals. *Salpiglossis* is tender, and the seeds are very fine. It is best started indoors 6 weeks before the last frost date, and transplanted into the open when the weather is warm. If the seed is planted directly in the garden, do not cover it. Keep the seed bed moist and the plants crowded until they are about 2 inches high. The plants will bloom all summer if they get a good start before the heat comes.

Salvia [sal'-vi-a].

Most people are only too familiar with red Salvia or Scarlet Sage. They are used frequently for bedding and gardens, and often so badly that they can be an eyesore, although they can also be very effective if used well. The green-leaved upright plants are topped with fire-engine red flower spikes. The number of varieties of red Salvia is confusing. Since the colors are more or less the same, the primary difference is in height, which can vary from 12 to 30 inches. Some recommended varieties are: dwarf, ST. JOHN'S FIRE, 12 inches, the earliest and most dwarf; BLAZE OF FIRE, 14 inches; medium, EARLY BONFIRE, 20 to 24 inches; tall, SPLENDENS, 30 inches—this is the Scarlet Sage. Park's has 5 pastel colors: lavender, purple, white, rose and salmon. *Salvia farinacea* is a perennial treated as an annual and is a beautiful plant. The foliage is greyish green, and the flowers are long fragrant spikes of pale true blue carried well above the foliage (which is true of all Salvias). *S. farinacea* is about 3 feet tall, and *farinacea* BLUE BEDDER is about 18 inches tall with deeper blue flowers, while *S. patens* has bright blue flowers. WHITE BEDDER is the white companion to BLUE BEDDER. *Farinacea* will live over

the winter with some protection, although in the northern
Zones E, F and G they had better be put in the coldframe.
They also self-sow. All Salvias are tender annuals which
take a long time to bloom from seed and must be started
early either indoors or in a greenhouse, and not planted
out of doors until all danger of frost has passed. Once in
flower they will continue blooming until frost.

Sanvitalia, Creeping Zinnia. See Zinnias, page 217.

Satin Flower, see Godetia.

Scarlet Runner Bean. *Phaseolus coccineus.*

Actually a vegetable grown as a vine for its decorative
foliage and attractive scarlet pea-shaped flowers. The
edible beans which follow are loved devotedly by English-
men, and are one of the reasons why English food is sometimes disparaged. It is a twining, tender vine which should
be sown about the date of the last frost where it is to
bloom. It will grow 10 feet long, and quickly. Stokes.

Schizanthus [sky-zan'-thus]. BUTTERFLY FLOWER. POOR
    MAN'S ORCHID.

Schizanthus is a most attractive plant. The flowers are
delicate and graceful, freely borne on long clusters, and in
full bloom look like tiny butterflies. The foliage is soft
light green and fernlike. The seed is available only in mixtures, as far as I know, but all the colors are good—white,
pink, carmine, purple, yellow, and apricot, all with a
golden blotch. This plant does not stand heat well and,
where the summers are warm, should be started early
indoors or in a hot bed so that it can bloom while the
weather is still cool. In cool summer climates, it can be
grown out of doors as a hardy annual. The plants will
bloom 6–8 weeks after seed is planted, but the flowering is

prolific and not too long lasting. Pinching the plants back when they are about 3 inches tall encourages branching and helps make a better shaped, less straggling, plant.

Snow-on-the-Mountain, see *Euphorbia*.

Statice [stat'-i-see].

Sometimes listed as *Limonium, Statice* is a peculiar looking plant but attractive in a way. The stiff flower stalks, 2½ feet tall, have flowers on one side that look papery and have a stiff papery texture. The flowers are everlasting, and look almost dried even while blooming. The flowering stalks are long and the plant a showy one. Several separate colors are listed: white, yellow, sky blue, dark blue, deep rose, and apricot pastels; the yellow is a clear lemon color and very nice. There is a dwarf variety, PETITE BOUQUET, 12 inches high, mixed, Park's and Harris. The seeds should be started early since they like cool weather.

Stocks. *Mathiola incana*.

Stocks are beautiful plants with attractive foliage and flowers of a heavenly fragrance, but are very definitely not easy to grow in most of the country. They not only like cool weather, they demand it, and if not started early and coddled they will not bloom. In California, Stocks are seen in many gardens blooming profusely in the middle of the summer. But in most of the country, and certainly where the summers are very hot, Stocks are not a safe bet for continuous bloom all summer. But if you start them early so that the buds can start forming before it is really warm, then you will have a display for a time at least, and worth it if you are partial to them. There are dwarf and tall types. The taller ones are grown primarily in greenhouses since this is a popular florists' flower. Two dwarf types are recommended for the home gardener. TRYSOMIC SEVEN

WEEKS is the earliest, starting to bloom when the central spike is only 6 inches high and eventually reaching 15 to 18 inches, with many branches. The mixtures have white, yellow, pink, rose, crimson, lavender, blue and purple flowers—typical Stock colors and all attractive. TEN WEEKS is a little later and Harris has 4 separate colors: white, pink, azure blue, and yellow. Their mixture has these 4 colors plus red, rose, and dark blue.

These two types are dwarf plants, 12–18 inches high, with the typical light greyish green foliage, and both bloom about 70 days after seed is sown. They need full sun.

Strawflower, see *Helichrysum*.

Summer Cypress, see Kochia.

Sunflower, see Helianthus.

Swan River Daisy, see *Brachycome*.

Swan River Everlasting, see *Acroclinium*.

Sweet Sultan, see p. 82.

Strawberries. Alpine Strawberries.

Normally Strawberries are bought as plants which produce runners and form matted rows. These annual berries are another instance of a perennial grown as an annual since it produces fruit from seed the first year. The berries are about half the size of the cultivated ones and twice the size of wild ones; they are very sweet and there are many of them. The plants are about 8 inches high, and form neat little clumps with good green leaves. Small ½-inch white flowers are followed by the fruit. Alpine Strawberries are native to Europe and the standard variety is BARON SOLE-MACHER. The seed can be started indoors about March 1st and transplanted into the garden about the last frost date. They will start bearing fruit in August and will continue until hard frost. The seed can also be planted outdoors after the soil can be worked but the plants will be smaller. These plants make a novel ornamental edging or pot plant, and, since they do not have runners, are ideal for one of those strawberry planters. They will live over, given a light mulch and some plant food the following spring.

Sweet William.

Sweet William is usually a biennial, but now there are varieties which bloom quickly from seed the first year, and in mild climates live over to bloom a second season. The individual flowers are about ¾ inch wide and grow in clusters of 4 to 6 flowers. The foliage is a good dark green. There are 2 varieties; 2 are mixtures and the other is a separate color. Since the mixtures have harmonious colors they are a good choice. The colors are red, pink, crimson, ruby, salmon and white, sometimes solid and sometimes zoned or edged with a contrasting color. The plant height varies from 4 to about 12 inches. WEE WILLIE is the dwarf variety, 4 inches high and about the same across. The plants start flowering when they are only 2 inches high, 7 weeks after sowing, and bloom abundantly. Ideal for edgings and rock gardens. SUMMER BEAUTY is the other mixture, 1 foot high with bushy plants and large single flowers, some starred and others with clear white eyes. RED MON-ARCH, an All-American Selection in 1966, has large scarlet flowers with white stamens. It blooms profusely with rounded clusters on upright sturdy 12-inch plants. It will flower in 2 months from seed. Nice bedding plant and excellent cut flower. Sweet William is hardy and so can be planted early.

Tahoka [ta-hoe'-ka] *Daisy.*

This most attractive long-blooming daisy is about 18 inches tall with very finely cut, bushy greyish green foliage. The 2-inch flowers are daisylike with a single row of bright lavender flowers surrounding a deep yellow center. The plant is full of petals which really do bloom a long time (so often in catalogues the period of bloom is fictitious). The seed should be planted while the weather is cool, about two weeks before the last frost date. It takes about 4 months to flower in our climate from an April 1st planting, but plants are still blooming in my garden in the middle of September and show no signs of stopping. In California I saw plants that had been blooming for three months and were still in full flower. Burpee, Park's.

Texas Bluebonnet, see *Lupinus.*

Thunbergia [thun-berj'-ee-uh] *alata.* BLACK-EYED SUSAN VINE.

This twining perennial vine is treated as a tender annual. It is about 4–5 feet long with 2–3-inch leaves. The flowers usually have black eyes, have 5 clearly defined petals and grow individually in the leaf-axils. The standard mixture is ALATA, and the 1-inch flowers are orange, yellow, buff and white. Two separate varieties are: GIBSONII with rich deep orange flowers twice as large as ALATA, Burnett, Stokes and Park's; and WHITE WINGS, with pure white 1½–2-inch flowers that are scalloped and overlapped with chartreuse throats, Park's. The vine is generally used for hanging baskets, window boxes, or low fences or banks. It can be planted outdoors after the last frost date but it is better to start the seeds indoors six weeks earlier.

Tickseed, see *Calliopsis.*

Tithonia [tith-oh'-nee-uh]. GOLDEN FLOWER OF THE INCAS.
MEXICAN SUNFLOWERS.

Tithonia is a very tall 4–6 foot plant. Elizabeth Lawrence in *A Southern Garden* says that the first year she planted seeds, the plants branched to the ground and every branch was tipped with a lacquer-red flower, that the plants were really too coarse for the garden, and that the flowers could only be reached by a stepladder when the plants were upright. The plants I have seen were not as tall as this, but were at least 4 feet high. The flowers are brilliant scarlet orange, 3–4 inches across, single and Dahlia-like, with large grey-green leaves. The only variety is TORCH, an All-American winner. *Tithonia* takes at least 4 months to flower, so in most parts of the country it should be started indoors. A Vermont gardener started seed indoors the first of April and the plants bloomed from August 15th until frost. Best use is as a background for the vegetable garden, or in a place where otherwise you might grow sunflowers.

Toadflax, see *Linaria.*

Tobacco, Flowering, see Nicotiana.

Torenia [tor-reen'-ee-uh] *fournieri.* WISHBONE FLOWER.

This annual has two very decided factors in its favor: it likes partial shade, and the flowers are exquisite. They are like tiny Snapdragons, violet-blue with a deep purple lip and yellow throat. The plants are about 10 inches tall, fairly bushy, with dark green leaves. This is the standard variety, FOURNIERI, listed by most seedsmen. Burnett has a pure white variety, and Park's a white one with golden throats. This tender annual can be started indoors or planted directly in the garden a week after the last spring frost date. The seeds are very fine and slow to germinate, but once the plants get started they grow quickly and bloom until frost. They self-sow freely in the South and to some extent in the North; the self-sown seedlings do not appear until the weather is warm. *Torenia* is one of the best annuals for semi-shaded positions.

Trachymene, see *Didiscus.*

Vinca [vin'-ka] *rosea.* MADAGASCAR PERIWINKLE.

Vinca plants are most attractive with very shiny laurel-like green leaves and flowers with good clear colors. They are single, round, 1½ inches across, and grow in the axils of the leaves. The plants are bushy and erect. There are two types: the standard one, which is about 18 inches tall, and a newer dwarf 10-inch type. The dwarf ones are available in 5 separate colors: rose-pink, pure white, white with rosy red eyes, and pale pink with red eyes; the fifth, less common one, is LITTLE LINDA, deep orchid, Park's. The taller Vincas are usually available only in mixtures, but that is all right since all the colors are attractive. Vinca is a tender perennial which is treated as an annual since it flowers the first year and doesn't like frost. However, it does have one drawback—it requires heat during all stages of growth and it takes a long time to flower. So it must be started indoors in March—be warned, it is a very slow grower—and the plants put into the garden when the weather is really warm (or buy plants). It will flower abundantly until frost, even in the hottest weather. Vincas make excellent colorful bedding plants or edgings. I really became acquainted with it in our Bermuda garden where it was one of the few plants that bloomed well during the hot humid summers—even Geraniums don't thrive then. In fact, there it is perennial and blooms all year, and I think it is beautiful.

Wallflower. Cheiranthus.

Anyone who has been in England in the spring knows how attractive the fragrant Wallflowers are. They are usually either biennials or perennials there, although now here there is an annual type. There is, though, a problem with this flower. Here we do not have the right growing conditions for them everywhere. They require cool nights and moisture in the air and grow best in cool moist areas near the ocean on the west coast. They also will not stand severe, cold winters. After this negative advice I must say that they are a welcome addition to any garden that can satisfy them. The plants are about 1½ feet tall and the colors in the mixture are golden yellow, coppery red, orange, citron yellow, and creamy white. EARLY WONDER is the annual variety, blooming in 4 to 5 months, Burnett.

Xeranthemum [zer-ran'-the-mum]. IMMORTELLE.

This is an old-time favorite everlasting, one of the prettiest of the lot. The silky, papery double 1½-inch flowers have attractive colors—white, shades of pink, bright rose, red and purple. The foliage is a light silvery green; the plants are 1½ to 2 feet tall. Available only in mixtures from Burpee and Burnett. It is a hardy annual so can be sown early. Plant where it is to bloom and it will flower from July on. Excellent for cutting and summer arrangements as well as for drying. To dry, see Everlastings.

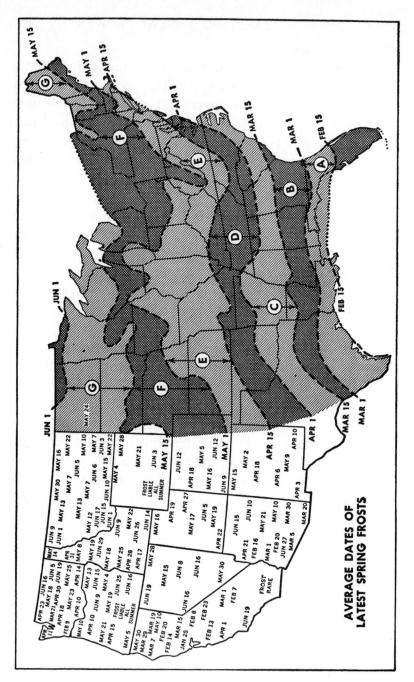

AVERAGE DATES OF LATEST SPRING FROSTS

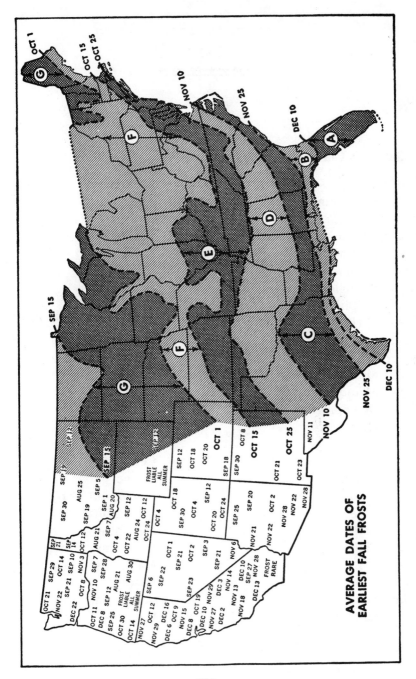

**AVERAGE DATES OF
EARLIEST FALL FROSTS**

Annuals Classified by Color

Blue

Ageratum
Anagallis
Anchusa
Browallia
Centaurea cyanus
Cynoglossum
Delphinium
Larkspur
Lobelia
Lupines
Morning-glories
Myosotis
Nemophila
Nigella
Pansies
Salvia farinacea
Statice
Stocks
Sweet Peas
Verbena
Violas

Lavender

Ageratum
Alyssum
Asters
Centaurea cyanus
Delphinium
Dianthus

Didiscus
Larkspur
Pansies
Petunias
Phlox
Salvia
Scabiosa
Snapdragons
Sweet Peas
Tahoka Daisy
Verbena
Violas
Zinnias

Orange

Calendula
Celosia
Cosmos
Dimorphotheca
Eschscholtzia
Helianthus
Impatiens
Marigolds
Nasturtiums
Pansies (apricot)
Petunias
Portulaca
Snapdragons
Sweet Peas
Tithonia
Zinnias

Pink and Rose Shades
  Ageratum
  Asters
  Balsam (Bush)
  Begonias
  Celosia
  Centaurea cyanus
  Cleome
  Cosmos
  Dahlias
  Dimorphotheca
  Dianthus
  Eschscholtzia
  Geraniums
  Godetia
  Gypsophila
  Hibiscus
  Hollyhocks
  Impatiens
  Jewels of Opar
  Nasturtiums
  Nigella
  Pansies
  Petunias
  Phlox
  Portulaca
  Salvia
  Scabiosa
  Shirley Poppies
  Snapdragons
  Statice
  Stocks
  Sweet Peas
  Verbena
  Vinca
  Zinnias

Purple
  Alyssum

  Asters
  Delphinium
  Dianthus
  Gomphrena
  Larkspur
  Nierembergia
  Pansies
  Petunias
  Salvia
  Sweet Peas
  Verbenas
  Violas
  Zinnias

Scarlet and Crimson
  Asters
  Balsam
  Begonias
  Celosia
  Centaurea
  Cosmos
  Cuphea
  Dahlias
  Dianthus
  Gaillardia
  Geraniums
  Hibiscus
  Impatiens
  Linum
  Lobelia
  Morning-glories
  Nasturtiums
  Pansies
  Petunias
  Phlox
  Portulaca
  Salvia
  Scabiosa
  Shirley Poppies

Snapdragons
Stocks
Sweet Peas
Sweet William
Verbena
Zinnias

White
Ageratum
Alyssum
Asters
Balsam
Begonias
Browallia
Centaurea
Chrysanthemums
Cosmos
Dahlias
Datura
Delphinium
Dianthus
Dimorphotheca
Eschscholtzia
Geraniums
Gypsophila
Hibiscus
Iberis
Impatiens
Larkspur
Lupines
Matricaria
Moonflowers
Morning-glories
Nicotiana
Nigella
Pansies

Petunias
Phlox
Portulaca
Salvia farinacea
Scabiosa
Snapdragons
Statice
Stocks
Sweet Peas
Verbena
Vinca
Violas
Zinnias

Yellow
Calendula
Celosia
Chrysanthemums
Cleome
Cosmos
Dahlias
Eschscholtzia
Helianthus
Marigolds
Nasturtiums
Pansies
Petunias
Phlox
Portulaca
Rudbeckia
Snapdragons
Statice
Stocks
Violas
Zinnias

LISTS OF ANNUALS FOR VARIOUS USES

Annuals that can be planted on sunny banks.

Alyssum
Anagallis
Brachycome
Dimorphotheca
Eschscholtzia
Gourds
Iberis
Mesembryanthemum

Nasturtiums
Phlox
Poppies
Portulaca
Sanvitalia
Verbena
Zinnia linearis

Annuals that can be fall sown to cover bulb foliage.

Calendula
Centaurea
Eschscholtzia
Larkspur

Myosotis
Phlox
Shirley Poppies

Annuals that are good for cutting.

Arctotis
Asters
Calendula
Canterbury Bells
Centaurea
Chrysanthemums
Cosmos
Eschscholtzia
Euphorbia
Gaillardia
Gypsophila
Helianthus
Hunnemannia
Lavatera
Larkspur

Marigolds
Mignonette
Nasturtiums
Nigella
Pansies
Petunias
Phlox
Salpiglossis
Scabiosa
Snapdragons
Stocks
Sweet Peas
Verbena
Zinnias

Annuals that do well in dry locations.

Alyssum
Calliopsis
Centaurea
Cleome
Eschscholtzia
Euphorbia
Gaillardia
Helianthus
Mesembryanthemum

Mirabilis
Morning-glories
Nasturtiums
Phlox
Poppies
Portulaca
Sanvitalia
Zinnia linearis

Annuals that are fragrant.

Alyssum
Calendulas
Candytuft
Carnations
Centaurea imperialis
Heliotrope
Marigolds
Matthiola

Mignonette
Nicotiana
Petunias
Snapdragons
Stocks
Sweet Peas
Verbena

Annuals that are good for temporary hedges.

Amaranthus
Bells of Ireland
Celosia
Cosmos
Datura
Helianthus
Hibiscus

Hollyhock
Kochia
Marigolds
Mirabilis
Ricinus
Rudbeckia
Tithonia

Annuals that can be naturalized (self-sow readily).

Ageratum
Calendula
Calliopsis
Centaurea cyanus
Cleome
Cosmos

Eschscholtzia
Euphorbia
Larkspur
Mirabilis
Nicotiana
Nigella

Petunias (small-flowered
  ones)
Poppies

Portulaca
Salvia farinacea

Annuals that can be used in a rock garden.

Ageratum
Alyssum
Anagallis
Iberis
Lobelia
Nemophila
Nierembergia
Petunias (dwarf
  varieties)

Phlox (dwarf
  varieties)
Portulaca
Sanvitalia
Snapdragons (dwarf)
Torenia
Zinnias (dwarf)

Annuals that will tolerate partial shade.

The three best ones
  are Impatiens, Balsam
  and Begonias.
Alyssum
Centaurea
Larkspur
Lobelia
Lupines
Myosotis

Nasturtium
Nemophila
Nicotiana
Pansies
Petunias
Snapdragons
Vinca
Violas

Annuals classified according to size.

Edging Plants up to 1 foot tall.

Ageratum
Alyssum
Basil, Ornamental
Begonias
Browallia
Capsicum
Celosia (dwarf form)
Centaurea cyanus
  (dwarf form)

Delphinium (DWARF
  CHINENSIS)
Dianthus
Iberis
Impatiens
Lobelia
Marigolds (French)
Nierembergia
Pansies

Petunias (dwarf form)
Phlox
Portulaca
Sanvitalia
Snapdragons (dwarf form)

Strawberries, Alpine
Verbena (dwarf form)
Vinca (dwarf form)
Violas
Zinnia linearis (and other dwarf forms)

Middle Border Plants 1–2 feet tall.

Ageratum (tall)
Alyssum maritimum
Anchusa
Asters
Balsam
Calendula
Celosia
Centaurea
Chrysanthemums
Cynoglossum
Dahlias
Eschscholtzia
Euphorbia
Geraniums
Gomphrena
Hunnemannia
Iberis

Jewels of Opar
Matricaria
Marigolds
Nasturtiums
Petunias
Phlox (tall form)
Salpiglossis
Salvia
Scabiosa
Shirley Poppies
Snapdragons
Stocks
Verbena
Vinca
Xeranthemum
Zinnias

Background plants 2 feet tall and over.

Celosia
Cleome
Cosmos
Helianthus
Hollyhock
Larkspur

Marigold
Morning-glories
Salpiglossis
Scabiosa
Statice
Zinnias

Vines

Canary Bird Vine
(*Tropaeolum peregrinum*)

Cardinal Climber
Cobaea scandens
Cypress Vine

Gourds
Moonflower
Morning-glories
Nasturtiums

Scarlet Runner
Sweet Peas
Thunbergia

Annuals that are good for window boxes.

Ageratum
Alyssum
Balsam (Bush)
Canary Bird Vine
   (*Tropaeolum pere-*
    grinum)
Geraniums
Impatiens
Lobelia
Marigolds (French)

Nasturtiums
Nierembergia
Pansies
Petunias
Phlox
Portulaca
Sanvitalia
Torenia
Verbena
Vinca

INDEX

A CATALOGUE OF SELECTED DOVER BOOKS
IN ALL FIELDS OF INTEREST

A CATALOGUE OF SELECTED DOVER BOOKS
IN ALL FIELDS OF INTEREST

THE DEVIL'S DICTIONARY, Ambrose Bierce. Barbed, bitter, brilliant witticisms in the form of a dictionary. Best, most ferocious satire America has produced. 145pp. 20487-1 Pa. $1.50

ABSOLUTELY MAD INVENTIONS, A.E. Brown, H.A. Jeffcott. Hilarious, useless, or merely absurd inventions all granted patents by the U.S. Patent Office. Edible tie pin, mechanical hat tipper, etc. 57 illustrations. 125pp. 22596-8 Pa. $1.50

AMERICAN WILD FLOWERS COLORING BOOK, Paul Kennedy. Planned coverage of 48 most important wildflowers, from Rickett's collection; instructive as well as entertaining. Color versions on covers. 48pp. 8¼ x 11. 20095-7 Pa. $1.35

BIRDS OF AMERICA COLORING BOOK, John James Audubon. Rendered for coloring by Paul Kennedy. 46 of Audubon's noted illustrations: red-winged blackbird, cardinal, purple finch, towhee, etc. Original plates reproduced in full color on the covers. 48pp. 8¼ x 11. 23049-X Pa. $1.35

NORTH AMERICAN INDIAN DESIGN COLORING BOOK, Paul Kennedy. The finest examples from Indian masks, beadwork, pottery, etc. — selected and redrawn for coloring (with identifications) by well-known illustrator Paul Kennedy. 48pp. 8¼ x 11. 21125-8 Pa. $1.35

UNIFORMS OF THE AMERICAN REVOLUTION COLORING BOOK, Peter Copeland. 31 lively drawings reproduce whole panorama of military attire; each uniform has complete instructions for accurate coloring. (Not in the Pictorial Archives Series). 64pp. 8¼ x 11. 21850-3 Pa. $1.50

THE WONDERFUL WIZARD OF OZ COLORING BOOK, L. Frank Baum. Color the Yellow Brick Road and much more in 61 drawings adapted from W.W. Denslow's originals, accompanied by abridged version of text. Dorothy, Toto, Oz and the Emerald City. 61 illustrations. 64pp. 8¼ x 11. 20452-9 Pa. $1.50

CUT AND COLOR PAPER MASKS, Michael Grater. Clowns, animals, funny faces ... simply color them in, cut them out, and put them together and you have 9 paper masks to play with and enjoy. Complete instructions. Assembled masks shown in full color on the covers. 32pp. 8¼ x 11. 23171-2 Pa. $1.50

STAINED GLASS CHRISTMAS ORNAMENT COLORING BOOK, Carol Belanger Grafton. Brighten your Christmas season with over 100 Christmas ornaments done in a stained glass effect on translucent paper. Color them in and then hang at windows, from lights, anywhere. 32pp. 8¼ x 11. 20707-2 Pa. $1.75

DRIED FLOWERS, Sarah Whitlock and Martha Rankin. Concise, clear, practical guide to dehydration, glycerinizing, pressing plant material, and more. Covers use of silica gel. 12 drawings. Originally titled "New Techniques with Dried Flowers." 32pp. 21802-3 Pa. $1.00

ABC OF POULTRY RAISING, J.H. Florea. Poultry expert, editor tells how to raise chickens on home or small business basis. Breeds, feeding, housing, laying, etc. Very concrete, practical. 50 illustrations. 256pp. 23201-8 Pa. $3.00

HOW INDIANS USE WILD PLANTS FOR FOOD, MEDICINE & CRAFTS, Frances Densmore. Smithsonian, Bureau of American Ethnology report presents wealth of material on nearly 200 plants used by Chippewas of Minnesota and Wisconsin. 33 plates plus 122pp. of text. 6⅛ x 9¼. 23019-8 Pa. $2.50

THE HERBAL OR GENERAL HISTORY OF PLANTS, John Gerard. The 1633 edition revised and enlarged by Thomas Johnson. Containing almost 2850 plant descriptions and 2705 superb illustrations, Gerard's Herbal is a monumental work, the book all modern English herbals are derived from, and the one herbal every serious enthusiast should have in its entirety. Original editions are worth perhaps $750. 1678pp. 8½ x 12¼. 23147-X Clothbd. $50.00

A MODERN HERBAL, Margaret Grieve. Much the fullest, most exact, most useful compilation of herbal material. Gigantic alphabetical encyclopedia, from aconite to zedoary, gives botanical information, medical properties, folklore, economic uses, and much else. Indispensable to serious reader. 161 illustrations. 888pp. 6½ x 9¼. USO 22798-7, 22799-5 Pa., Two vol. set $10.00

HOW TO KNOW THE FERNS, Frances T. Parsons. Delightful classic. Identification, fern lore, for Eastern and Central U.S.A. Has introduced thousands to interesting life form. 99 illustrations. 215pp. 20740-4 Pa. $2.50

THE MUSHROOM HANDBOOK, Louis C.C. Krieger. Still the best popular handbook. Full descriptions of 259 species, extremely thorough text, habitats, luminescence, poisons, folklore, etc. 32 color plates; 126 other illustrations. 560pp. 21861-9 Pa. $4.50

HOW TO KNOW THE WILD FRUITS, Maude G. Peterson. Classic guide covers nearly 200 trees, shrubs, smaller plants of the U.S. arranged by color of fruit and then by family. Full text provides names, descriptions, edibility, uses. 80 illustrations. 400pp. 22943-2 Pa. $3.00

COMMON WEEDS OF THE UNITED STATES, U.S. Department of Agriculture. Covers 220 important weeds with illustration, maps, botanical information, plant lore for each. Over 225 illustrations. 463pp. 6⅛ x 9¼. 20504-5 Pa. $4.50

HOW TO KNOW THE WILD FLOWERS, Mrs. William S. Dana. Still best popular book for East and Central USA. Over 500 plants easily identified, with plant lore; arranged according to color and flowering time. 174 plates. 459pp. 20332-8 Pa. $3.50

MANUAL OF THE TREES OF NORTH AMERICA, Charles S. Sargent. The basic survey of every native tree and tree-like shrub, 717 species in all. Extremely full descriptions, information on habitat, growth, locales, economics, etc. Necessary to every serious tree lover. Over 100 finding keys. 783 illustrations. Total of 986pp.
20277-1, 20278-X Pa., Two vol. set $8.00

BIRDS OF THE NEW YORK AREA, John Bull. Indispensable guide to more than 400 species within a hundred-mile radius of Manhattan. Information on range, status, breeding, migration, distribution trends, etc. Foreword by Roger Tory Peterson. 17 drawings; maps. 540pp.
23222-0 Pa. $6.00

THE SEA-BEACH AT EBB-TIDE, Augusta Foote Arnold. Identify hundreds of marine plants and animals: algae, seaweeds, squids, crabs, corals, etc. Descriptions cover food, life cycle, size, shape, habitat. Over 600 drawings. 490pp.
21949-6 Pa. $4.00

THE MOTH BOOK, William J. Holland. Identify more than 2,000 moths of North America. General information, precise species descriptions. 623 illustrations plus 48 color plates show almost all species, full size. 1968 edition. Still the basic book. Total of 551pp. 6½ x 9¼.
21948-8 Pa. $6.00

AN INTRODUCTION TO THE REPTILES AND AMPHIBIANS OF THE UNITED STATES, Percy A. Morris. All lizards, crocodiles, turtles, snakes, toads, frogs; life history, identification, habits, suitability as pets, etc. Non-technical, but sound and broad. 130 photos. 253pp.
22982-3 Pa. $3.00

OLD NEW YORK IN EARLY PHOTOGRAPHS, edited by Mary Black. Your only chance to see New York City as it was 1853-1906, through 196 wonderful photographs from N.Y. Historical Society. Great Blizzard, Lincoln's funeral procession, great buildings. 228pp. 9 x 12.
22907-6 Pa. $6.00

THE AMERICAN REVOLUTION, A PICTURE SOURCEBOOK, John Grafton. Wonderful Bicentennial picture source, with 411 illustrations (contemporary and 19th century) showing battles, personalities, maps, events, flags, posters, soldier's life, ships, etc. all captioned and explained. A wonderful browsing book, supplement to other historical reading. 160pp. 9 x 12.
23226-3 Pa. $4.00

PERSONAL NARRATIVE OF A PILGRIMAGE TO AL-MADINAH AND MECCAH, Richard Burton. Great travel classic by remarkably colorful personality. Burton, disguised as a Moroccan, visited sacred shrines of Islam, narrowly escaping death. Wonderful observations of Islamic life, customs, personalities. 47 illustrations. Total of 959pp.
21217-3, 21218-1 Pa., Two vol. set $7.00

INCIDENTS OF TRAVEL IN CENTRAL AMERICA, CHIAPAS, AND YUCATAN, John L. Stephens. Almost single-handed discovery of Maya culture; exploration of ruined cities, monuments, temples; customs of Indians. 115 drawings. 892pp.
22404-X, 22405-8 Pa., Two vol. set $8.00

THE BEST DR. THORNDYKE DETECTIVE STORIES, R. Austin Freeman. The Case of Oscar Brodski, The Moabite Cipher, and 5 other favorites featuring the great scientific detective, plus his long-believed-lost first adventure — 31 New Inn — reprinted here for the first time. Edited by E.F. Bleiler. USO 20388-3 Pa. $3.00

BEST "THINKING MACHINE" DETECTIVE STORIES, Jacques Futrelle. The Problem of Cell 13 and 11 other stories about Prof. Augustus S.F.X. Van Dusen, including two "lost" stories. First reprinting of several. Edited by E.F. Bleiler. 241pp.
20537-1 Pa. $3.00

UNCLE SILAS, J. Sheridan LeFanu. Victorian Gothic mystery novel, considered by many best of period, even better than Collins or Dickens. Wonderful psychological terror. Introduction by Frederick Shroyer. 436pp. 21715-9 Pa. $4.00

BEST DR. POGGIOLI DETECTIVE STORIES, T.S. Stribling. 15 best stories from EQMM and The Saint offer new adventures in Mexico, Florida, Tennessee hills as Poggioli unravels mysteries and combats Count Jalacki. 217pp. 23227-1 Pa. $3.00

EIGHT DIME NOVELS, selected with an introduction by E.F. Bleiler. Adventures of Old King Brady, Frank James, Nick Carter, Deadwood Dick, Buffalo Bill, The Steam Man, Frank Merriwell, and Horatio Alger — 1877 to 1905. Important, entertaining popular literature in facsimile reprint, with original covers. 190pp. 9 x 12. 22975-0 Pa. $3.50

ALICE'S ADVENTURES UNDER GROUND, Lewis Carroll. Facsimile of ms. Carroll gave Alice Liddell in 1864. Different in many ways from final Alice. Handlettered, illustrated by Carroll. Introduction by Martin Gardner. 128pp. 21482-6 Pa. $1.50

ALICE IN WONDERLAND COLORING BOOK, Lewis Carroll. Pictures by John Tenniel. Large-size versions of the famous illustrations of Alice, Cheshire Cat, Mad Hatter and all the others, waiting for your crayons. Abridged text. 36 illustrations. 64pp. 8¼ x 11. 22853-3 Pa. $1.50

AVENTURES D'ALICE AU PAYS DES MERVEILLES, Lewis Carroll. Bué's translation of "Alice" into French, supervised by Carroll himself. Novel way to learn language. (No English text.) 42 Tenniel illustrations. 196pp. 22836-3 Pa. $2.00

MYTHS AND FOLK TALES OF IRELAND, Jeremiah Curtin. 11 stories that are Irish versions of European fairy tales and 9 stories from the Fenian cycle — 20 tales of legend and magic that comprise an essential work in the history of folklore. 256pp. 22430-9 Pa. $3.00

EAST O' THE SUN AND WEST O' THE MOON, George W. Dasent. Only full edition of favorite, wonderful Norwegian fairytales — Why the Sea is Salt, Boots and the Troll, etc. — with 77 illustrations by Kittelsen & Werenskiöld. 418pp.
22521-6 Pa. $3.50

PERRAULT'S FAIRY TALES, Charles Perrault and Gustave Doré. Original versions of Cinderella, Sleeping Beauty, Little Red Riding Hood, etc. in best translation, with 34 wonderful illustrations by Gustave Doré. 117pp. 8⅛ x 11. 22311-6 Pa. $2.50

EARLY NEW ENGLAND GRAVESTONE RUBBINGS, Edmund V. Gillon, Jr. 43 photographs, 226 rubbings show heavily symbolic, macabre, sometimes humorous primitive American art. Up to early 19th century. 207pp. 8⅜ x 11¼.
21380-3 Pa. $4.00

L.J.M. DAGUERRE: THE HISTORY OF THE DIORAMA AND THE DAGUERREOTYPE, Helmut and Alison Gernsheim. Definitive account. Early history, life and work of Daguerre; discovery of daguerreotype process; diffusion abroad; other early photography. 124 illustrations. 226pp. 6⅙ x 9¼. 22290-X Pa. $4.00

PHOTOGRAPHY AND THE AMERICAN SCENE, Robert Taft. The basic book on American photography as art, recording form, 1839-1889. Development, influence on society, great photographers, types (portraits, war, frontier, etc.), whatever else needed. Inexhaustible. Illustrated with 322 early photos, daguerreotypes, tintypes, stereo slides, etc. 546pp. 6⅛ x 9¼. 21201-7 Pa. $5.00

PHOTOGRAPHIC SKETCHBOOK OF THE CIVIL WAR, Alexander Gardner. Reproduction of 1866 volume with 100 on-the-field photographs: Manassas, Lincoln on battlefield, slave pens, etc. Introduction by E.F. Bleiler. 224pp. 10¾ x 9.
22731-6 Pa. $4.50

THE MOVIES: A PICTURE QUIZ BOOK, Stanley Appelbaum & Hayward Cirker. Match stars with their movies, name actors and actresses, test your movie skill with 241 stills from 236 great movies, 1902-1959. Indexes of performers and films. 128pp. 8⅜ x 9¼. 20222-4 Pa. $2.50

THE TALKIES, Richard Griffith. Anthology of features, articles from Photoplay, 1928-1940, reproduced complete. Stars, famous movies, technical features, fabulous ads, etc.; Garbo, Chaplin, King Kong, Lubitsch, etc. 4 color plates, scores of illustrations. 327pp. 8⅜ x 11¼. 22762-6 Pa. $5.95

THE MOVIE MUSICAL FROM VITAPHONE TO "42ND STREET," edited by Miles Kreuger. Relive the rise of the movie musical as reported in the pages of Photoplay magazine (1926-1933): every movie review, cast list, ad, and record review; every significant feature article, production still, biography, forecast, and gossip story. Profusely illustrated. 367pp. 8⅜ x 11¼. 23154-2 Pa. $6.95

JOHANN SEBASTIAN BACH, Philipp Spitta. Great classic of biography, musical commentary, with hundreds of pieces analyzed. Also good for Bach's contemporaries. 450 musical examples. Total of 1799pp.
EUK 22278-0, 22279-9 Clothbd., Two vol. set $25.00

BEETHOVEN AND HIS NINE SYMPHONIES, Sir George Grove. Thorough history, analysis, commentary on symphonies and some related pieces. For either beginner or advanced student. 436 musical passages. 407pp. 20334-4 Pa. $4.00

MOZART AND HIS PIANO CONCERTOS, Cuthbert Girdlestone. The only full-length study. Detailed analyses of all 21 concertos, sources; 417 musical examples. 509pp. 21271-8 Pa. $4.50

BUILD YOUR OWN LOW-COST HOME, L.O. Anderson, H.F. Zornig. U.S. Dept. of Agriculture sets of plans, full, detailed, for 11 houses: A-Frame, circular, conventional. Also construction manual. Save hundreds of dollars. 204pp. 11 x 16.
21525-3 Pa. $5.95

HOW TO BUILD A WOOD-FRAME HOUSE, L.O. Anderson. Comprehensive, easy to follow U.S. Government manual: placement, foundations, framing, sheathing, roof, insulation, plaster, finishing — almost everything else. 179 illustrations. 223pp. 7⅞ x 10¾.
22954-8 Pa. $3.50

CONCRETE, MASONRY AND BRICKWORK, U.S. Department of the Army. Practical handbook for the home owner and small builder, manual contains basic principles, techniques, and important background information on construction with concrete, concrete blocks, and brick. 177 figures, 37 tables. 200pp. 6½ x 9¼.
23203-4 Pa. $4.00

THE STANDARD BOOK OF QUILT MAKING AND COLLECTING, Marguerite Ickis. Full information, full-sized patterns for making 46 traditional quilts, also 150 other patterns. Quilted cloths, lamé, satin quilts, etc. 483 illustrations. 273pp. 6⅞ x 9⅝.
20582-7 Pa. $3.50

101 PATCHWORK PATTERNS, Ruby S. McKim. 101 beautiful, immediately useable patterns, full-size, modern and traditional. Also general information, estimating, quilt lore. 124pp. 7⅞ x 10¾.
20773-0 Pa. $2.50

KNIT YOUR OWN NORWEGIAN SWEATERS, Dale Yarn Company. Complete instructions for 50 authentic sweaters, hats, mittens, gloves, caps, etc. Thoroughly modern designs that command high prices in stores. 24 patterns, 24 color photographs. Nearly 100 charts and other illustrations. 58pp. 8⅜ x 11¼.
23031-7 Pa. $2.50

IRON-ON TRANSFER PATTERNS FOR CREWEL AND EMBROIDERY FROM EARLY AMERICAN SOURCES, edited by Rita Weiss. 75 designs, borders, alphabets, from traditional American sources printed on translucent paper in transfer ink. Reuseable. Instructions. Test patterns. 24pp. 8¼ x 11.
23162-3 Pa. $1.50

AMERICAN INDIAN NEEDLEPOINT DESIGNS FOR PILLOWS, BELTS, HANDBAGS AND OTHER PROJECTS, Roslyn Epstein. 37 authentic American Indian designs adapted for modern needlepoint projects. Grid backing makes designs easily transferable to canvas. 48pp. 8¼ x 11.
22973-4 Pa. $1.50

CHARTED FOLK DESIGNS FOR CROSS-STITCH EMBROIDERY, Maria Foris & Andreas Foris. 278 charted folk designs, most in 2 colors, from Danube region: florals, fantastic beasts, geometrics, traditional symbols, more. Border and central patterns. 77pp. 8¼ x 11.
USO 23191-7 Pa. $2.00